Urban Economics: a set approach

Urban economics:

a set approach

J. Parry Lewis

Edward Arnold

© J. Parry Lewis 1979

First published 1979 by
Edward Arnold (Publishers) Ltd
41 Bedford Square, London WC1B 3DQ

British Library Cataloguing in Publication Data

Lewis, John Parry
   Urban economics.
   1. Urban economics
   I. Title
   330.9′173′2   HT321

   ISBN 0–7131–6236–8
   ISBN 0–7131–6237–6 Pbk

Text set in 10/11 pt VIP Century, printed and bound in Great Britain at
The Pitman Press, Bath

To

BRINLEY THOMAS
who taught me when and how to be discontented
and how to turn discontentment into understanding

Contents

Preface

This book arises out of my discontent with my own lectures. I began to teach urban economics around 1963, treating the subject as essentially an application of standard economic theory to a variety of urban problems. As time went on I became increasingly uneasy about the application of a theory developed with individuals, firms or national economies in mind to the behaviour of not very well defined sets of people whose decisions might be made for reasons, or by methods, that the theory did not embrace. I also became uneasy about the ways in which we were neglecting so many of the interdependencies of the urban system.

While this unease was constantly nagging me, other forces were at work. I was building a model of an artificial town, in which various groups of people made decisions about various things, and so produced changes in land use, rents, house prices, wages, employment patterns, traffic densities, and so on. It was designed to provide a basis for an examination of the consequences of policy decisions. At the same time I was mingling increasingly with town planners, surveyors and property developers. On both counts I was forced to consider constantly the processes of urban change. Doing so increased my unease.

It was not until September 1976, when I was marking some examination papers in economics at Khartoum University, and thinking about the housing problems there, that I suddenly saw the real reason for my unease. At the same time I realized that to some extent most of us who teach and write about urban economics have fallen into the trap that lies in wait for all who seek to extend the application of theory. How we have done so, and how to avoid the trap, is the subject of this book.

If we are to avoid the trap we have to go right back to basic ideas, and try to say what we mean by 'the urban economy'. We then have to consider the extent to which this 'economy' can be analysed. It turns out that the amount of economic theory that is necessary for an examination of urban economics, and for the development of an understanding of the economic causes and consequences of various urban activities and phenomena, is very little. What matters is not the development of complicated theory, but the correct application of a few very simple ideas. It is this that makes this book both a contribution to economic analysis and an introductory text book. The student of economics should have no difficulty with it, even though the treatment may be new to him. The student of planning, surveying or urban affairs will probably find that, while a knowledge of elementary economics will be useful, he can nevertheless read and understand the argument without this prior reading.

As so often happens, now that the book is written I would like to rewrite it, with different emphases: but that is a process that can be interminable. My hope is that it will help students and others to understand towns, and that it may stimulate discussion not only about the urban issues that are involved, but also about the application of the same basic approach to other areas of economics.

My colleagues in the Department of Town and Country Planning at Manchester University, my research students there, and above all my undergraduate students have contributed more than they realize both by their comments and by their patience. In particular, I must thank Mr A. L. Traill, Mr M. J. Bridges, Professor R. H. Kantorowich and Professor D. G. Robinson. I have also to thank Professor J. N. Wolfe of Edinburgh University for his encouragement, and the anonymous publisher's reader for some very constructive criticism of an early draft. My greatest debt, however, is to Professor Brinley Thomas, whose interest in this field so long ago directed me towards it.

Finally I must thank Mrs Margaret Barrow and Mrs Linda Johnson for their patient and painstaking care in producing the typescript, and Alan Johnson for practical assistance.

J. Parry Lewis
5 November, 1978.

1

An introductory survey

Most economic theory has been developed with an individual, a firm or a nation in mind. In this book we shall be looking at towns, and we have to acknowledge that while certain economic concepts developed for other purposes are useful in the analysis of towns there may be others that will mislead us in that context. Consequently, we shall begin by considering certain features of towns and the application of economics to them.

'The urban economy' is an impressive term that invites confusion. If we mean that part of the economy that is urban rather than rural we immediately have problems of definition and disentanglement. If, instead, we mean the economy of a specific town we must, at least, define the town, and then consider what we mean by its economy. Towns are defined for administrative purposes by boundaries, and there are normally town councils or other legally recognized bodies with responsibility for various administrative and executive functions within those boundaries. Having both income and expenditure, with problems of choice, the municipal authority has an economy, but it would be a very narrow approach to urban economics if we restricted it simply to the economics of local governments. If we try a wider approach we must pay some attention to the urban boundary, and it is tempting to define the economy of the town as the economy of its residents. This presupposes that 'residence' can be defined, but this is a comparatively minor problem. A more difficult consideration is the one illustrated by trends to be observed in the City of London. Despite the fact that the ancient city is entirely surrounded by a vast urban area, it has its own identity, status and administration. Today the great majority of those who work there do not live there. If we consider simply the economy of its residents we could not possibly say that we are looking at the economy of the City of London. If the depopulation con-

1

tinued the City could have no residents at all, but it would still have an economy centred on the businesses operating in and from it. Yet just as the economy of the citizens of a town cannot be called the economy of the town, no more can the collective economy of its businesses, for there may well be people living in the town but earning outside it, and a study of the town's businesses will pay incomplete attention to these. Similarly we need to take account of the economic characteristics of the ownership and occupation of property, and of the operation of services in the town. In short, the economy of the town is the economy of several different sets of people and firms often overlapping in their membership, and all with economies that interact with each other.

In this book we are going to keep constantly in mind this approach to urban economics – the approach that stresses the existence of different sets, and examines their interacting economies. Since the study of set economics does not seem to have been developed to the degree that this approach requires, we begin by presenting some of the basic ideas, for application in later chapters. We do so without attempting, at this stage, to focus on urban sets, since our purpose is to present certain definitions and analytical ideas. Their use in the study of towns will become apparent in the rest of the book.

After introducing some of these basic ideas in Chapter 2, we turn in Chapter 3 to an analysis of some problems of urban macro-economics. We consider certain relationships between the imports and exports of the residents of a town, and of those who work in it, the level of urban employment and investment, and other matters that can be usefully analysed in broad aggregates at the level of the individual town. It is an analysis that depends on some of the ideas introduced in Chapter 2.

These ideas are used even more in Chapter 4 where we begin to consider the economics of the town's governing body – the municipal authority. This involves an examination of sources of municipal revenue and the implications for various sets of people of different forms of local taxation.

Taken together, Chapters 3 and 4 set the principal economic and financial constraints within which urban activity must take place. The remaining important constraint is the spatial one, and it is this that must distinguish urban economics from a hotch-potch of housing economics, transport economics, and various other subjects of respectability in their own rights but capable of being bonded into the subject of urban economics only if developed in a way that takes full account of spatial relationships, which may have economic causes and consequences.

Every activity requires space. Human activity requires people and space. The ways in which people use space sometimes result in certain spaces being more or less permanently devoted to particular uses, such as housing and the activities associated with houses, offices and the employment and services they provide, recreation, and so on. In other cases certain spaces may experience a variety of uses at different times. Each occupation of space means that during the time that it is occupied in that way, either by a person or by some physical object or animal or vegetable it cannot be occupied by any other person or object, animate or otherwise. In a sense space is thus like any scarce commodity, and consequently its use has economic aspects. But one of the factors that makes it unlike scarce commodities, and of greater interest and difficulty for economists, is that every unit of space has unique relationships with every other unit of space. Some of these relationships may change over time. Moreover, while space may be used and is limited it is never used up. It may be adapted but never created; wasted but never destroyed.

Every human use of space has economic and social implications, as well as implications for the use of other spaces. To assess the importance of these implications we need to know the spatial requirements of various activities, not only in quantitative terms but also in terms of locations relevant to other spaces, used and unused. If we are to know these we must know something about the activities themselves.

Consequently, in Chapter 5, we turn to one of the principal land uses of towns – housing. This is not a chapter on housing economics but on selected economic problems of urban housing. In this chapter spatial matters are ignored. Our purpose is to present those matters that can be analysed in a non-spatial context and to provide a basic background that will facilitate the examination of housing as a land-user in later chapters, especially Chapters 8 and 10.

In Chapter 6 we present a similar non-spatial analysis of some economics of retailing and warehousing, again with the intention of helping to prepare for the spatial analysis of urban activities that comes later.

Although there are, of course, other users of urban land, they do not require the same kind of non-spatial treatment for reasons that will emerge in the text. There is, however, need to consider certain economic aspects of transport in this way, and this is done in Chapter 7.

Chapter 8 considers the locational requirements of urban activities. More precisely, it considers the determinants of the demands by different sets of people for the location of a specified activity in a specified place or kind of place. These demands are to a large extent dependent on economic factors, and in studying them we draw upon what we have learned in earlier chapters, and especially Chapters 5 and 6.

They are demands that conflict with each other, and we have to consider the resolution of this conflict. Before we can do so we have to consider certain aspects of the development processes. Demand for the occupation of a space for a certain purpose is likely to be important in the land-use conflict only if there is a realistic possibility of the land being put to that use. In some cases this will depend not so much upon the wishes of potential occupiers of that land as upon the ideas of those who are able to provide a certain kind of building (or other artefact) in that place.

Accordingly in Chapter 9 we discuss some of the factors, and especially the economic factors, that affect the decisions of property owners and developers. This includes some comment on the provision of public utilities.

In Chapter 10 we bring together our studies of locational requirements and development decisions in the context of land values, urban rents and other factors, as they operate in a free market with no public intervention.

Chapter 11 discusses reasons for public intervention in the land market and land-use decisions. It raises questions of inefficiencies and social costs, and discusses various ways of intervening. In particular, it looks at various forms of taxation.

Those who intervene in the use of land often use professional advice. In Chapter 12 we consider some of the techniques that are used by these professional advisers. In particular we look at cost-benefit analysis.

We then turn in Chapter 13 to the ways in which urban decisions are made. Here we develop a framework that helps us to explore the consequences, economic and otherwise, of various kinds of urban decisions. It also helps us to see how various sets may influence each other, sometimes through the exercise of economic or other power. In short, it enables us to place a study of urban economics into its context. Chapter 14 briefly summarizes some of the points that emerge from this wider look at the subject.

2

The economics of sets

Basic definitions

We have argued in Chapter 1 that the urban economy has to be viewed as a collection of economies – the economy of the residents, the economy of those who work in the town, and so on. This is a point that we develop in later chapters. Now we consider some fundamental economic propositions that will be true of all sets of people. Before we develop them we must discuss the meaning of 'set'.

In this book we shall often refer to 'sets' of people. It would perhaps be more in keeping with normal English usage if instead we referred to 'groups' of people or 'collections' of people. The word 'set' sometimes has social connotations that we intend to disregard. By it we mean any specified collection. The residents of a street will form a set. So will all those people who do not live in that street. An individual may belong to the set of residents of his street, to the larger set of residents of his town, to the set of all who work in the same place as him, to the set of all who have the same colour hair as he does, to the set of all who were born on the same day as him, and so on. These are ideas we consider more formally shortly, but before doing so we must explain our choice of the word 'set'.

It has been chosen mainly because it conforms with the use of that word in mathematics. Although we shall not do so, the ideas in this book can be developed and extended by the use of the mathematical theory of sets. If we had used the word 'group' we would have been using it in a way that mathematicians would have found unwelcome, because the mathematical theory of groups (as defined by mathematicians) is very different from that of sets. And what we would be calling a group would be what they call a set, rather than what they call a group. If the reader cares to think of a group of people (in the non-mathematical sense) when we refer to a set of people he

5

will make no mistakes: but to facilitate mathematical development we shall use the word 'set'.

We now turn more formally to definitions. We define a *set* in terms of people, firms and other legally recognized entities that are capable, in law, of owning goods, making payments, making decisions, and being held legally responsible for their actions. Any one person, firm or other such entity will constitute the simplest of all sets – the one-member set. A two-member set will consist of any two persons, firms or other entities who have some stated attribute in common. Two people living in the same street will constitute a two-person set. As there are other people living in the street, the attribute is not unique to them. The number of two-person sets capable of being defined from the n residents of the street will be $n(n - 1)/2$. A particular two-person set drawn from this collection of sets may be defined in terms also of other attributes, which appear in their entirety for only two persons, but it need not be. The two members could be distinguished simply by their names. Indeed, any two persons whose names are listed as being members of a set become, by that very process, a two-person set. We may also have a two-firm set, consisting of two firms having some stated attribute in common.

In these cases the two persons and the two firms are called members of the set. We should note that a two-member set may have a person as one of its members and a firm as the other. For example, there may be two land owners in a certain part of the country, one a person and the other a property company. Together they constitute the set of land owners.

We now extend the definition, in an obvious way, to a set of n members, where n may be any positive integer. The n members may be identified by listing them, or by stating some attribute, or collection of attributes, that they have in common.

There are certain relationships between sets or their members that occur so frequently that it is useful to define them precisely and to give them special names. A discussion of these is aided by the use of a diagram in which every person is represented by a point in a two-dimensional space, such as the dots and crosses in Figure 2.1.

Suppose that certain people represented by the dots in the parallelogram A belong to a set which we call set A. Some of them also lie within the circle B – and we call

them the members of set B. Others also belong to set shown
by the rectangle C.

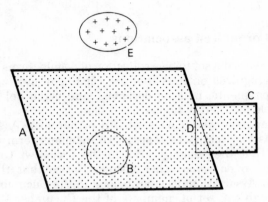

Figure 2.1

We say that A *contains* B, which is said to be a *sub-set*
of A because membership of B necessarily implies membership
of A.

Sets A and C have some members in common. These form
the *intersection* of A and C, and are shown by the triangular
area D.

The shape bounded by the heavy line contains all points
that are in A or C (or possibly in both A and C). This
defines the *union* of A and C.

No member of set E belongs to the set A, and so these
sets are said to be *distinct* (from each other).

Note that all the people represented by either a dot or
a cross belong to the *union* of A and C and E (as they
necessarily belong to at least one of A or C or E), even
though E is distinct from both A and C.

Finally we may note that any set that is divided into
two sub-sets in such a way that every member belongs to
one, and to only one, of them, is said to be divided into
complementary sub-sets; and one sub-set is the complement
of the other. The set of residents of a street is divided into
two sub-sets – those who have university degrees and those
who do not. Those with degrees complement those without
them and vice versa.

These definitions can be developed more rigorously through
the use of mathematics but we shall not do so. Since, however,
we shall need to refer to these words, and especially to

union and intersection, we need to be familiar with their meanings.

Sets and organized associations

We have defined a set to be a collection of people, firms or other legally recognized entities that are capable of owning goods, making payments, making decisions, and being held legally responsible for their actions.

Consider now the Cwmscwt Anti-Anarchist Association which has two members. These two members form a set. It happens that they belong, also, to the Cwmscwt Cucumber Club, but so do some other people. Notice that the Anti-Anarchist Association does not belong to the Cucumber Club, even though the set of members of the Cucumber Club contains the set of members of the Anti-Anarchist Association. The point is that there is a distinction between the Association and the set of all its members. The Anti-Anarchist Association is itself a legal entity and constitutes a one-member set. This is also true of the Cucumber Club. We can, if we wish, think of a three-member set defined to be the Association (as a legal entity) and its two members. This set would intersect with another set defined to be the Cucumber Club and all of its members.

This distinction will turn out to be an important one. For example, the interests of an association may at times differ from the interests of the set of its members. One case where this could be so is when all the members of an association that is pledged to the preservation of public footpaths finds that a 'forgotten' footpath runs through their own very private rose-gardens. This clash of interests can be important in the making of urban decisions.

Set decisions

A great deal of economic theory assumes that decisions are made rationally. Amongst other things this means that when alternatives are compared, then if A is preferred to B and B is preferred to C, A necessarily will be preferred to C. If this were not so the decision process would imply a contradiction. If I prefer coffee to tea and tea to beer and beer to coffee, how can I choose one drink if I am offered a choice from these three?

Whatever I choose, at least one of the others would be preferred by me.

This assumption of the transitivity of preferences (A preferred to B, and B preferred to C, imply A preferred to C) is basic to the derivation of indifference curves and other concepts of economic theory. In urban affairs most decisions are made by sets of people or firms, so we now consider some ways in which a set could make a decision about its preferences, in order to see whether we can assume rationality.

The simplest possibility is that every member of a set has exactly the same preferences about everything. In this case, every decision will be unanimous and if any one of its members is rational then all of its members will be, and the set will make rational decisions. But few such sets exist, other than one-member sets.

Another possibility is that the set adopts the rule that all decisions must be majority decisions. It is easy to see that this cannot be guaranteed to lead to consistent decisions, even when all members of the set are individually consistent. Consider, for example, a set of five members who rank three alternatives in the following way:

	A	B	C			
P	1st	2nd	3rd	A>B*	B>C	A>C
Q	3rd	1st	2nd	C>A	B>C	B>A
R	1st	3rd	2nd	A>C	C>B	A>B
S	2nd	3rd	1st	C>A	A>B	C>B
T	3rd	1st	2nd	B>C	C>A	B>A

Clearly A is preferred to B by P, R and S (which is 3 out of 5)

B is preferred to C by P, Q and T (which is 3 out of 5)

C is preferred to A by Q, S and T (which is 3 out of 5)

We thus have a majority preferring A to B. There is also a majority preferring B to C. These imply that, if the set decisions are consistent, then A is preferred to C, but in fact a majority has expressed preference for C over A. Thus, although all five individuals are consistent in their preferences, they will not enable the set to reach consistent decisions

* A > B is here to be read 'A is preferred to B'.

by majority vote. The transitivity of preferences does not necessarily apply to majority decisions, and so consistency of choice is not guaranteed.

To pursue this argument through the various alternatives would be tedious and logically not very satisfactory since it has been shown with elegance and rigour that there is no decision process (other than obedience to a dictator) that will guarantee the rationality of set decisions. For this reason we shall invoke economic theory that assumes rationality only when there is justification for doing so. In particular, indifference curves will not be used in the analysis of the behaviour of sets.

Another common assumption in economic analysis is that decisions are (or should be) made in a way that aims at optimization, and that this is achieved by using concepts of marginalism in a rational way. For example a producer who wishes to maximize his profit will employ labour (and other factors of production) up to the point where the marginal cost of labour is equal to the value of its marginal product* – in other words, if the employment of one more man adds more to the total value of output than it adds to the costs of labour then that man should be employed.

In most cases one can expect either the value of additional output to fall as the number of employees rises above a certain level, or the cost of obtaining more labour to rise, or both of these. Thus if the marginal output does not exceed the marginal cost at a specified level of employment it would be rational to increase the labour force, but one would have to be careful not to overdo it, as further additions to it would eventually add less and less to the excess of output over costs, and could eventually increase costs more than output. The point to stop is where this is just about to happen.

When we consider set decisions in this context three problems arise. One is that some members of the set may feel that the problem before them is not 'purely economic'. A second is that even those who do consider it to be an economic problem may view it differently, possibly even seeking to optimize different things. The third is that members may have different ideas about the costs and other values associated with the decision. All of this means that we could have a situation in which every person advocates a rational decision in light of his aims and the facts as he sees them, but that when the set

---

* The 'marginal' product is the additional product due to the ('marginal') addition of a small quantity of labour, provided at a (marginal) additional cost.

decision emerges it appears to many of the members of the set, and to a detached observer, to be wrong in the sense that it is not an 'optimal' solution.

This does not mean that it is wrong to explore urban decisions with concepts of optimality and marginalism in mind. But it does mean that we should not assume that decisions will (or should) always be reached in this way.

Possession and ownership

We are concerned with the economics of sets of people, firms or other entities and must consequently decide upon some of those properties of a set – rather than the properties of the members who constitute it – that enable us to discuss it in an economic context.

We shall say that a set 'possesses' everything that is owned by any of its members, but that these 'possessions' are completely at the disposal of the members who own them. This means that 'ownership' has its common meaning but 'possession' is given a special meaning that will become clear as we proceed but is contained in the definition just given.

Thus, for example, the set of all old-age pensioners in the famous Welsh village of Cwmscwt may 'possess' ninety cars, but whether this number grows or declines will depend upon decisions taken by individual pensioners, and no member of the set has, as a consequence of his membership of the set or this definition of its possessions, the right to use a car owned by another member. In short, 'the possessions of a set' is simply a convenient shorthand statement meaning 'the belongings of all individual members of a set'. Since a member of one set will also be a member of other sets, every item owned by him will be possessed by many sets.

The Anti-Anarchist Association, a legal body in its own right, forming a one-member set, owns a typewriter, to which no member has exclusive rights and which can be sold only by a resolution of the Association.

Mr Jones, its President, owns a bicycle, while Mr Evans, its only other member, owns a greenhouse. The two-member set of persons who form the Association possesses a bicycle, a greenhouse, and everything else belonging to Mr Jones or Mr Evans, including whatever legal claims they may have on the typewriter owned by the Association to which they belong. The Association itself owns the typewriter but it does not own or possess the bicycle. The three-member set consisting of the

Association and its two members possesses the typewriter and the bicycle but owns nothing – because it is not an entity legally capable of owning. A set possesses all that is owned by its members, but owns only that of which it is the legal owner. This can be the case only if the set is itself a legally recognized entity.

Imports and exports

If Mr Jones, President of Cwmscwt Anti-Anarchist Association, sells his bicycle to Mr Evans, its other member, there are two changes in possession. The set consisting of Mr Jones has depleted its possessions by a bicycle, while the set consisting of Mr Evans has added to its possessions. The set consisting of Mr Jones and Mr Evans has experienced no change in its possessions.

If, on the other hand, Mr Jones sells the bicycle to his wife, who is not a member of the Association, the set consisting of the members of the Association has reduced its possessions. The Association, as a one-member set, has experienced no change in its possessions, for it still possesses only its typewriter.

When a member of a set sells something owned by him to a non-member, both he and the set of which he is a member will be said to export that item. More precisely, if an item owned by X passes to Y then all sets of which X is a member but Y is not a member export that item to all sets of which Y is a member but X is not a member. Sets of which a member receives an item from a non-member are said to import that item. The imports and exports are owned by members and form part of the possessions of the sets. We should note that in the sense that we are using these words, imports and exports are related to physical boundaries only in so far as these may help to define a set.

While a set may export, or import, goods it may also export and import services. It exports services when any of its members work for one or more non-members, be these non-members their employers, clients or customers. Similarly, if any set member employs the services of a non-member those services are imported by the set. An important service in this respect is that of shelter or accommodation, which the tenant buys from the landlord. If the tenant is a member of the set and the landlord is not then the set imports this service.

Members of the set engage in various transactions amongst themselves. These do not at present concern us for they involve neither imports nor exports. What do concern us are those transactions with non-members, and normally these involve not only flows of goods or services but also flows of money. When the set exports it receives payment from outside the set. More precisely, the member who exports receives payment and so adds to his stock of money. But everything that he owns, including his money, is possessed by the sets to which he belongs. Consequently all the sets of which the exporter is a member and the importer is a non-member increase the money in their possession by the amount that the exporting member receives. Similarly, all of the importing sets, being the sets of which the importer is a member but the exporter is not a member, suffer a reduction in their monetary possessions.

We should note that people who are members of many sets help to determine the imports, exports, payments and receipts of all those sets.

Few sets are able to mint money of a kind that is acceptable both to members and to non-members. This means that a set that regularly imports more than it exports experiences a continuous reduction in its stock of money.

Unless it is able to augment this stock by increasing its exports or receiving gifts it will have to reduce its imports. This is a point that we must examine further.

It means, first, that all one-person sets must export at least as much as they import, or receive gifts. We have defined 'exports' and 'imports' as sales and purchases. Gifts have identical effects on ownership and possession of items but differ from exports and imports in that they have no associated flow of money, unless, of course, it is a gift of money. When we say that a one-person set must export at least as much as it imports or receive a gift we imply that some other set may be able to donate that gift. This implies a reduction in the possessions of that set without a compensating payment, or a reduction in its money stock.

Every time that anybody (considered as a one-person set) buys anything he imports, and in most cases the export that provides the money for the purchase of the import is the service of labour. The statement that a one-person set must export at least as much as it imports means quite simply that the person's income must be high enough to pay for his purchases. There is nothing, however, to prevent him from saving, or from always importing (or purchasing) less than he exports (or receives in income). Thus, at least for a one-person set, there is no need for a set to balance its imports and exports. Many one-person sets, such as children and other dependants, and those in receipt of assistance or presents, may import more than they export.

When we consider larger sets the detail is a little different. If a set imports more than it exports then it means that the total of imports by its members from non-members exceeds the total of exports by members to non-members. Transactions between members do not matter in this context. If every member importing from non-members exported at least as much then the total imports could not exceed the exports. It follows that if a set has net imports – i.e., imports exceeding exports – then at least one member must be importing from outside the set more than he is exporting to outside the set.

There may be several such members, forming the sub-set of net importers from the outside world. It is easy to see that either this sub-set has a net surplus of imports with everybody else taken together – (i.e., its total imports from the outside world and from the complementary sub-set of those who are not net importers exceed its total exports) or the complementary sub-set imports more from this sub-set than it exports to it. More specifically, if the residents of Cwmscwt import more than they export, and those of Upper Cwmscwt have a net surplus of imports with the outside world, then either Upper Cwmscwt residents have an overall net surplus of imports or they export more to the residents of Lower Cwmscwt than they import from them.

To take a non-geographical illustration, if trade unionists as a set import more from non-trade unionists than they export, then this must be true of at least one trade unionist. Let him and all like him be called The Lucky Ones. Then either The Lucky Ones have total imports from all sources exceeding total exports, or they export more to those remaining trade unionists called The Unlucky Ones than they import from them. A similar result holds for surplus exports.

Power

Before leaving this subject of imports and exports of a set we must introduce a concept that has had little attention in economics. If a set has a long-standing surplus of imports over exports and sustains it by running up debts or receiving gifts it is obviously becoming to some extent indebted to, or dependent upon, the creditors or donors. Even if the creditors or donors have assumed that role unwittingly, or with only altruistic motives, the set of creditors or donors will have acquired some influence or power over the recipient of its largesse. Perhaps the debtor set will feel grateful, or fearful that credit or aid will be withdrawn, or hopeful that more will come. In some cases, too, the aid may be provided partly with the intention of creating one of these feelings, and perhaps of adding substance to them. The creditors are acquiring power over the debtors, and the greater the accumulated imbalance between imports and exports becomes the greater this power is likely to be. Whether this power is used, and whether its use tends to use it up, are mattters that have to be considered in more specific cases. In some urban contexts it becomes very important, as we shall see in later chapters.

The set multiplier

Now we consider a different but related aspect of set economics – the multiplier. It has been widely considered in a spatial context, and there are good reasons for this, but here the emphasis will be on the sets involved.

Suppose that there is a set of people X, with some members being out of work but wishing to work, while other members of X are working and producing goods and services.

Let us also suppose that for some reason or the other, there is an increase in the demand for the output of X. It may be possible to meet this rise in demand in a way that causes no rise in employment, as when goods are sold out of existing stocks, but if the rise in demand is sustained then sooner or later some of X's unemployed may become employed. In return for their efforts, the newly employed workers of X receive some pay, directly or indirectly from other members or elsewhere. In normal circumstances this will lead to increased expenditure by members of X. If they direct some of this to buying goods and services made by other members of the same set X, then this will constitute a further increase in demand for X's product, with the same result as before (provided that it is still possible). The larger the fraction of the increased expenditure by members of X that is spent on X products, the greater will be the number of unemployed now put to work. This second increment of new workers will, in turn, demand products that can be supplied only if there is a third increment, and so on.

Eventually, however, this process will either cease or become insignificant. If all of the unemployed are found work – in this or some other way – then obviously the process must cease. On the other hand, unless every new increment of employed members of X spends all of its money in a way that causes an equal increment of unemployed to join them (which would mean not only spending all of it on the products of X but also ensuring that any profits or other sums not paid out in wages would, with equal speed, be spent on X products) then successive increments of newly employed persons will decline. It is easy to show that eventually the increments become trivial. In fact, if a fraction a of increment of X's income arising in the creation of one increment of employment is spent on the products of X, the successive increments of income arising in this way will eventually be β times as large as the original increase in spending on X's products where

$$\beta = \frac{1}{1-a}.$$

This means that, provided there is sufficient unemployment amongst members of X, a sudden sustained increase in demand for their product amounting to, say, £1000 per day, will eventually lead to an increase in demand of £10,000 if 90 per cent of the new spending remains within the set, but to an increase of only £2000 if only half of it remains within the set. We call

$$\frac{1}{1-a}$$

the set multiplier, and a the marginal propensity to spend on products of the set.

If the set X is small, or highly specialist in its output, it is quite likely that none of the newly created income (arising out of newly created employment) will be spent on products of the set, and in that case the employment level in X will have no further increments. The importance to any set of an increase in the demand for its product depends, when there is unemployment within the set, on the extent to which the set imports or saves. If it imports and saves little, but spends considerably within itself the increase will be multiplied many times. In urban economics we will often have to consider how much money received by a set subsequently circulates between its members, giving a high multiplier effect.

Preserving the usual terminology of economics, we will say that when the members of the set spend some of their money purchasing imports from non-members there is an income-leakage. This may also arise in other ways. A high leakage will mean a low multiplier.

In this chapter we have considered certain aspects of the economies of sets of people (or other legal entities). In particular we have noted that it is unwise to assume that decisions taken by sets are consistent, or even compatible with concepts of optimality. But there has to be regard for some kind of balance between imports and exports, and the set multiplier can be important. All of these ideas will be more readily appreciated when applied in an urban context. We begin to do this in the next chapter.

3

Some urban macro-economics

In introducing the economy of sets we concentrated on the balance of payments and on the multiplier effect. We now turn to a fuller examination of certain sets of people who are of particular interest to us – especially the set R of residents of a town, and the set W of people who work in the town. The two sets are obviously different. Some residents will be at work only outside the town, and some will be non-workers. Membership of R does not therefore imply membership of W. Similarly, some of those who work in the town will live outside it, so that membership of W does not imply membership of R.

While we denote the set of residents by R, we will denote the complementary set of non-residents by R. Some of these non-residents have the right to derive income from land or buildings within the town. We can call them non-resident landlords. If we use L to denote the set of people who between them own all of the land and buildings in the town, we can denote the locally resident of these landlords by RL and the non-resident landlords by RL. We shall not make much use of this extension of the notation, but the reader may care to employ it himself when considering some of the arguments that follow.

Another set consists of non-residents who are employers in the town. They may be direct employers, or they may be shareholders in a firm that employs locally. In either case, like non-resident landlords, they do not (as members of that set) work in the town, and by definition they do not live in the town, but they are entitled to receive income that is generated within the town. We can denote this set of non-resident employers by RE, and use RE to denote resident employers.

We now consider some of the macro-economic relationships that affect these sets. They will all be subject to what we have already said about the balance of payments and multipliers.

18

Goods, services and balance of payments

It is usual to divide production into the production of goods and the production of services. There are occasions when it is difficult to distinguish between them, but in general the distinction is clear. Somebody who makes, or in any way alters or transforms some material is producing goods, but the teacher, bus driver, architect, doctor, and office worker are all performing services. So is the hairdresser, despite his working upon material that he alters, and so is the shoe-black. In urban economics one of the big differences between goods and services is that the former are more easily, and more obviously, capable of being imported and exported: but this is a difference that can be too easily exaggerated. Before we go further we must consider some of the ways in which services may be exported. We shall do so by thinking of the set R of residents.

First we must note that, by definition, the set receiving the exports of R must be identical with or be contained by the set of non-residents R. Any service performed by any member of R for any member of R is exported.

There are four ways in which R may export services to R. If a member of R buys from a shopkeeper who is a member of R, then the shopkeeper exports to his customer the service of obtaining, stocking and selling the good that is bought. Similarly, if a member of R visits a hairdresser or lawyer who is resident, there is an export of services. The second way of exporting services is to do so via the post or the telephone, as may accountants, stockbrokers and so on. A third way is for members of R to travel to places outside the town, and to perform services for members of R. An example is the teacher or office worker who travels to work in a neighbouring town. The fourth way is when a member of R allows a member of R to use something that he possesses in return for payment. For example, the landlords RL, living in the town and owners of property in it, and the landlords RL, who also live in the town but own property outside it, will both be exporting if they have members of R as tenants.

We will now consider a few points about how residents R and workers W may balance their payments, taking first the set R.

It is unlikely that R will import no goods. Indeed, this could happen only if the town's residents grew all of their own food, used no fuel, metal or other material not produced by themselves, and so on. It would mean a primitive existence even for the residents of a country, while for a town it would lead to a degree of restriction that probably exists nowhere. On the other hand, the set R could enjoy a fairly high standard of living without importing any services. Its doctors, lawyers, teachers and shopkeepers could all belong to it. Of course, if the residents were in a country that had an army then, even if they never met, the residents would still be benefiting from the existence of the army, and would also probably be contributing towards its cost through taxes. In any realistic account of urban life we have to suppose that both goods and services are imported by R, although the import of services may be very low.

In order to pay for these imports, R has to export, but there is no compulsion to export goods. It could pay for its imports simply by exporting services, in any of the ways we have already described. A plausible instance would be the residents of a town built around a major airport, where all of the exports would be services performed for the airline companies, the users of the airport and other visitors. Another would be the dormitory town, with no manufacturing activity, whose residents travelled to work in neighbouring towns, where their employers would be non-residents. Yet another is simply when, wherever the residents' place of work may be, in the town or outside it, the employers are all non-resident.

Equally, there is no compulsion upon R to pay for its imports by exporting services. Indeed, one can envisage a set of residents who produce no services even for trading amongst themselves. All that matters as far as the balance of payments is concerned is that exports of some kind pay for imports.

The other set to which we will often refer is the set W of those who work in the town. This is a set that could not conceivably fail to produce some services, for that would mean that no services would be provided in the town. There could be no shops, banks, schools, postal services or police. On the other hand, like R, the set W could concentrate exclusively on the production of services, and depend on the export of some of them to pay for its imports of goods.

It follows that the composite set, consisting of those who live in the town (R) augmented by the non-residents who work in it (*R*W), (which is another way of describing the union of the two sets R and W), could produce no goods yet exist through exporting services; but it would necessarily produce services, even though it could have a balance of payments deficit in this sector.

Base/non-base theory

A common approach to urban or regional economics is to divide employment into 'base' and 'non-base'. The former produces for export, thus providing the 'export base' for the economy. The latter produces for home consumption. It is a useful concept, but consideration of the arguments we have just presented will show us some of the dangers of the casual application of base/non-base theory, especially in quantitative work. It may be possible to describe some industries as 'export-orientated' and others as 'providing for the town's needs' but there will be very few that come entirely into one of these categories even if the set of people whose imports and exports are being considered has been defined – and often it has not. A factory or office may employ both residents and non-residents. If we define our set to be R then we have to determine how much of the output of the factory is due to its resident employees, rather than its non-resident employees, and how much of it is purchased by residents. If we extend the set to include all workers in the town we still have to consider the residents who work outside the town. These are matters that present problems that are soluble but tedious. Moreover, there are likely to be errors in the solutions, and these errors can become of importance when they enter into ratios, turning

$$\frac{x}{y}$$

into

$$\frac{(x \pm a)}{(y \pm b)}.$$

Another source of possible error is the ease with which the import or export of services can be underestimated.

Yet another, to which this is closely related, arises out of the places of residence of employers, especially when the legal employer is a de-personified firm that has shareholders living both in and out of the town. If a firm is owned entirely by residents then transactions between its owners and its resident employees do not affect the balance of payments of the resident set. But if some of the profit is distributed to non-residents then there is a balance-of-payments effect. This can be of importance even in a town that produces only services. Where do the shopkeepers, or people with shares in retail firms, live? And what are the profits ascribable to the shops?

Despite these problems of precise definition and measurement, there is still much merit in the concept of the economic base. Given that every set of people will need to import some of the goods and materials that it uses, and possibly some services, it follows that a set that produces very little that is exportable cannot afford to import much. At the other extreme, a set producing highly exportable items will find it easier to pay for its imports. On the other hand, if it exports much it may need to import much, either in the form of materials used in its exported manufactures or in order to provide itself with substitutes for what it exports. The import content of exports, the 'home' demand for the exported goods, and various propensities to consume, all come into the equation.

The set that produces little that is exportable needs further attention. Let us imagine a town whose residents make goods and perform services that are bought almost entirely by other residents. It can import only to the very limited extent that can be paid for with its meagre exports. But this is probably not the result of a collective decision. The town's residents are individuals, and unless there is a law prohibiting the import of goods in excess of a certain quantity they will make their individual decisions about what to purchase. Whether the good is made locally or not will be of little concern if an individual wants it, especially if he has no substitute to choose in its place. The consequences of spending on imported goods in this way are easily analysed. The individual spenders have less money left with which to purchase the output of their fellow residents. This means that either the price of that output has to fall (which will lead to lower wages for those who provide it) or the volume of output will fall with consequent reductions in employment or wages. At the same time, local employers will be making less profit, because they will have reduced activity. The reduced employment or wages will lead to a further decline in spending, with a second round of reductions in employment, wages and profits. This is a process that cannot continue indefinitely, simply because other decisions will intervene. The employer whose profits are declining will, perhaps, decide to try to sell to non-residents, thereby increasing exports. Alternatively, he may go out of business, increasing the number of unemployed. Some of those who are unemployed (for this or some other reason) may decide to emigrate from the town or to seek work outside it for non-residents, thereby exporting their labour. Another possibility is that a non-resident, seeing the extent of resident unemployment or the lowness of wage rates, will open a factory in the town.

These or some other reactions may reduce the demand for imports, or raise the achievement of exports, sufficiently to restore the balance of payments. If they do not then the decline in resident employment and incomes will continue until one of the processes we have just described restores stability, or charity is received, or the residents either emigrate or accept a lower standard of living.

When we consider such matters as economies of scale and the division of labour it seems reasonable to suggest that while the residents of no town will be able to produce all of their wants, the residents of a large town are probably able to satisfy a greater fraction of their needs than are the residents of a small town. (A source of possible error in this assumption is that in a large town there may be greater difficulty in providing fresh food from the residents' own resources, but this seems likely to cease to be significant after a certain size has been reached, while in the approach to this size there could be sufficient factors operating in favour of the assumption for it still to be valid.)

If this is so, it suggests that the residents of small towns are more likely than those of large ones to need to have high per capita imports, if they are to enjoy the same variety of choice, and consequently to have high per-capita exports if they are to afford this standard of living. Yet because of their comparative smallness their diversity of product, and even their scale of manufacture, will tend to make exports less varied and possibly more expensive (unless wages or rents are low, which they may well be). In short, the smaller town may need to have higher per-capita exports but have difficulty in providing them. There are, of course, many factors other than size to be considered. But the argument just summarized could well explain why the residents of some small towns have a comparatively low standard of living.

We must also note that the residents of a remote town will have difficulty in exporting services unless, for example, many of them work in offices with clients in more distant places. In general, the residents of the town will need to produce exportable merchandise, or have amongst them people with pensions, dividends, or other incomes that arise from outside the set of residents, or to receive some form of subsidy.

Stability of employment

A question of some importance concerns the extent to which the employment offered to residents of a town is stable. May jobs suddenly appear, or disappear, because of events elsewhere? Does a rise in the national unemployment rate probably mean an even greater rise in the local rate? These two questions are a little different from each other and need to be considered separately. The first point to note is that if the residents of a town export largely to a single set of people, be they the residents of another town, the deaf, or any other set of people who may more or less simultaneously be influenced in the same way, then those residents are vulnerable. If the importing residents of the other town experience a fall in income then they will buy less. If a new deaf-aid vastly superior to existing ones suddenly appears, the residents who make the existing ones for export will soon be out of work. If there is great dependence on exports to one country then war or international balance-of-payment factors may intervene. Any specialization in market or in product makes the set of residents highly vulnerable to particular fluctuations in demand. The way to avoid them is to export a wide range of items to a wide spread of places. The other question concerns the relationship between local and national levels of unemployment. The national level of unemployment may be high if either the foreign or the home demand for the nation's product declines without a compensating increase in the other sector; or if the labour force grows faster than demand; or if technological change causes labour redundancy. There may be other reasons, but these are probably the principal ones. Whatever the reason may be, high unemployment will tend to breed itself once it has appeared, as the purchasing power of the unemployed falls and so home demand declines. If the residents of the town that we are considering have products that are sensitive to these income-induced demands then they are likely to feel the national decline in purchasing power. If, on the other hand, they produce and export mainly items for which demand declines very little in times of national unemployment, or in response to falls in income, the residents of the town will be cushioned against the national decline. This may also be true if home demand forms only a small part of their market.

Towns whose residents produce luxury goods of a kind whose demand depends substantially on income levels may be less fortunate, but the story is more complicated. If national unemployment rises there may still be people of a certain kind who are comparatively unaffected – and it is possible that these are the people who buy the luxuries that are made by the residents. The other important point is that if the residents are employed largely in factories that are owned by firms who make the same products in other places, and especially if the parent factories are in some of these other places, a trade recession may result in decisions to close branch factories, and so lead to particularly high unemployment in towns dependent on the branches.

The prescription for stability of employment therefore has several ingredients. The goods and services exported by the residents should be as diverse as possible and directed to a wide range of markets. They should, as far as possible, be necessities rather than luxuries, but if they are luxuries they should be of a kind whose demand is unlikely to be affected by recessions. If possible the parent factory or office should be in the town. Another desirable feature, not so far mentioned, but highly important, is that the employment structure should be highly adaptable, so that if the demand for one product falls the men and machinery may be used to produce something else. All of this is more easily said than done.

Wages

Another aspect of employment is the income that it brings to those engaged in it, mainly as wages but also as profits, for employment needs to be looked upon not only as an activity of the employee but also as an activity for the employer. We look first at wages.

The wages paid to an employee in a specified job in a given town will be determined by many factors, especially in the more organized societies. In some countries the wage rates paid may be determined by purely local demand-and-supply considerations. Within a town all the employers who require a particular skill or type of employee will be competing with each other to acquire as cheaply as possible sufficient employees of that kind. If the demand for a skill is low compared with its supply it will not command a high wage – but a lower limit may be set by comparison with wages being paid to other workers or rewards to or some other factors. If many people of that skill are unemployed then some of them will look elsewhere for work, and possibly for residence. Some of them may seek jobs not related to their skills. And in some cases the availability of surplus and cheap labour of that type will attract new employers.

If, on the other hand, a skill is in short supply locally then wages will tend to rise. At the same time people from other towns will tend either to commute daily into the town or to migrate into it, provided that they benefit by doing so. There will also be a tendency to migrate into that skill. Either form of migration will raise supply and tend to reduce the wage differential.

Despite all of this, if labour of a certain kind is sufficiently available in a town only at a price that exceeds that at which it is available elsewhere, there will be a tendency for prospective employers to choose different locations and for existing ones to move. If the product of this skill is for sale in a local market substantial inter-town differences in wage rates may exist. In each town the wage will be determined mainly by the local supply of that skill and the local demand for its product. Wage rate differences may also exist if the skill has to be related to other local factors, such as the existence of coal seams or oil or the demand for new houses. But if the product is for general availability the demand for that skill in a town where its price is high will tend to be low. Since merchandise is more easily exported than services, there will thus be a tendency in unorganized societies for inter-town differences in wage rates to be more apparent in services, and construction, than in manufacturing industries, providing that one is comparing jobs of the same kind.

As society becomes more organized the effects of trade unions and national legislation become more apparent, and there is a greater tendency for wages for a specified job, or for a man of a specified skill, to have regional or national minima enforceable by law or by trade-union sanctions. These will sometimes be determined more by the bargaining strength of a trade union at national level than by consideration of local labour markets. In these cases the ability of a union to withdraw the labour of some of its members who are in key posts, or working in one area, may lead to a wage rise for all of its members. Effectively, unionization alters both the position and the slope of the supply curve for labour of that kind.

When a wage rate has a legally or industrially enforceable minimum it may mean that certain kinds of labour cannot be profitably engaged in certain towns, because for those particular kinds of job the other operating costs, or the selling price of the product do not then enable an acceptable profit to be made. This is a possibility that deserves a fuller examination.

Suppose, for example, that pine furniture is made in various towns in a country where pine wood is not grown. The timber is imported into the country at various ports, and by the time that it reaches the widely dispersed furniture factories the carriage charges will mean that these factories have raw-material costs that vary from place to place. We will suppose that all factories operate equally efficiently, and that the labour has a standard wage rate all over the country. This means that the cost of making pine furniture will be higher in some places than in others. In towns remote from the ports the manufacturers of furniture will have to accept lower profits, or to charge higher prices, than would be the case if they produced on the same scale elsewhere.

Local demand curves will also vary, because of differences in tastes, incomes and other factors. Moreover, they will change over time in different ways in different towns. There are regional and local fashions and changes of fashion, as well as regional and local changes of prosperity. Consequently the price that equates supply of locally produced furniture to the demand for it will vary from place to place.

If there is now a national decision to raise the wages of furniture workers then every manufacturer will have increased costs, which will tend to result in higher prices being charged to the public. Unless there are simultaneous and adequate increases in the incomes of the purchasers this is likely to cause some fall in demand. In some towns this will be more severe than in others, and if these happen to be towns where the manufacturers' costs are high the continued local manufacture of pine furniture may cease to be profitable.

The furniture manufacturers may react by using different techniques, replacing men by machines, but in some cases they may decide to close down, because they are no longer making enough profit and are unable or unwilling to involve more capital. In that case the furniture makers lose their jobs. If no other suitable jobs are available for them locally they may offer to continue to produce furniture for their old wage rates, but it may be illegal for the employer to accept the offer. The enforceable minimum wage rate will have led to unemployment in that trade or industry in that town. Possibly some of the skilled workers will then emigrate to another town where there is a demand for them, thereby increasing the supply of labour there and so reducing the wage rate that a fictitious free labour market would produce. It would also help to concentrate the labour force, and the industry, with economic and industrial consequences whose further consideration would take us too far from our theme. The point for us to notice is that enforceable minima may result in income being increased but can also result in local unemployment. On the other hand, in some towns the enforceable minima are quite unimportant simply because market conditions compel employers to offer wage rates that are well above them.

Profits and industrial investment

We must now look at profits. These may be defined as the money left in the bank account of the firm after payment of wages, suppliers' bills, interest on loans, local taxes and all other expenses. Usually such profits are subject to national taxation, leaving some 'net profit after tax'. Anything that tends to increase the revenue of the firm more than its costs will tend to push up the profits. If, on the other hand, higher wages or local taxes (for example) increase costs more than revenue increases, profits fall.

From the viewpoint of the urban economist, there are three interesting ways in which the profit may be used. One, which we have already mentioned, is in payment of national taxes, which transfers money to the central government where it no longer has a specific association with the town. The second fate of profit is that it may be distributed amongst the shareholders. Unless all of these live locally, this too will transfer money to non-residents, and even to people who have no other association with the town than a share in the ownership of a factory that happens to be there.

The third possibility is that the profits are retained by the firm, either to act as a buffer against possible subsequent losses, or in order to facilitate some investment in buildings or machinery. If the firm's activities are not restricted to one factory then, of course, profits made in one factory may lead to investment in another, and once again there may be no benefit to the residents of the town. But another possibility is that the profits made in the factory are used to enlarge, modernize, or re-equip it. This may be done in a way that causes more labour to be used, or it may lead to a decline in the demand for labour. Whichever it may be, the use of profits in order to finance local industrial investment is likely to have local consequences.

Yet investment need not be financed out of profits made by the firm concerned. The industrialist may borrow money. If he is considering this he will be influenced by the cost of the investment and the financial return that it brings him. He will always need to consider the rate of interest that he has to pay for any money he borrows, or could get by lending his cash instead of using it to finance his own investment. Only if his expected addition to annual profit exceeds the interest charge on the cost of the investment does it make sense to carry it out. He will normally tend either not to invest (because it does not make sense to do so or because he cannot borrow money in any case) or to invest in that way that seems to him to be the most profitable. Even then he will have to keep in mind that capital is but one of the factors of production, and that it may be more profitable to employ more labour, in association with the existing stock of capital, than more capital with the existing volume of labour. It depends on the marginal additions to his profit that can be attributed to marginal additions to his capital and labour costs. This last point means that if wage rates rise there will be a tendency for industrialists to invest in less labour-intensive techniques, replacing men by machines. Similarly, if prices of machinery rise or the rate of interest rises, there will be a tendency to use more labour rather than to use more machines, or to replace those that wear out.

All of these are questions to be asked by the industrialist who already has a factory somewhere. The loans are likely to come from a widely spread set of people, and may provide employment in two ways. There will be some addition to employment, not necessarily in the town, at the time of the investment. Building a new factory will certainly mean that some people are employed locally, but buying a new machine may not. The other way of providing employment is in the productive process for which the investment has been undertaken. We have already seen that the investment may need extra labour if it is to be used, but may instead reduce the demand for the labour. In either case, the industrialist has to pay back the loan, largely to non-residents.

From the standpoint of the urban economist, a more interesting question is the one that results in a location decision.

Where does new investment take place? Here we have to remember that although there is a great deal of literature dealing with where different kinds of industry have located, and where it should locate if certain objectives are to be achieved, there is much less that is devoted to the question at the level of aggregation that is also the level of decision making. It is firms, and individuals, rather than industries, that make the decisions.

Those firms and individuals already in the town that have made a decision to invest will be predisposed towards investing locally, even though they may decide to invest somewhere else instead. The quality of locally available labour, its rates of pay, the costs of obtaining raw materials in an adequately regular way, accessibility to markets, land prices and site availability, local taxation levels, the availability of houses for immigrant managers and other workers, and the existence of schools, sports facilities, shops and other amenities for them, all play a part in the decision. Money spent in providing these amenities may have an important economic impact on the town simply through the quantity and quality of industrial investment that it attracts.

Investment, loans and interest

It has been convenient to consider private industrial invest-ment at the same time as we have considered profits. Before we turn to the other forms of investment, both private and public, we should consider the way in which different investments compete with each other for their finance.

Money that is invested in machinery or buildings employs resources that, at that time, are producing nothing that satisfies current consumer needs. At the same time, the money that is spent in employing these resources cannot be used to buy goods and services. Investment is undertaken in the hope of future productions of goods and services at the expense of not having resources now to produce, and money now to buy, goods and services to satisfy current requirements or fancies.

In a closed economy, such as that of a country with no foreign trade, or a primitive town with none, then the resour-ces involved in investment must come from unemployed re-sources or resources that would otherwise be satisfying current consumer needs. Payment would have to come out of current or accumulated savings or taxes, unless new money can be created (which would lead to inflation). In urban or regional affairs this equating of investment with savings, (including some taxes, which are forced savings but may not be devoted to investment) which forms an important part of national and international macro-economics, ceases to be necessary as long as there is a well organized capital market. For example, the residents of a town could borrow money from non-residents, and employ non-residents to build roads for them, without having any accumulated savings and without making any current savings. But they and their successors would need to reduce their future spending in order to repay the loan, probably with interest on it. On the other hand, if there is not a well organized capital market the residents may be able to invest only out of their own accumulated and current savings.

The matter of interest is important. Basically interest is the payment made to the lender by the borrower, for the use of the lender's money. If the total demand for loans at any one time exceeds the amount that people are willing to lend, then the borrowers compete with each other by offering higher rates of interest. Some borrowers then drop out, or reduce their demands, while the prospect of a higher interest rate persuades other people to make more loans available. Eventually a single interest rate is reached at which the demand for loans equals the supply.

But it is not quite as simple as that. Lenders recognize that a borrower may default. Consequently they expect 'bad-risk' borrowers to pay higher rates of interest than 'good-risk' borrowers, and so there will be a spectrum of interest rates around the 'single interest rate' just mentioned. Furthermore, they will consider whether the money they lend is likely to be losing value during the period of the loan. If it is, then they will seek more compensation for this expected loss by seeking a higher interest rate.

A detailed discussion of these matters is beyond the scope of this book, but one point implicit in what has just been said must be emphasized. Every demand for a loan competes with other demands. It increases the total demand for loans and so tends to push up interest rates in a way that will squeeze out some of the demands. This is true even when the 'loan' takes the form of the sale of a share in a business. If an industrialist persuades some people to give him £1000 each in return for a share in the control of his business and in its future profits he is attracting money that might well otherwise have been available to borrowers. Even investment financed out of accumulated profits uses money that would otherwise be on loan to a bank (and earning interest); and the bank would take account of this in lending to others. Every investment competes with every other for its finance, just as it also competes for physical resources.

Public investment

There are different forms of public investment. One is public investment in such things as hospitals or certain kinds of roads at the expense of the national taxpayer through a decision by the national government or some organization that acts for it. Another is locally financed public investment, which we divide into two kinds. One is housing and to some extent shops and offices, provided by a locally taken public decision, and intended to earn revenue through rents; the other category of local authority investment expenditure provides services but has to be financed out of local taxes except for comparatively small revenues or contributions from other sources.

We turn first to nationally financed public investment. The whole cost may be paid directly out of current national taxation, of which the local residents will pay a part, but it is more likely to be financed by government borrowing. In this case the immediately needed money will come out of savings by somebody somewhere, while the cost of repayment with interest over several years will be borne by future national taxpayers. The investment will generate a demand for both local and non-local labour during its period of formation, and if the local labourers would otherwise have been not fully employed, and spend largely within the set R, it will have a multiplier effect. After the completion of the investment there may still be demands for labour. (A hospital will need nurses and cleaners.) These, too, could have their multiplier effects, and this is an important point when such matters as the 'rationalization' of government-financed services is being discussed. While there may be many advantages in the closure of small hospitals or schools, the local employment effect, and its possible multiplier-type consequences, should enter into the decision making. Often, however, the terms of reference of the decision-maker prevent him from allowing this.

The principal difference between this type of investment and locally financed public investment is that in the latter the burden of repayment is carried by local taxes. As we will see in Chapter 4, much of this may be shunted onto national taxes, or in some other way lifted from the shoulders of the residents:

but some of it will remain. The decision made by the municipal
council is essentially one that produces an investment from
which services will flow to future residents (and perhaps
others) and be paid for in part by future residents (and other
payers of local taxes) and in part by the national taxpayer.
Whether the future payers include all, many, few or none of
the future beneficiaries, and vice versa, depends on the detail
of the investment, its operation, the tax structure and other
matters.

The exact implications of some of these municipal investment decisions are not always appreciated. One aspect of them
is illustrated in Figure 3.1. The decision will be made by a set
D, normally contained within, and in some way responsible to,
a larger set E, which may be the electorate, or the residents, or
some other large set identified with the town. Not all of the
members of E, or of D, will, in fact, be contributing to the cost
of the investment, partly because their age, income or other
circumstances will exclude them from the list of taxpayers,
and partly because some of them may die before payments
begin. Those who pay belong to the set P, which includes
people who pay as national taxpayers, or only indirect payers
of local taxes, and those who will be paying in the future but do
not at present belong to E. Those who benefit, shown by B, may
include some members of all the sets mentioned by us, but also
some who are affected only in that they will derive benefits,
especially if the life of the investment greatly exceeds the
period of payment. In a democracy, operating in the name of E,
the members of D require members of P to provide benefits for
B. In most cases E and B will contain only residents, while
some of P will be non-residents. If members of D wish to
emphasize their concern for residents they will try to include
as many non-residents as possible in the set P. One way of
achieving this is to attract shops and industry (especially the
latter) that cause some of the local taxes to be paid by
customers and others (including business owners) who are
non-resident. This is a matter considered further in Chapter 4.

The fact that so much municipal investment may be paid for
with borrowed money that has to be repaid later becomes
especially important in times of high interest rates, especially
if the municipality has borrowed at a variable rate, when its
repayment charges increase in a way that is outside its control.
This is a possibility too often disregarded in cost-benefit
analysis. In practical everyday terms it can mean that the
present wishes of the set of electors E may be incapable of

being given expression because of the repayments they have to make, with unexpectedly high interest charges, of loans borrowed by their predecessors.

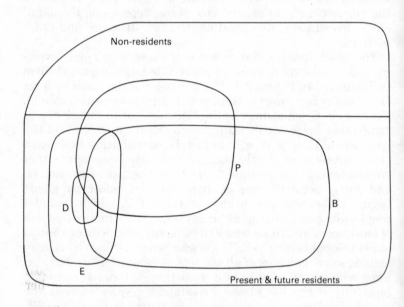

Figure 3.1

The one kind of municipal investment to which this argument may not apply is the kind that earns revenue. Frequently, the most notable example is municipal housing, for which the rent may be raised if interest charges increase. We discuss this further in the chapter on housing. The important point is that, except when there is a policy of subsidy, the sets of payers P and beneficiaries B tend to coincide with the set of tenants. There is not complete coincidence, for the existence of municipal housing has consequences in the private housing sector and elsewhere, bringing benefits to some (such as by reducing rents paid by private tenants) and imposing costs on others (such as by reducing rents received by private landlords). Nevertheless, if interest rates rise the whole of the increase can, in principle, be imposed on the tenants who occupy the houses.

Non-industrial private investment

In the private sector there are two forms of investment: in houses, offices, shops and other buildings that provide services, and in industrial buildings and machinery that combine with labour to produce goods. This latter form of investment has already been considered by us.

Offices, shops, hotels and other commercial buildings differ from housing in that they provide employment other than in their construction and maintenance. Like factories, they may be built out of profits or with borrowed money, and (also like factories) they may be owned or rented by their occupiers. We say more about these matters in later chapters, but here we must note that the level of investment in these commercial buildings is determined by several factors, including interest rates, construction costs, and expectations of local business and trading levels, on the part either of the intending owner occupier or of the building developer, who will base his expected rental income on his view of the trade that a prospective tenant would expect to do. The implications for employment are similar to those of factories, but in that they provide services rather than goods the implications for the balances of payments of the set R and the set W will be slightly different, in the way that we have already seen. We must also note that if the property owners do not belong to R then the rental payments will not accrue to its members.

Finally, we turn to housing. This, too, is discussed in more detail in later chapters. Employment is provided at the time of construction, and to some extent in later years through demands for maintenance workers of various kinds. Once again the level of investment will depend on the price of a loan – the rate of interest – but there are, of course, other factors also. An important point here in relation to our principal theme is that while owner-occupiers will be, or will become, residents, and finance part of the housing investment out of their accumulated savings, the loan is not dependent on the level of savings by the town's residents, except to a very small degree, unless the capital market is very localized. On the other hand, this means that while the resident borrows in order to have a house built, and thereby creates employment in the town,* he will have to pay it back with interest over the life of the loan: and

---

* If he buys from a speculative builder he is encouraging the builder to repeat his exercise. The employment consequences are much the same.

the money that he pays in this way is a leakage from the circular flows of money of the set of residents and such composite sets as residents plus workers. The same point would be valid if tenants paid rent to a non-resident landlord, with the difference that in this case the houses would never become the possessions of the set. Owner-occupied houses do, and normally continue to provide services for members of the set after their purchase has been completed.

Here we are brought up against an interesting point. If the residents of a town have finished paying for their houses then their income is less committed, and there can be (but may not be) a higher level of spending by them upon other goods and services of which some may be locally produced. If some of these residents sell their houses and move to other towns, taking the proceeds of the sale with them, then some of the new residents are likely to have borrowed money in order to make the purchase, and so to have repayments to make. Thus, even if the new resident has the same income as the old resident, the transfer of ownership will result in a renewed leakage from the system, with consequences for local employment.

The inner-city fallacy

While we have developed certain ideas with the town in mind we must remember that most of them are valid for sets of people associated not so much with the town as with part of that town, such as the inner city. Unfortunately the vast interest in 'the problems of the inner city' produces a great deal of muddled thinking because this point is not appreciated. Putting it another way, we fail to recognize that it is people, not areas, that have problems. It is true that in the inner city the extent of urban decay, unemployment and social disorder will sometimes be more apparent than elsewhere. But if we are attempting to reduce these we may well end up with a rag-bag of confused, contradictory and inefficient measures unless we consider carefully the identities of those involved, and the economic laws that will apply to them.

In particular we have to ask questions about those who reside in the inner city, those who work there, those who own property located there, those who rent such property, and those who provide jobs located there. As we know, these sets will overlap, and some of their members will also belong to other sets. The nature and extent of overlapping, and membership of other sets, may well vary from town to town; and for this reason, if for none other, a policy that may 'solve' the problems 'of the inner city' in one town may well fail in another. If, for example, much of the shop property in one inner city is owned by inner city residents, who may spend part of their rental incomes in inner city shops, the economic effects of any change in incomes of the residents will be different from what they would be if all of the shop property were owned by non-residents.

The set approach also encourages us to ask another question, to which we could be led by other routes, but which is not often asked. How do we expect our policies to affect the membership of the sets we are considering? For example, if the tenants of inner-city houses receive special rent subsidies then, quite apart from questions about the sources of the subsidies, the balances of payments of various sets of people, and multiplier effects, we have to ask whether the subsidy will cause some existing tenants to cease to be tenants, or entice others to seek to be tenants. In certain circumstances the subsidy could allow a tenant to augment his savings sufficiently for him to accumulate a deposit payable on a house purchase. In others it could so swell the demand for tenancies that either rents would rise or some kind of black market would develop. The important point is that in some circumstances these or other changes of membership of the tenant set, the landlord set, or some other set, would have important impacts on the consequences of the subsidy, and the extent to which the policy achieves its stated objective.

People associated with the inner city are inevitably members of sets with wider associations. Policies or accidents affecting them may have widely spread consequences; and some policies or accidents that appear to be geographically remote may lead to physical or social change in the city. 'No man is an island' should be inscribed on the doors to the inner city lobby. In this book the term 'town centre' embraces 'inner city'.

4

Municipal expenditure and revenue

Probably every town has some form of government. In some towns it will be an elected council. In others it may be a governor nominated by the national government, or a local notable who has acquired power by force, money or personality. Whether the urban government is in the hands of a one-person set or a multi-person set does not at present concern us, nor are we interested in how that set has acquired its responsibilities and powers. We are concerned simply with considering certain points about its duties and costs, and with methods of raising revenue to cover these costs.

Municipal powers and responsibilities

At the outset we must note that the urban government has two essentially different functions that in principle define two sets of people. That these sets may be identical in their membership is a consequence of accident, politics or convenience, but not of necessity. Tasks performed for the community as the result of a community decision, and in some way or the other financed at least in part by members of the community, could, for example, be undertaken by private contractors chosen by a ballot; but neither could the contractor be certain of payment nor could the community be certain of the service unless some kind of legally binding contract existed between the private contractor and some identifiable representatives of the community endowed with that authority and responsibility that enables them to enter into legal contracts on behalf of the community. Few people would agree to be representatives in this way unless they knew that they had power to enforce the collection of sufficient money for them to be able to honour their contracts. The set responsible for paying those who perform the services, as employees or as contractors, may or may not also be required to ensure that the services are performed, and may or may not be given discretion about how much to spend on each service. But the set that undertakes to manage urban services in these ways is not necessarily the set that decides (possibly after spending some money) upon planning applications, local road-traffic legislation, and other matters of local government of a kind that is more concerned with setting limits to activity than with providing a service that costs money. It is with this former 'management' set that we shall be concerned most, even though decisions by the other set may have profound economic consequences. It will be convenient if we take the two sets to be identical. Whether this bi-function set is selected or nominated by central government, or in authority by the use of force or threats does not matter, provided that it has the power to raise money from members of the community, the power to spend this money, and some kind of responsibility to the community or to a higher level of government for ensuring that certain services are provided. We may, for convenience, call it the Municipal Council, or simply the 'Council', without implying anything about its composition or origin.

Like all other sets, the Council has to have regard for its balance of payments. The more common idea that it must balance its budget, by not spending more than its income, and not imposing local taxes in excess of what it needs, is but another way of saying the same thing. In balance-of-payments terms, the group called the Council has to balance its imports against its exports. The Council imports labour and material from other sets, especially the set of its own employees. It exports its administrative services and other services such as road cleaning, education and so on. It does not sell these services, except in rare cases, but it receives income from a variety of sources on the understanding that these services will be provided. It is this income, derived from its exports, that the Council can use to pay for the imported goods and services used by it. If it spends less on imports than it receives for its exports then those who pay for the exports will reduce their payments to prevent the Council piling up credit balances at the expense of local taxes or other sources. If the Council spends more on imports than it receives in revenue from its exports it runs into debt, with all of the problems that that implies.

Unlike other sets, the Council has powers to raise finance through taxes, and it may be required to spend money in ways of which it does not approve. If we are to consider its economics we have to look not only at ways of raising money but also at the impacts on other sets, both of revenue raising and of the ways in which the money is spent.

Provision of services

A Council may provide goods and services in response to two totally different kinds of decision. The decision may be taken by the Council, or, at least, be within the power of the Council to rescind. Alternatively, it may be taken by a national government or some other body that can require the Council to act in a certain way. Moreover, while the national government may ordain that the municipal councils provide certain services, there may be instances in which the standard of that service provided by certain municipalities is higher than the minimum that complies with the law. The service is provided because of a statutory obligation, but there is a voluntary decision, made locally, to 'top-up' the level of that service. We will find it convenient to divide the services provided by municipal councils into 'statutory services' and 'optional services', with the understanding that the latter name includes the topping-up of statutory services.

Statutory services require a little examination. The national government finances some such services from the national revenue. In this case the national government is responsible for both the decision to provide the service and the decision to raise the necessary money. In other cases, however, the national government may decide that the municipalities shall provide the services but leave them with the problem of finding all or part of the cost. This has certain consequences that must be spelt out. We are not here concerned with any ethical or moral judgements, but as we are looking at the economics of urban sets we need to identify the economic consequences of a national set requiring a local set to provide itself with a specified service apparently at its own cost.

The first matter that we have to consider is why we have said 'apparently'. As we shall see later, the extent to which locally levied taxes are ultimately borne by local residents or employees, rather than by others who have little or no direct relationship with the town, depends very much on the detail of both local and national taxation measures. On the whole, the purely local burden of local taxes is probably less than most people perceive. This is a matter that can be properly appreciated only when we have considered local taxation in greater detail. At this stage we simply note that it is a more complicated problem than it appears to be.

Independently of the ultimate incidence of the taxes, the fact remains that if a municipal council is required by law to provide and to finance a certain service then either it must increase its revenue or it must reallocate its existing revenue. There is a limit to its ability to raise more, and in some cases local opposition could effectively prevent this. In any case, if more revenue is raised for one purpose it makes it more difficult to raise additional revenue for some other purpose. This means that, whether the Council decides to reallocate or to raise more revenue, there is an implied reduction in the amount of money available for the financing of present and contemplated optional services. At a general level there is not much more that can be said. The Council's decisions, reached by majority vote, are not necessarily consistent and so the usual analysis of consumer behaviour with a diminished budget cannot be relied upon. In practice, in any case, savings are likely to be made where they can be made most easily, and with least public outcry. These are the factors that are likely to dictate preferences for pruning. There is, in fact, a degree of asymmetry in the formation of preferences by the Council, for if it is able to spend more it will perhaps favour an expansion of service A to an expansion of B on grounds of popularity, social justice, or what you will. But if it has to save money it may cut A before it cuts B simply because it is easier to do so. Alternatively, it may cut B, if this is easier. (This asymmetry may, of course, also exist in the behaviour of other sets, including, indeed, the one-person set: but conventional indifference-curve analysis usually assumes perfect reversibility.)

Another question that we have to consider is how a national decision to compel a municipality to provide a certain service, and to finance it out of local revenue, differs from a decision to compel its provision but to finance it out of national revenue. This, again, depends on the detail of taxation schemes, but there is one other aspect of the question: would the same service be provided?

If the service were administered throughout the whole country, or a region, as a national service it would probably be less sensitive to local conditions and complaints than one administered entirely by the municipality. On the other hand, the national government could arrange for the municipality to provide the service and to reimburse its costs. In this case some municipalities would probably depart from national 'guidelines' or incur extra costs in some way, and the national government would need to find some formula for protecting its exchequer against the more profligate municipalities. Nevertheless, the national government and the municipalities could normally find an acceptable way of ensuring that the cost of implementing the national decision at an acceptable basic level could be calculated for each municipality.

Raising revenue

With these preliminaries about the services provided we turn to the other side of the question – to the raising of revenue. A municipality may obtain money in many different ways. There can be taxes imposed by the Council, grants or gifts (with or without conditions) from the national government or other bodies, revenue from charges for services or from lotteries, and so on. Many of these matters were considered in the context of Great Britain by a Committee that reported in 1976, and we may begin our own analysis by summarizing some of its views. In the Layfield Report* on local government finance in England, Scotland and Wales, eight desirable features of a system for raising local revenue were suggested. We will comment on these later, but it will be useful for us to summarize them now.

1 *Accountability:* that 'whoever is responsible for deciding to spend more or less money on providing a service is also responsible for deciding whether to raise more or less taxation.' Those who say 'spend less' have to say precisely how to do so, while those who say 'employ more staff' have to find their pay.

2 *Fairness between Individuals:* 'The result should be fair in the sense that people in similar circumstances should be treated alike.' The Report describes this as a desirable principle that is very difficult to interpret and to apply.

3 *Fairness between Areas:* 'Where services are provided and taxes are levied by local authorities, fairness between individuals living in different places can be achieved only by redistributing resources between areas.' But how this should be done is never an easy decision, and at times it

* Report of the Committee of Enquiry into Local Government Finance, HMSO 1976, Cmnd 6453.

may 'have the effect of impeding the achievement of greater economic efficiency and growth'.

4 *Consumption and Investment:* Sometimes if we spend more now we will need to spend less later, while economies now may lead to large bills in the future. It is also true that current expenditure may be financed out of loans to be repaid, with interest, in the future. 'Individuals make similar choices in their daily lives . . . affected by their expectations . . . and their preferences about how they wish the benefits they can have to be spread over time. Public authorities should take decisions in a way which reflects the preferences of their electors. But the choices . . . have important economic implications . . .'.

5 *Efficiency:* 'The standard of service desired should be provided at the minimum reasonable cost.'

6 *Stability:* 'Taxpayers, local authorities and the government should know where they stand. They should be able to rely on reasonably firm expectations about future commitments. . . . The sources of revenue available to local authorities should enable them to absorb fluctuations in expenditure arising from factors outside their control, for example, changes in interest rates, while maintaining reasonably stable tax rates.'

7 *Flexibility:* 'The system should be flexible enough to accommodate a wide range of economic circumstances, such as varying rates of (national economic) growth, and varied political preferences about local expenditure, without politicians and administrators having to spend an inordinate amount of time in reorganizing the administrative components of the system.' We cannot keep on introducing new forms of revenue raising. We need forms that can lead to changes in income through decisions that are easy to implement, such as simple changes in tax rates.

8 *Comprehensibility:* The system should be easily understandable by those who make decisions about revenue raising and expenditure, and by 'serious commentators and interested members of the public'.

One principle, once thought to be important, but, in Britain at least, inviolable, is not listed:

'*No Taxation without Representation*' can apply only when all groups who are taxed are represented on the group who levies the taxes. In Britain local-authority taxes are levied on occupiers of business properties who have no vote in the local elections unless they happen to be residents.

There is obviously merit in stating at the outset a list of desirable features of a revenue and spending system, but there is also a danger. The financial system used in local government is part of at least two other systems – the broader national (and even international) financial system and the whole urban system. Judged by a limited list of tests of restricted coverage a revenue raising device may seem to be very acceptable, yet when its implications for the wider financial system, or for other aspects of urban life, are considered it may have to be rejected. In other words, yet another desirable feature of the urban financial system, left unconsidered by the Layfield Report, is that:

Minimum adverse consequences should arise from it.

The serious student of local finance will read the Layfield Report himself and we make no attempt here to summarize it. Instead we will look at a few forms of local taxation and other revenue-raising devices for ourselves, in the knowledge that there is an easily accessible fuller treatment.

Property tax

The first tax that we consider is a property tax. There are many possible forms of it, and in some cases the term is used in an ill-defined way. Here we are going to be concerned with a tax paid by either the owner or the occupier of a building or a piece of land simply because of his ownership or occupation. We are not, at present, concerned with any tax on the activity of creating a building, on selling it, or on incomes derived from it.

Land and buildings are easy to identify. They cannot be moved from place to place and they normally have a lengthy existence. Thus they can provide the basis for a tax that is difficult to evade and has a stable and predictable yield at any specified tax-rate. At one extreme there can be a flat levy on every property, or on every property of a specified kind, independent of its size or value. At the other extreme the tax may depend on a detailed valuation of the property and vary between properties of the same value but different types or locations (even apart from the way in which these factors are reflected in the value).

To consider the economics of several slightly different kinds of property tax would be tedious and repetitive. Instead, we will here concern ourselves with the economics of a property tax that reflects the essential features of the British rating system. Some more specialized aspects of the British system will be considered later in the book.

In the system that we now consider all properties are given 'ratable values', which are determined by the authorities, subject to the right of appeal to an independent tribunal. These ratable values reflect in some way, and possibly inadequately, either the selling price of the property or the rent that could be obtained for it. The important point is that they increase as the market value of the property increases. Perhaps the best way of describing them is to say that they are notional annual rents.

If the municipality wishes to raise £18 million in property tax and the total of the ratable values of property within its boundary is £20 million, it can do so by levying upon every occupier a tax (or rate) of 90p for every single pound of ratable value, so that the occupier of a house of ratable value £300 pays £270 in local property tax. If the sum needed by the municipality is, say, £24 million it could levy a rate of £1.20 in the pound, so that the house occupier would pay £360. Occupiers of other kinds of property, such as shops, factories, offices and universities, would also pay taxes, determined in the same way, but, as we shall later see, not necessarily at the same rate. Before we consider this in more detail we shall examine how these taxes affect different sets of people.

The tax paid by house occupiers is essentially a part of their expenditure on accommodation. It is not related directly to the extent of the benefit they derive from the services, for although the total to be raised by local taxation depends on the total cost of the services, the tax paid by the individual depends simply on this total and on the fraction of the total ratable value of properties in the town that is represented by the ratable value of his house. The amount paid by him in rates may vary from year to year and in inflationary times, or when there are changes in the organization or provision of services, the annual variation can be very considerable. It is known a month or two in advance, and may be paid in instalments spread over several months. In that it reflects the value of the house that he occupies it is likely to be related to some degree to his income, but more accurately it is related to the amount that he spends on housing. It is, in short, a tax on an approximation to his housing expenditure, and most people will be aware of this when they consider buying or renting new accommodation. They ask not only about the price or the rent but also about the ratable value. A lower-than-expected ratable value can result in the seller or landlord obtaining a higher price or rent than he would otherwise obtain, while a higher ratable value may depress market values.

For the same reason, an increase in the rates levied, causing an increase in the tax on all houses in the town, may lead to a depression in newly negotiated prices and rents. People have to apportion their income or other means between various forms of expenditure. If they are not on the point of moving then an increase in their rates bill means that they have less money available for other purposes. But if they are about to move they can take some account of this increase when they make their decision.

An important consequence of this kind of local tax is that occupiers of comparable houses in different towns may be called upon to pay different levels of tax. Even if the two houses have identical ratable values the annual rates to be paid may differ substantially. There can be three reasons for this. The amount that one town needs to raise by local taxation may be less than that needed by the other town (in relation to its size) because of a poorer level of service, a greater efficiency, or some other source of income. Alternatively, the total ratable value of one town may be greater not because it is a bigger town but because it contains larger and more expensive houses. The third reason is that the two towns may have similar total ratable values but the division of value between houses and industrial/commercial properties differs, and so if these latter properties are taxed at a higher rate than houses the domestic rate in one town can be lower than in the other. This is a point to which we return.

If occupiers of comparable houses in different towns are required to pay different rates there can be important consequences, especially if the towns are close to each other. A particular instance of this is when an old town has expanded beyond its boundaries, so that some of its functionally related suburbs lie in another authority's area. The housing in the old town is likely to be older, smaller and less attractive than the new housing in the suburbs, and so, unless there is a compensating amount of commerce or industry, the total ratable value is low in relation to the number of households. Since the level of services to be provided is determined more by the number of households than by the value of their property this means that the rates that have to be levied in the old town are higher than they would be if the more expensive houses were within the boundary – for in that case ratable value would increase faster than local-authority costs. The new houses in the suburbs, on the other hand, would be in an area where the costs of municipal services would tend to be low, partly because they would be unhampered by factors such as central-area congestion and partly because the costs that arise out of the age of a town, including the renovation of housing and service installations, would be low. This combination of comparatively low costs and the inclusion in its total ratable value of comparatively costly houses would result in a lower rate in the pound being levied.

A result of this fall in rates as one crosses the boundary of the old town is that a person working in the centre of the old town is tempted to live outside it, for although he has travelling costs to pay, once he passes beyond the boundary a greater proportion of his housing costs will be for things that he can see. A given total expenditure on housing will provide him with a better house. Similarly, a newcomer to the area will tend to look more favourably upon the suburbs. In extreme cases the drift from the old town may lead to empty properties and a reduced total ratable value at a time when more money than ever is needed in order to maintain services and to engage in urban renewal. The contrast between rates levied then tends to increase, and the municipality is caught in a 'rate-trap'. It has to put up rates, and by doing so causes the ratable value to decline. Moreover, it is the poor, unable to afford the better houses of the suburbs, who remain and have to pay the higher rates, unless there are special income transfers of a kind that we consider later.

Rates are also paid by occupiers of non-residential property. To illustrate the impact of this we consider three cases – government buildings, shops and offices, and factories.

The occupiers of national government offices pay rates to the municipality. These rates are, of course, paid by the national exchequer out of the receipts of national taxes. If the rates rise then the exchequer has to pay more and so, in ordinary circumstances, to raise more from national taxes. Thus the presence of government buildings in a town means that some part of the cost of local services is borne nationally. If the town has 'more than its share' of government buildings then the consequent contribution of the national government to the costs of municipal services is likely to exceed the related part of the national taxes paid by its residents. On the other hand, the residents of a town with no government offices are paying, through their national taxes, part of the cost of services provided in towns where government offices are well represented.

Rates paid by shopkeepers present a totally different story. An increase in the rates demand represents a legally enforceable, and virtually unavoidable, addition to costs. If the shopkeeper does nothing about it this addition to his costs will cause an equal reduction in his net profits, and if these are small it could turn a net profit into a net loss – as could any other increase in costs. Except in this extreme case, where the taxation consequences would need more detailed examination, the reduction in net profits will result in a lower assessment for national taxes. This means that the increase in rates is partly offset by a lower contribution to the national exchequer. In other words, some fraction of the increase in rates is passed on to the national taxpayer. The rest of it is borne by the shopkeeper, who may be a resident of the town, may reside elsewhere, or may be a partnership or a company with few or many shareholders living locally, all over the country or even abroad.

It is likely however that the shopkeeper will not 'do nothing about it' when an increase in rates is announced, especially if it represents a significant increase to his costs. He may decide to reduce its impact on his profits by increasing his revenue, and he can try to do this either by selling more or by raising his prices. If the municipality has raised his rates it is likely that the rates to be paid by his customers, as house occupiers in the town, will also have been raised, and so they are unlikely to increase their spending in shops. While some shopkeepers may manage to sell more it will be through capturing trade from others. Unless it is possible to save costs in other ways, such as reducing staff, or in one of the ways discussed in Chapter 6, the shopkeeper will probably have to choose between bearing the whole loss of profits after taxation or raising his prices. As we shall see later on, this will not always increase his profits, but in many cases it will, and if he chooses this solution some of the increase in rates will thereby be transferred to his customers. In most cases these will be mainly local people, but in towns that attract purchasers from further afield part of the cost of municipal services will be borne by these visiting shoppers. On the other hand, if there are not similar increases in rates elsewhere the shopping centre could become relatively expensive, and so tend to lose trade.

Thus an increase in the rates demanded from shopkeepers will be borne partly by the shopkeeper (who may or may not be a local resident), partly by national taxpayers, and partly by the customers, of whom many will normally be local residents. It may also lead to some local unemployment if staff are dismissed in an attempt to reduce costs.

Before we turn to offices and factories we have to mention another aspect of the rating of shops.

So far we have considered some of the effects of an increase in the rates demanded of an existing shopkeeper. An effect that we have not considered is that he will close his shop, possibly to reopen elsewhere. This brings us to the more general question of how the rates will affect the choice of shop, and consequently the rents paid to the owners of shop property, the numbers of empty shops and the extent of shopbuilding. These are matters that are analysed in later chapters. What we have to note now is that, like the level of employment in retailing, they are capable of being affected by the level of rates.

Offices are affected in much the same way as shops. The balance between the various alternatives open to the office tenant will depend on the service he provides, but basically the rates will be borne partly by him, partly by the national taxpayer and partly by his clients, and he will consider his rates when deciding where to locate.

Factories are differently affected, simply because their customers are likely to be more widely spread. As with shops, part of the rates bill will be passed to the national exchequer through a reduced liability to national taxes, but if the factory puts up its prices, so that part of the burden falls on the customers, the effect may be very widely dispersed. Some of the factory's product will be sold to other factories or establishments who can set the increase in price against their own taxation liabilities, while the individual customers are likely to live over a wide area. Thus the fraction of the increase that will be borne locally is likely to be low. On the other hand, if location costs become high because of high rates the factory owners will consider moving to another place, or cutting down their labour costs.

We have said sufficient to indicate that the precise incidence of local taxation of the occupation of non-domestic property is very difficult to determine, yet this tax may well have a yield exceeding the total yield on houses and flats. In the United Kingdom this has certainly been the case in recent years, with domestic property accounting for only 42 per cent of the total rates in 1974/75 and expected to account for 43 per cent in 1975/76. Thus the view that this is a local tax is open to some question. It would be more correct to describe it as a locally determined tax of semi-local incidence. The householders on whom it partly falls have a vote in electing the set that has responsibility for determining its level within the constraints imposed by the law, including requirements about the provision of certain services. The others on whom it falls directly, such as shopkeepers, at one time had a vote in the local authority elections in the United Kingdom but now have not. They can influence through persuasion but not through direct representation.

Sales tax

Two other forms of local taxation call for comment. One of these is the idea of a local sales tax. Whenever alternative taxes are considered we need an idea of the level at which they have to be levied if they are to make a useful contribution to revenue. In this case it may be obtained from the fact that in 1975/76, when the average rate of Value Added Tax in the United Kingdom was about 10 per cent, the yield of this tax on goods and services was about £3,300 million. Property rates yielded £4,200 million. Thus, in the United Kingdom, a local tax on sales and services of about 13 per cent would raise a sum roughly equivalent to the yield of property rates (on the assumption that the abolition of rates would have a positive income effect sufficient to offset the negative effect on sales of the price elasticity of demand).

A local tax on sales and services could thus yield a useful income. It would be paid by customers and clients. Whether these would be significantly non-local would depend on the detail of the tax. A tax falling simply on shop sales would be borne by the residents of the market area, and fall most heavily on residents of the town. It would thus be both more local and less useful than a tax of wider incidence and greater yield. Yet a locally determined value-added tax would mean that a shop or manufacturer in one town wishing to buy stock or semi-manufactured goods would find the tax element in his purchase price would depend on the town of origin, unless the tax paid depended on the address of the purchaser.

In commenting on a sales tax, the Layfield Report stated:

> . . .such a tax fails to meet the tests of local accountability and perceptibility. Indirect taxes are included in the price of goods and services bought by local electors and others – both businesses and people from outside the local-authority area. If the variations in price between areas were large, there would be an incentive to reduce the tax paid by making purchases elsewhere. If the variations were small, then very few taxpayers would be aware of the amount of local tax in each transaction, let alone the total amount paid during the year. Special arrangements would have to be made for purchases for commercial and industrial purposes, particularly by companies from outside the area, to avoid substantial local taxes falling on organizations with no direct influence on local affairs.
>
> In its administration a local sales tax would be complex, particularly if levied in addition to VAT. Depending on the scale and scope of exemptions, it would mean annual assessments of between half and one million tax returns from traders. The different tax levels in different areas would lead to severe complications, particularly for businesses with outlets in several taxation areas. For mail-order firms and manufacturers selling directly, accounting for tax at different rates according to a customer's address would be a formidable task.

Local income tax

The other form of local tax that calls for special comment is a local income tax. The Layfield Report implies that in Great Britain a local income tax of about 11p in the pound would be needed in order to raise the present equivalent of property rates. In principle one could introduce a tax according to place of residence or place of origin of income, but normally the former would be very much the easier to administer. The tax could be imposed as a fixed sum independent of incomes, when it would share costs evenly over all earners, or it could be a fixed percentage rate. Such a local income tax, at a fixed percentage of income, would redistribute incomes within the town, in the sense that those on high incomes would be paying a higher share of the costs of the services without necessarily benefiting any more than those on lower incomes who would pay less. If, as in many national income-tax schemes, the percentage rate itself increased with income the degree of redistribution would be greater. There is thus scope for making the tax as redistributive as the municipal council wishes, within any constraints imposed by the national government.

Because a local income tax is so similar to a national income tax, in which variations are a major instrument of economic and social policy, there are obvious dangers of local decisions tending to nullify or dangerously to exaggerate the effects of national policy. It may be argued that if local income tax replaces, in whole or in part, a property tax, then the municipality will increase or decrease it only if it would otherwise have been increasing or decreasing the property tax, and so it is no more likely than the property tax to offset national policy. On the other hand, while the total tax levied may be in accord with national policy, its incidence may not. In times when the national government is pursuing highly redistributive policies, a municipality of different political views could use local income tax to make the total taxation less redistributive and vice versa. This would have both social and economic consequences, partly because different income groups have different marginal propensities to consume. One way round this objection would be for the national government to impose some constraints on the pattern of marginal local income-tax rates. Even then, however, if local income tax existed alongside the property tax the municipality could affect the distribution of income after tax by deciding how much to derive from the progressive local income tax and how much from the less progressive property tax – unless there, too, the government set limits.

A related, and perhaps more fundamental, question is to what extent the tax-raising powers of a municipality should enable it to pursue social and economic policies of its own. Every tax that it imposes, and many of its other actions, have economic and social consequences; but just as some would argue that every municipality should have very great powers to impose the economic and social policy of its majority set on others, some will argue instead that their powers should be minimal. What we, as economists, should keep in mind is that if different economic or social policies are pursued in different towns then sooner or later these will exert an impact on the migration of people and firms to or from those towns. They may also, as we have seen, make the control of the national economy more difficult. Neither of these observations necessarily implies an objection to, or a welcoming for, the pursuit of local economic and social policies.

There are, of course, other possible ways of raising revenue ostensibly from local sources. The important question that must always be answered is on what sets of people they ultimately impinge.

Direct grants

Direct grants from the national government need some mention. These can arise in various ways but the principal cases are illustrated by two possibilities, which we now consider.

The first is the specific 'earmarked' grant intended to pay for the whole or part of a specified service. In most cases this will be paid by the national government to all municipalities. It has the effect of increasing the total taxes paid by those whose marginal national tax rates exceed their marginal local tax rates; and of decreasing the total taxes paid by the complementary set. Here the meaning of 'marginal' has to be carefully noted. It relates to the change in tax paid by a person as a result of a decision by the national or local taxing authority to change its revenue from taxes. A person paying a high rate of income tax, and subject to even higher rates as his income increases, will in our context not necessarily have a high marginal national tax rate. It would depend on whether the next increase in national revenue was to be made by raising income tax, or say, the tax on tobacco. If local taxes are of few kinds it is easier to identify those with high marginal local tax rates, but certainly the marginal national tax rates have a distribution very much at the whim of the authors of the next budget.

One cannot, therefore, say that if a town has a low average income per resident, then those residents will pay only a low fraction of the cost of a new service financed out of national revenue. They may be abnormally heavy smokers, for example, and the service may be financed by an increase in tobacco duty.

On the other hand, as time goes on it becomes less easy to relate a service to a specific tax. A government may decide at times simply to rearrange the incidence of taxes rather than to vary their total yield, and historic decisions to increase certain taxes specifically to pay for certain services cease to be relevant, even though they were highly relevant at the time they were taken.

The second possibility considered by us is that the national government may decide to give grants to municipalities who could otherwise meet their obligations only by levying taxes that are unacceptably high compared with those of other municipalities. This is very similar to the grant that may be provided when otherwise the increase in local taxes would be too high. In both cases the recipient municipalities are enabled to charge lower local taxes than would otherwise be the case. As we have seen, not all of this is of purely local incidence, and some of the national taxes that go to finance the grants will be paid out of company and other taxes that otherwise might have yielded less, because of national tax relief on, for example, local property rates. Nevertheless, the set of local tax payers benefits at the expense of the overlapping set of national tax payers. If the municipalities concerned have only a small fraction of the total population it is likely that on average their local tax payers will benefit.

Before leaving the subject of municipal finance we should note that the municipal council is almost exclusively concerned with providing services for the residents of the town. Putting this into other words, we can say that the residents are the principal importers of the services produced by the council, and these imports have to be purchased (through taxes) out of the sale of exports to non-members of the resident set. Some of the residents are wholly employed by the council in helping to provide these services, and consequently it is the non-council-employed residents who have to produce and export sufficient goods and services to pay for the municipal services. Every time a decision to spend more on some service is made by the set consisting of the municipal council, acting voluntarily or at the command of the national government, there is an implied requirement that the set of local taxpayers should export more, or import less from outside the union of the set of residents and the set of councillors, unless the council is to receive financial assistance. There may also be a multiplier effect if the provision of the service makes use of unemployed residents.

5
Housing: mainly non-spatial

Introduction

In most towns more land is devoted to housing than to any other use, and few questions in urban economics arouse such interest and emotion as those that relate to it. This is not surprising. A person's house (or other living accommodation) is the physical focus for his household. It provides shelter and privacy, and a place where he may keep his own possessions and lead his own life with a minimum of interference, except, perhaps, from other members of the same household. If that becomes too great the usual answer is for the household to split, with a demand for two dwelling places rather than one. It is a building, or part of a building, in which the family group expresses itself, and which each family will decorate, adapt and use in its own way, so that its members will not 'feel at home' even when housed together comfortably in some other place, until that, too, has been given its personal characteristics. To its occupiers a house is a framework for a home. At times it will seem to be the wrong framework, preventing the family from expressing itself as it wishes to do, or it may be considered to be insufficiently insulated from neighbours or neighbouring activities. At such times the possibility of change is considered, and questions of cost arise, just as they do when for some reason or the other the existing house is considered to be too expensive. If cost, or anything else, prevents a household from living where it would wish to live there will, at times, be a tendency for emotions to be aroused, either on the part of those who wish to move or on the part of others who feel that movement should be possible for them. Such emotions are not morally wrong, ignoble, or a cause for shame; and at times perhaps an emotional approach to a problem will in some sense be better than an economic one. But we should recognize the nature of the approach.

In this chapter we will be concerned with only some aspects of the economics of housing. There are two reasons for this. One is that some of the economic problems of housing are not especially urban problems. Rural areas have some housing problems of little concern to urban economists. There are also some problems of housing economics that are more the concern of the national economy than of the urban economy. The borderline is often very fuzzy, but as a general principle we shall normally consider the economic problems of housing in a town, taking the centrally made decisions about the national economy as data that help to set a context.

The other reason for not considering certain aspects of housing in this chapter stems from the fact that housing is but one form of land use. So far as the existence and price of housing may be determined by the availability and price of land, the economics of housing is part of the wider subject of the economics of land use, in which different potential users of land compete with each other, and affect each other both in that competition and through the pattern of land-uses and spatial relationships that emerge from it. This wider consideration of housing economics in a spatial context comes later in the book when we have considered some of the other land users. Here we will be concerned mainly with the non-spatial aspects of the subject, but even here we need to draw attention to the relationship between the house and the land on which it stands.

Some housing is mobile. The house, caravan, tent, or other form of accommodation is moved from place to place and its owner has only a transitory interest in the land that it occupies at any one time. Fixed housing is built in such a way that moving it means destroying it (except in rare cases involving great expense). The land on which it is built may belong to the owner of the house. In Britain we use the term 'freehold ownership' in such a case, and without implying any exact identity between systems of ownership and tenure we shall use this phrase throughout the book.

Another possibility is that the land belongs to somebody other than the owner of the house, in such a way that on a specified date the house will pass automatically to the landowner. In short, even the ownership of the house is for only a limited period. We call this 'leasehold ownership', and refer to the owner of the land as the 'ground landlord'.

A third possibility is that the land belongs to somebody else, or possibly to the State, who may be entitled to annual rent but has no existing right to terminate the occupation of the land or to take ownership of the house. There is a 'perpetual lease'.

Finally, we may note the existence of houses 'owned' by people who have built them illegally on land that does not belong to them, as is typified in 'shanty-town' developments.

If the owner of the house is also its occupier then we call him an 'owner-occupier'. Another possibility is that the house is owned by the state or the municipality and occupied by tenants who pay rent. This form of 'public sector' housing is very common in some countries but virtually non-existent in others. The contrasting form of tenancy is in the private sector where the owner is a private person or a non-state-owned firm that rents the accommodation to a tenant. In both sectors the house may be rented furnished or unfurnished. We call its non-resident owner 'the landlord'. Finally, we must note that in some cases the tenant has a special relationship with the landlord and that his tenancy may cease when that relationship ends. In particular, the owner may employ the tenant, and wish to keep the house for occupation by an existing employee. Examples are when a farm worker lives in a house owned by the farmer for whom he works, and when a policeman, minister of religion or government official has a house provided for him during his tenure of that post or office. We call these 'tied' houses and tenancies.

The economics of housing depends very much on the extents to which these different forms of land-tenure and house-tenure exist in the area that is being considered. We shall be able to appreciate this more fully when we examine urban land markets. To some extent, most houses are imperfect substitutes for most others; and if a person can occupy the house that he really wants only by paying a price in excess of what he would have to pay for some other acceptable (but less desirable) house then he may decide to take his second best, which may mean living in a place whose main virtue for him is that land values are low. Certainly he will be prompted to compare the prices that he has to pay. This will be true not only if the houses are for sale, but also if they are for rent, and if one is for purchase and one is for rent. In this and other ways the economics of owner-occupation is to some extent interlinked with the economics of private and public-sector rented housing. While it is convenient to consider the different sectors of housing separately in a first analysis we must constantly keep this interdependence in mind.

We must also keep in mind the fact that a large part of the economics of housing must be concerned with problems arising out of the maintenance and allocation of an existing stock. There are also economic problems associated with changes in that stock. Although these two sets of problems are interlinked, a failure to distinguish between them (such as when we speak loosely of 'the supply of housing') may lead to a faulty analysis.

In an attempt to deal with all of these matters in an integrated way we shall begin with a consideration of different kinds of housing market and then try to pull them together. In doing so we will make use of the set approach where this is helpful, but not in a slavish way. Our purpose is to present some background for use in later chapters, and to set a context for later analysis.

There are two very different kinds of housing provision to be considered. A typical European or American town will normally have a number of flats or houses that equals, to within a few per cent, the number of families or households. In many developing countries, however, the phenomenon of a single room being shared by two or more households may be fairly common in some of the towns. The more interesting economic problems arise in the former case, and we concentrate on this. Later in the chapter we shall return to the intense overcrowding that characterizes so many developing countries, and is of considerable social importance. A similar phenomenon is also to be observed in some cities in developed countries.

Privately rented housing

We begin by considering a town in which all accommodation is rented unfurnished from private landlords who have no other relationship with their tenants. We will also suppose that these landlords are all acting individually and making no collective decisions. Finally, we suppose that the population of the town is growing because of natural increase, migration from other areas, or both of these.

We may imagine that at a given time the landlords own a stock of accommodation, not all the same, of which most is currently let at a variety of rents. Newly formed, or newly arrived, households will wish to obtain accommodation. There may also be existing tenants who wish to move within the town, and although they cause an empty accommodation to appear when they have moved from it, at the time that they are intending to move they, like the new households, are prospective tenants of the places that are already empty. (There can, of course, be straight exchanges of tenancies but to consider them complicates the argument without leading to conclusions that are different in any important respect.)

The prospective tenants will not all be aware of all of the vacant property, and will not have identical requirements. If a landlord and prospective tenant reach agreement about the rent and conditions of tenancy and accommodation is let, and the number of prospective tenants falls by one. Whether the number of empty properties also falls depends on whether he is an immigrant or present tenant of elsewhere in the town. Unless he is motivated by charity or one of the other consider-ations mentioned in Chapter 2, the landlord will try to obtain the highest rent that he can, taking account of rents paid by existing tenants of both similar and different shelter, and of what he believes is to be the pressure on the housing market. If accommodation of that kind is scarce in relation to the demand he will know from the number of enquiries and will normally wait until he has a clear enough indication of this before agreeing to a tenancy. If there are few enquiries, or nobody agrees to his suggested rent, he is faced with the problem of whether to let the accommodation at a lower rent or to leave it empty in the hope of letting it later.

Several factors influence or are influenced by the decision that he makes. At some time he has had to build, buy or otherwise acquire the property and he will normally expect the rent to provide him with an income that is not derisory when he considers his expenditure. His views on this will be affected by the rate of tax that he pays on rental income, whether he has to pay municipal or other taxes as the owner of empty property, whether he has a liability in law to maintain and repair the property, and by current repair costs. There will also be other factors, including not simply the present answers to the questions just listed but his expectations of future answers. He will be influenced by whether, and on what conditions, he has a right to alter the rent and the right to terminate the tenancy. His tenants' rights will also be taken into account.

It is at this stage that the landlord's decisions about rents of the existing stock have to be related to decisions about changes in the level of that stock. In order to see this we may consider Figure 5.1, in which we suppose that only three different kinds of rented accommodation exist. To avoid awkward language we shall refer to this accommodation as 'housing', and speak of the number of 'houses' with the understanding that 'house' means an identifiable unit of accommodation. The curve S1 shows the number N of existing houses (tenanted or empty) of type 1 that landlords are willing to let at rent R. Curves S2 and S3 show similar relationships for houses of two other types. We suppose that the types are numbered in descending order of quality and value. The curves D1, D2 and D3 show the numbers of households willing to occupy these houses at various rents. The numbers of the three types of houses that are actually let, and their rents, are shown by the coordinates of the points of intersection A1, A2 and A3.

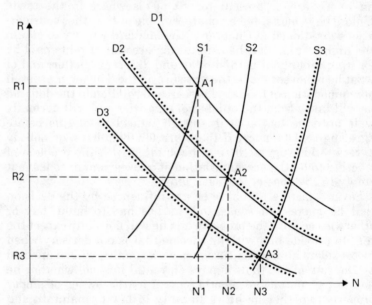

Figure 5.1

Unless some households are sharing accommodation (which is a matter we consider further, below) the numbers N1, N2 and N3 have to add up to the total number of households.

Consider now what happens if, possibly because of some change in laws about taxation, or because of a disaster leading to demolitions, the supply curve S3 moves to the left, with landlords offering fewer houses at any given rent. This would take time to have any effect but eventually existing tenants would be under pressure to pay higher rents and new tenants would have no choice – other than between accepting and rejecting a tenancy.

In such a case the gap between the rent R3 for 'poor' housing and the rent R2 for 'medium' housing would narrow, and some people would consider that the gain in accommodation standards obtainable by living in type 2 housing rather than type 3 would more than offset this reduced gap in rent levels. The result would be that some previous demanders for type 3 would become demanders for type 2. The demand curve D3 would shift to the left to a position such as the dotted line shows (tending to bring down the rent of type 3 housing) while the curve D2 would shift to the right (causing rents of type 2 to increase). This increase in rents of type 2 housing would similarly lead to some transference of demand to type 1 housing. Eventually a new 'equilibrium' would be reached with fewer people housed in type 3 housing but more in types 1 and 2 (taken together, and probably when taken separately). All rents would be at higher levels than previously. Possibly the total $N_1 + N_2 + N_3$ would be less than previously, implying a growth of sharing or an emigration.

The same diagram can be used to examine the consequences of a change in the position of any of the demand or supply curves. The broad conclusion is that if any supply is curtailed or any demand increased then all rents are likely to rise, while increased supply or reduced demand will have the opposite consequence.

If rents rise then two further consequences have to be mentioned. One is that, unless the amounts of money that some tenants have available for rent increase then probably some households will share accommodation or try to find housing elsewhere. The other is that landlords may be induced to order the construction of some new houses. This is a matter to which we turn shortly.

If rents fall then there may be a tendency for new household formation, or migration, to occur, causing some reversal of the fall. Landlords will also in some cases have to reconsider their finances and decisions.

So far we have looked upon landlords and tenants as individuals making their own decisions in such a way that collective demands and supplies arise. There are times, however, when economic or social events will tend to affect all tenants, or all landlords, in much the same way. For example, an increase in the tax payable on rental income will mean that all landlords will be worse off, and so the whole set of landlords will find that the balance of payments *vis à vis* non-landlords is upset. This means that landlords will either have to decrease their spending, or to reduce their saving, or to increase their income. The last alternative is likely to be the most attractive, and one obvious way of attempting to do it is to increase rents, which will pass some of the effect of the tax on to the set of tenants, with consequences on their balance of payments. They, too, will have to decrease their spending, or to reduce their saving, or to increase their income, and since not all of the impact on the landlords of this tax will be passed on to the tenants we find that both tenants and landlords have the problem of restoring their balances of payments with firms and people who belong to neither set. This important consequence becomes clearer if we consider Figure 5.2, which also compels us to ask about the place of residence of the landlords. This figure has been drawn in a way that implies the existence of some owner-occupied housing, since some residents are not tenants. This is an implication that is contrary to our simplifying assumption in this first analysis. The contradiction can be eliminated by considering the sets 13 and 14 to coincide, but it is convenient for us to present a single diagram that covers the more general case.

The diagram shows corporate bodies on the left and people on the right. Some corporate bodies have employees working in the town. Some of them (including some of these) are landlords of housing in the town or elsewhere. The totality of corporate bodies is shown by the sum of the sets 1, 2, 3, 4, 5, 6. Those with employees in the town are represented by the areas $2 + 3 + 4$, of whom the set 4 will also be landlords in the town, and so on.

Other landlords will be people. Some of these will live in the town, possibly as tenants. For example set 10 consists of people who are tenants of houses in the town and owners of houses elsewhere. Set 9 are owner-occupiers of property in the town who are landlords of houses elsewhere, while set 11 are owner-occupiers who also own other houses in the town.

The diagram shows 15 different sets of people and corporate bodies, as well as the Exchequer. Every one of these sets has a balance-of-payments problem. We may not, in the present exercise, be very interested in the balance of payments of corporate bodies that employ nobody in the town and are landlords nowhere; yet some of these bodies may be paying important dividends to tenants in the town. The point is that between the sixteen sets shown there may be 240 different flows of money (in one direction or the other), with each flow affecting two balances of payment. How important these may be will vary from town to town. For example, in a popular retirement resort a high fraction of the tenants may derive substantial income because they are landlords of property elsewhere. (In other words, set 10 in Figure 5.2, is important).

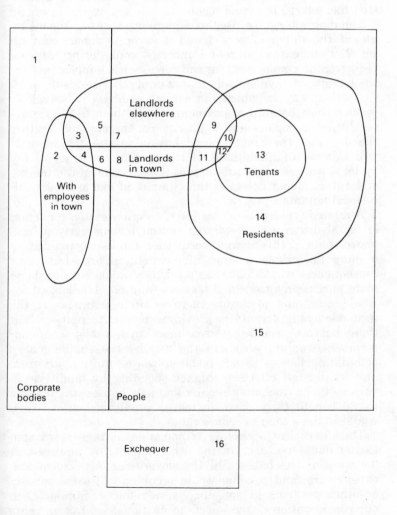

Figure 5.2

In general, however, if landlords react to a tax by raising rents then both landlords and tenants will tend to reduce their spending with other sets of people or try to increase their income from them. The spending by tenants will normally be more localized than spending by landlords (except perhaps for spending on the property itself), and consequently the ability of landlords to pass on taxes as rent increases may have a strong downward multiplier effect in a town that has a large tenanted sector.

The diagram can be used to explore other cases. For example, if the union of sets 3 and 4 is large compared with set 2, then a tax on rental incomes could bring about a reduction of employment in the town, with implications for the balance of payments of tenants (and other residents).

Another way in which the set of landlords may seek to restore their balance of payments is for them to reduce expenditure on repairs and maintenance, thereby accelerating the decay of the property and hastening the day when it will become uninhabitable. If repair work is done mainly by local workers then this implies a reduction in the income of local residents (who, in this simplified example, will all be local tenants).

A related problem concerns the consequences of a reduction of (or abolition of) an existing tax on income derived from house rents. If this were to occur then landlords would have a more favourable balance of payments. Three important consequences would follow: as a set they would tend to spend more purchasing goods and services from non-landlords; they would also tend to devote more of their resources to the income-earning activity of providing houses to rent, so that their balance would be even more favourable; and non-members would try to join the set, by the simple means of building houses to let. In other words, quite apart from any locally felt effects of higher spending by landlords on various items (including repairs and new houses) the tenants would benefit through an increased supply of houses which would in itself tend to reduce rents.

Thus one way of easing a housing shortage is to stop taxing house rentals. On the other hand, this would upset (or worsen) the balance of the government's taxation and expenditure, and possibly would occur only if some subsidy or other government spending were reduced. Similarly, in our consideration of the effects of an increased tax on rents we have to keep in mind the unknown consequences of any government spending that is financed out of the proceeds of that tax.

In this examination of certain aspects of the privately rented sector, we have said very little about the process by which landlords add to the stock of housing. This is because to do so requires some consideration of the house-building industry. Before we turn to that we shall look at public-sector rented housing, and at owner-occupation, of which both give rise to competing demands for house-building resources.

Public-sector rented housing

We must now consider rented accommodation that is owned by the state or municipal authorities. This may arise for several reasons. In Britain municipal housing was introduced late in the nineteenth century, in order to provide rented houses for low-paid workers who could not afford the rented accommodation available from private landlords. Later it was continued on the basis of various assertions including that it ensured a fair distribution of resources, that it was more efficient and that it was immoral for the private landlord to be allowed to make large profits. These are assertions that need not now concern us. All that we need to note is that municipal housing may exist for several reasons and that what matters at any one moment is a combination of the consequences of past decisions and the current motives and policies of people with the power to make decisions. It is the legacy of history rather than the motives of the past that affects the present most.

In our discussion of the privately rented sector we assumed that the landlords would be influenced by prospects of profit. Publicly owned rented accommodation has to be analysed with the aid of less clearly cut assumptions. Publicly provided housing is, in the last resort, subject to the decisions of those politicians who may keep or lose power by the political voting of an electorate whose members will hold views about it.

At times they will be motivated more by a wish to retain power than by a desire to have a 'sound', 'fair', 'rational', 'business-like', or 'humane' housing policy. But whatever the policy and motives may be, certain economic and accounting truths remain, and force the decision makers to face certain problems.

The existing stock of municipal housing has probably been provided or acquired with the aid of borrowed money on which interest is still being paid. Only if the houses are built out of current tax revenue, or acquired through some form of nation-alization, confiscation or other compulsory transfer of owner-ship, is this likely to be untrue. If it is true then the housing account is faced with repayment and interest charges. Unless the houses are to decay, the housing authority has also to pay for management, maintenance and repair.

It is unlikely that the housing authority will charge rents that cause its revenue to exceed the sum of these costs. In some countries the law does not permit it, but in any case if it became known that municipal housing was making a profit there would be a strong public and political demand for a reduction in rents. More commonly the rents are not high enough for the revenue to equal these costs, and this means that subsidies of one kind or another are being paid. They have to come from central or local taxes, for even if they are stated to come from state or municipal trading profits or other non-tax revenues, the fact is that if these subsidies were not being paid the profits or revenues would be available for the reduction of taxes. Since most voters do not like paying taxes the decision makers have to strike a balance between charging rents that are so high that they become unpopular with the tenants and their champions, and so low that they become, instead, unpopular with almost everybody else.

Decisions to increase the stock of municipal housing can be of two kinds: to acquire existing houses for the municipality and to build new houses. In the former case there is a change in the absolute sizes of the public and private sectors, with consequential changes in the relative importances of the different decision and management procedures, but no new houses are created. Even so the new owners have to consider what rents to charge and what relationship these should have to the rents of other municipal houses.

This is the difficult question that confronts the decision makers when they build new municipal houses. The decision to build may be made for a variety of reasons. There may be associated schemes of compulsory purchase and demolition in order to provide a site, which will reduce the stock of houses and add to costs. If prices are generally rising the costs of the newly built houses may already be so high that if their tenants are charged the same rents as existing tenants the housing account will increase its deficit. Existing rents, based on building costs of some years ago when the capital was bor-rowed, and only to a small extent on current repair costs, cannot be expected to cover repayment and interest charges arising from current inflated costs. Every time that interest rates or repair costs rise there is an argument for changing the rents of existing tenants, for the costs currently being incurred on their behalf are changing. What the authorities now have to consider is whether to change the rents of existing tenants in order to reduce the gap between what they pay and what tenants of new houses pay. Either the tenants of new houses pay the full economic rent of those houses, and so pay more than those who secured houses a year or several years earlier, or they pay less than the full economic rent with an increased subsidy out of taxes, or existing council tenants have their rents raised sufficiently to make this increased subsidy unnecessary.

The position, and its comparison with the private sector, are complicated by the fact that in the private sector rents are determined essentially by market forces subject to various controls, but in the public sector they cannot be determined in this way unless the housing authority is allowed to make profits in time of housing shortage with which, perhaps, to create a fund out of which to build more houses and, perhaps, to finance a deficit in other years.

Whichever solution is adopted there are welfare implications. If the rents of new houses are subsidized out of taxes there are clearly income redistributions. Whether it is strictly correct to emphasize the redistribution when rents of existing tenants are raised to help to pay the rents of new tenants is doubtful, for if a market mechanism were at work every household would expect to pay the market rent. From this standpoint there is an income redistribution in favour of existing tenants if their rents are not raised. A redistribution has to be from a starting point, and if one chooses to start from the middle one must expect to reach different conclusions than if one starts from the beginning, if, indeed, that can be found.

A common assertion is that people occupying essentially identical houses in essentially identical localities (or even in very different localities) should pay the same rent. This means adjusting existing rents in the way that we have described. It also means that one way of keeping rents down is not to build new houses, despite the presence of excess demand. In that case the families not already housed by the public sector could turn only to the private sector. If legislation prevents the operation of a market mechanism there, and so restricts the landlords' profits in a way that

discourages them from providing additional rented accommodation, these families are forced to buy, to share with others, or
to move to another town.

A different solution to this problem is to leave the rents of
existing tenants unchanged, but to charge new tenants of all
houses, old and new, higher rents. In time this will allow all
rents to rise. It is, however, a very slow process, with not easily
predicted revenue effects (since we cannot accurately predict
how many tenants will move). It also acts as a deterrent to
mobility, which may have undesirable economic and social
consequences.

Although they complain about it, most people have come to
accept that prices rise, and that more has to be paid for the
same amount of food, fuel or clothing. They know that farm-
workers, miners and factory workers have wage increases
which put up costs. But the house in which they live has
already been built. Why should they have to pay more for
continuing to occupy it? If they are told that new housing now
costs more they can rightly assert that if this argument is
applied in the private sector many landlords of old houses who
have no intention of building new ones will have windfall
gains at their expense. If these rent increases in the private
sector are not permitted, are municipal rents to rise above
private rents? They may also point out that old owner-
occupiers are not expected to subsidize new ones, although in
some countries it has been suggested that this should be
effected through changes in taxation allowances. Yet people
who bought furniture or other household durables when prices
were lowere are not expected to subsidize those who have to
make these purchases now.

In reporting on these arguments we have not attempted to
correct wrong arguments or to resolve the muddle, but now it
is time to emphasize a few points. The first is that fairness is
not an economic concept, and that people have different views
about what is fair. When the concept is introduced into
economic arguments one has to tread very warily. The second
point is that several of the problems on which we have touched
are due entirely to inflation, and indicate some of the many
ways in which this affects some people more adversely than
others. In particular it affects the 'have-nots' more adversely
than it affects the 'haves'. At this stage emotions arise. Let us
remember that many *have* as a result of their own honest
efforts and prudence, just as many *have not* because they are
young. Attempts to reduce disparities by transferring from the

haves to the have-nots are not necessarily 'fair', and in some cases can even add to inflation. Until one can find an effective way of arresting inflation, one must seek a housing policy that minimizes its undesirable consequences but takes full account of the complexities of the housing situation. Such a policy is likely to vary from country to country, or even from town to town.

Tied houses

Tied houses present a different kind of problem. The essential feature of the tied house is that the tenancy ceases when employment ceases. In defence of the system it is argued that by its design, furnishing or location the house is particularly suited to the needs of the employee, and either that an employee living elsewhere could not do the job so well or that a replacement employee could not be attracted without the offer of accommodation. The principal arguments against the system are that an employee may feel that he would like a different job in the same locality but cannot take it because he would be homeless, and that some employers take advantage of this by treating their employees badly. Examples of tied houses have already been given.

The system has its economic features. For the employee/ tenants concerned it reduces the journey to work and certainly in some cases contributes to the efficiency of the operation. A farmer whose employees all live some distance away would have considerable difficulty if he could not call upon somebody at very short notice when the weather changes or an animal becomes ill. On the other hand, it also reduces economic and social mobility. Its importance is greatest when housing stress is greatest. If it were easy to find alternative accommodation it would have fewer critics. We consider it further in our discussion of the inner city in Chapter 10.

Owner-occupation and speculative house-building

The importance of the owner-occupied sector varies from country to country. In some countries all housing is state-owned. In others very little rented accommodation exists. The nature and processes of owner occupation also vary, but in all cases there are two interacting markets, which interact further with the markets for rented housing. There is a market in existing 'second-hand' housing, and a market for either new (never previously occupied) housing or for the resources needed to build such houses. In some countries people will acquire land (legally or otherwise) and build their own houses, possibly with the help of friends, buying materials only when they must. Others will employ builders directly, and possibly even require them to buy the materials on their behalf. In both of these cases the house is built directly in response to a decision by its intending occupier. A different process, known as 'speculative building', is when somebody else takes the initiative in constructing houses that will be offered for sale during and after the process of construction. Some may be left unsold for some time.

We must begin with a word about the finance of house purchase. Once again the detail will vary between countries, and, indeed, between different kinds of housing. In some cases the intending purchaser has to have cash drawn from his own savings or loans from friends. In other cases there are institutions of one kind or another that lend money to approved applicants for housing loans. These institutions may derive their money from the government or by borrowing from private persons, or by drawing upon investment or pension funds. There may also be tax advantages for borrowers (which we shortly consider). For our present purpose the detail does not matter provided that we note that typically a house purchaser will need to make an immediate payment of some fraction of the purchase price and then to make regular payments over a long period. These regular payments may be partly repayment of principal and partly interest, or entirely interest until some date when the whole principal can be repaid (usually through the maturing of an associated life-insurance policy). Obviously the availability of loans, and the terms on which loans may be had, will affect the demand for house purchase.

In some cases people form associations that may operate in various ways but have the effect of building houses for occupation by their members, sometimes with payments spread over a very long period. The members may never become individual owners but their financial obligations and interests vary considerably. For present purposes we exclude them and consider that all houses are built to the order of landlords in the renting sector, and either for specific individuals or for speculative builders in the owner-occupier sector.

Let us now suppose that either some immigrant households with sufficient access to finance, or existing tenant households, wish to buy houses for their own occupation. The houses that they consider buying will include not only any newly built houses that have not been sold but also other houses advertised for sale. Some of these may be empty but in most cases they will be occupied by their present owners who will be depending on the sale of those houses in order to purchase other houses. There may well be half a dozen transactions all dependent on each other in this way, and if anything prevents the sale of one such house the whole chain of transactions may collapse. Thus the supply of houses for owner occupation consists of empty houses, mainly newly-built, available without doubt on payment of the agreed price, augmented by the occupied houses advertised for sale but normally not available until the existing owner has bought another house. Except with very rapidly growing or changing towns the 'second-hand' house market is likely to be larger than the market in new houses. There will also be new houses that are built to order for the intending owner who, if already an owner-occupier, will have a house to sell on completion of the new one. It is a sale of which he will have been aware for some months and may have already effected.

Few markets are as imperfect as the housing market. No two houses are identical, in identical locations with identical neighbours and views. This existence of differences is especially true with second-hand houses and the seller is likely to emphasize the peculiarities that appear to be desirable, but for newly built houses on a speculative estate the prices sought are likely to be the same for more or less identical houses on the same estate unless some are in clearly more desirable positions. The builder sets his advertised asking price at the highest figure at which he thinks he can sell all the houses in a reasonable time. He knows that if they sell too slowly he can lower the price of all or some of them. But if he underprices them he can raise his price only with difficulty and almost certainly not for all of them.

In ascertaining this price the speculative builder has three considerations in mind. He has had to buy the freehold or leasehold of the land. Possibly he did this several years earlier so that he could secure a supply of sites on which he could build. If he did then probably the land cost him less than it would have cost him more recently, although he has had capital tied up in it. He will want to recover the land cost and the interest charges on that capital.

He will also want to recover what he has paid out for wages, materials and management and other charges, and to make some profit for himself after paying taxes.

However, the builder who operated simply in this way would soon be out of business, especially in inflationary times, since he would have insufficient money either to buy more land or to pay for wages and materials during the construction of further houses. His selling price has to contribute towards his future operating costs. It is for this reason that some builders seek to buy land freehold but to sell it leasehold, charging each purchaser an annual rent for the land and thereby securing a guaranteed annual income, useful in itself or as a security for a bank loan.

The speculative builder does, however, know the prices at which other new houses have been selling and those obtained (or asked) for second-hand houses. He can also see how rapidly houses sell. It is part of his job to keep in touch with his market, and he uses his knowledge of the market first to decide on where to build, and how many houses to start and then, nearer to the date of completion, on the price at which he will try to sell. It will obviously be influenced by the prices at which other houses, old and new, have been selling, and by rents being obtained in that locality.

The price asked by the owner of his occupied house will also be influenced by the prices of new houses in his locality, but he has other matters also to consider. If he still owes money to some financial institution to whom he has mortgaged the house he is unlikely to sell it for less than that debt. If the mortgage is fairly young and there has not been rapid inflation of house prices this will tend to act as a lower limit preventing him from selling the house for much less than it cost him, even though he has enjoyed its use for a few years. Only if he is moving to a cheaper house, or more or less compelled to sell in order to move to a new locality is he likely to consider selling at a loss, and even then he will be disinclined to do so.

A second factor that he considers is the prices of other houses in his locality and of similar houses in other places. He will be particularly influenced by the price of the house he hopes to purchase, and by whether it is leasehold or freehold. In the former case he will tend to reduce his offer if the lease has only a few years to run. In this way the asking and actual selling prices of houses affect each other, with imperfections in knowledge, differing skills in bargaining and luck, in various ways, all influencing the outcome and so establishing another price to influence others. If a seller waits even an hour before agreeing to a price he may find somebody willing to pay more. Alternatively, he may find that the offer is withdrawn, because the purchaser has found a house that suits him better, or is cheaper. Even professional house agents can do no more than estimate a price based on their detailed knowledge of actual recent house prices in the area where they operate. Their advice is often to ask for a certain figure but to accept even a 10 per cent reduction if one is in a hurry to sell.

Despite these imperfections, the basic laws of demand and supply continue to apply. If there is a high unsatisfied demand for four-bedroom houses in a certain area then the people who seek them will tend to offer higher prices. These will entice some existing occupiers to sell, and speculative builders to provide more such houses, if sites are available. In an area where the existing large houses are unwanted, but there is a demand for flats, the owners of the large houses will tend to convert them in order to maximize their rental or selling value. But these are changes that take a long time and during the adjustment period the continued high demand may cause prices to rise very appreciably. When the new supply begins to appear the builders will only very slowly allow prices to fall, unless problems of liquidity force them to sell.

Before taking an overall view we must deal with one point on which we have already touched. In some countries people who borrow money in order to buy a house may deduct their interest payments from their income before being assessed by tax. It has been argued that in the British case, and possibly some others, this means that house purchasers are being subsidized, in that part of the cost of purchase is met at the expense of the taxpayers. It is instructive and important to see how the application of set analysis leads us to a different conclusion.

First we may note that almost everybody is either a net payer of taxes or a net recipient of a subsidy. In many cases it is very difficult to determine into what category a person falls. When it is said that house purchasers are subsidized by non-purchasers the implication is that house purchasers pay less tax, or receive greater subsidy, than they would if they were not purchasers. The argument continues that in fairness to non-purchasers, tax relief to purchasers should be abolished.

Let us now look at this more closely. In Britain the bulk of house purchase is effected through building societies. These organizations receive loans from people whom we will call lenders, and they pay interest to these lenders. They, in turn, pay tax on this interest to the government. (Here, as elsewhere in the story, there are certain administrative devices which impinge less fairly on some than on others, but they do not detract from our broad analysis.) The building societies lend the money they receive from lenders to borrowers for house purchase. The borrowers pay interest to the societies, and are able to claim a reduction in the amount they pay in taxes. Building societies are required to be essentially non-profit making, and the difference between the interest rate they pay and the one they charge is intended to cover their costs.

The four sets who are party to this system of house finance are thus the lenders, the societies, the borrowers and the government. The flow of interest and tax payments is as shown in Figure 5.3.

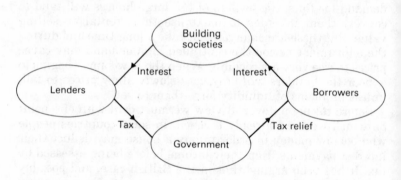

Figure 5.3

It happens that the tax received by the government from interest accruing to lenders more or less balances the tax relief granted to borrowers. Consequently the government's exchequer is virtually unaffected by the activity of financing house purchase through building-society loans.

Suppose now that the tax relief is abolished. The government will be a net recipient of additional tax revenue because people borrow money to buy houses. It will, in fact, be taxing the financing of house purchase. It is important for us to note that it is the activity of financing, rather than some party to that activity, that is taxed. As we illustrate in Chapter 11, the person from whom tax is collected is not necessarily the person, or the only person, on whom it falls. In practice almost all taxes are on activities, usually involving the purchase (and sale) of goods, services, labour, land, ideas or rights: and any tax falls to some extent on all who are party to the activity.

In the case we now consider, the tax on the activity of house financing would be collected from the lenders who receive interest. If it were increased then lenders would seek higher interest payments in order to be nearer to their former net position, and this would compel the building societies either to borrow less (and so be able to lend less) or to raise the rate charged to borrowers. In short, the tax collected from the lender would affect lenders and, through the societies, the borrowers.

Let us now suppose that in an attempt to escape from the political odium of taxing the activity of financing house purchase, the government decided not only to end tax relief for borrowers, but also to stop taxing interest received by lenders.

In that case the net income of lenders to building societies would be very attractive compared with income from other forms of loan. But borrowing from building societies would be less attractive than now. More people would offer loans to the societies at current interest rates, now free of tax; and fewer would wish to borrow at these rates. To maintain equilibrium the societies would be forced to reduce their interest rates and eventually they would reach their present post-tax levels. Lenders would receive, free of tax, what they now get after tax. And borrowers would pay, without tax relief, what they now pay after tax relief. The government would get no revenue from the activity, which is more or less its present position.

Who would then be subsidizing whom? Nobody would be better or worse off than now, and the government would be neither paying nor receiving money. It might be answered that the activity of house-purchase financing is in fact being subsidized because it is exempted from tax. But not all activities are taxed, and in most industrial cases borrowers receive exemption on tax payments when lenders are taxed on receipts. To argue that the absence of a tax implies a subsidy is to forget that between positive and negative lies zero.

It may still be possible to argue that those who obtain large tax relief do better than those who obtain little. But that is a different argument.

An overall view

In any real town there will, of course, be interplay between the rented and owner-occupied sectors. A shortage of rented accommodation will drive up rents, causing some owner-occupiers and speculative builders with empty houses to consider letting their property rather than selling it. At the same time some actual or prospective tenants decide that it is financially worthwhile to purchase. Thus there is a tendency for the supply of vacant property available for sale to fall (because some of it is being let) at the same time as the demand for it rises. House prices go up and induce an increase in supply through new building. The effects of excess supply in one sector will similarly be transmitted, but we must remember that in all cases there are also spatially transmitted effects, which we will have to consider later.

We now look in a little more detail at some of the non-spatial characteristics of housing economics. We have discussed several aspects of the demand for, and supply of, various kinds of accommodation. Four require more specific attention. On the demand side we must look at incomes, demographic factors, and credit, while on the supply side we must look at the building industry and, as it happens, once again at a demographic factor and credit.

Other things being equal, a family with a high income will spend more on housing than a family with a low income. It would, however, be wrong to think of expenditure on housing in the same way as expenditure on food, clothes or even cars. There are important reasons for this.

A change in housing expenditure has a degree of permanence in it. One does not often have an occasional extravagance of housing expenditure and then a period of comparatively low spending. This is partly because people know that at times some are forced by changes in income to seek less expensive rented accommodation, or to sell a house in order to buy a cheaper one, or to rent one, and they do not wish to be so unfortunate themselves. If the existing accommodation is furnished there are moving costs, although these can be reduced considerably by hiring a self-drive van or using one's own or borrowed animal transport. More important, in some cases, are non-monetary costs. There is a loss of prestige and a fall in housing standards. If a severe decline in income arises (or even a slight decline if the household budget is strained), and it is expected to last for some time, the household may decide that the most acceptable (or perhaps the only) way of adjusting to this decline is to move, but a more common reaction to declining income is, where possible, to reduce spending on other items. In periods of high unemployment in the nineteenth century the cotton workers of England would sometimes sell their furniture in order to pay the rent, but a prolongation of poverty would lead to their moving into poorer accommodation, sharing with relatives, or emigrating. In some cases they negotiated rent reductions.

Thus a decline in the incomes of existing households is likely to affect their spending on accommodation very slightly, unless it is a more or less permanent decline. But there is one way in which it may have a more substantial effect. Many existing households will be on the point of moving. They will have been saving for a deposit on a house, or completing the purchases of other items that have priority over an improvement in housing, or possibly expecting another child and planning to move shortly before or after its birth. A reduction in the income of these people will cause them to reconsider their intentions. They may leave them unchanged, but in other cases they will either postpone their move or seek less expensive new accommodation.

A similar, but not exactly identical, phenomenon exists when incomes rise. While a slight but prolonged fall in income may force a household to move if it is already on a strained budget, a slight increase may be quite insufficient to encourage a household to seek better accommodation, although it may enable it to accept better accommodation if it happens to find it. The point is that while a slight fall may sometimes compel a search for cheaper housing, a slight rise will not compel a search for something better and may not even encourage one. In some cases the rise will be spent on consumer items or household durables. In other cases it may be saved, possibly in order to acquire a deposit for house purchase. After some time it may enable sufficient to be saved for the household to seek a house of its own.

A larger rise may have a different effect. If it is expected to be permanent it may appear to be sufficient to enable the household to buy for the first time, or to move to a bigger house, or one in a preferable neighbourhood.

In countries where house prices are expected to rise faster than the general level of prices some people will be influenced by the thought that they should spend as much as they can on buying a house, partly so that they may, in old age, sell it and buy a cheaper one but still have a useful capital gain to add to any pension that they may have. Even if other prices are rising faster than house prices a household may feel that a bigger house-purchase commitment is the best means of saving, and preferable to a deposit in a bank. Households that are in any case on the point of moving are likely to contemplate increasing their housing expenditure more than they originally intended.

In both cases, however, the household is likely to have in mind the question of permanence. There will be a reluctance to incur greater financial obligations if it is at all likely that before long some change will compel the household to consider moving once more, to less expensive accommodation.

We should also note that income changes can affect the rates at which new households are formed, and so affect the demand for dwellings indirectly.

Some idea of the income elasticity of demand* for housing is important for two reasons associated with prediction. We may need to know how a general change in income levels will affect spending on various items, including housing. Alternatively, our main interest may be in the extent to which the demand for new houses will be affected, so that implications for the house-building sector may be gauged. In some studies income changes appear as one of the several variables in a time-series analysis. Others rely on cross-section studies in which actual housing expenditure is related to actual income. If the remarks just made are correct then both of these methods may at times be misleading, since the existence of any income effect, its magnitude and its timing vary considerably between different sets of households; and if changing demographic, economic or other factors cause the circumstances of people to change in such a way that the relative numbers in these different sets alter, then the average elasticity of demand estimated by such methods will alter. Very detailed cross-section studies are needed, with attention to shifts between sets, as well as to questions about the expected degree of permanence in the income changes.

The importance of demographic factors in determining demand has been emphasized by some writers but strangely neglected by others. Obviously fifty thousand people forming ten thousand households will have different housing requirements than the same number of people forming twenty thousand households. Both the number of households and their sizes affect housing demand, and both economic and purely demographic factors determine these. A rise in the number of people in the age groups when marriage is most common will normally increase the rate of creation of new households,

* This is a measure of the responsiveness of housing demand to changes in income. Its precise definition needs not concern us here.

although abnormally good or bad economic conditions may advance or retard the timing. Similarly, a rise in the number of elderly people can be expected shortly to lead to an increase in the number of households disappearing through deaths, merging with young households, or movement into some kind of institution. Here, too, economic factors can have their effects. The point to note is that this disappearance of households adds to the supply of available second-hand houses. Other changes in the numbers of households will arise from migration, which can be affected by economic and social conditions in the town of immigration and in the town of emigration.

The size of a household affects housing demand in two ways that interact in an important manner. On the one hand household size affects the demand for space. A growing household will want more or bigger rooms, while a declining one may eventually feel that smaller accommodation would be welcome. On the other hand, the size of the household affects both its income and its expenditure. A large number of young children will reduce the per capita income of the household and in many cases compel it, despite its needs, to live in poor accommodation. As the children grow the space-needs increase, and so do their food and clothing requirements. But eventually the children start to earn, or to leave home, and the per capita income of the household rises, facilitating higher expenditure on housing. The phenomenon has been discussed at greater length elsewhere. Demographic and economic factors combine in a way that frequently produces long cycles of about twenty years duration in construction and urban development.

Credit is the third factor mentioned above as needing further attention. When credit is abundant and cheap it is easier for house purchasers, and for those who build, be it for speculation or as landlords, to borrow. Credit scarcity and high interest rates work in the opposite direction. Rents may also reflect current borrowing rates, especially if the houses are financed with long-term borrowing. A point that is less frequently appreciated is that a rising volume of building activity is likely to drive up interest rates, and to be accompanied by other activities that have the same effect. This is a matter examined in detail in another book. What we must now remember is that credit is supplied by people who have choices before them – the choices of whether to lend, to whom to lend, and on what terms to lend.

New houses come from the building industry. While very large house-building firms exist, probably no industry is easier to enter, and so in most countries there are very many small house-building firms or a great deal of do-it-yourself house building. In times of high activity shortages tend to appear, as the total demand for some material or skill exceeds the amount that is currently locally available. Apart from the important seasonal element, the factors we have already discussed can lead to very great changes in demand over a very short time. The availability of skilled labour is an obvious source of one constraint, especially since, while it may take a long time for a man to become skilled as a joiner, there is little to compel him to remain a joiner if he cannot find work, and in times of low building activity there may be a loss of skilled workers of whom only some will return when activity revives. Building materials present problems for other reasons. Many materials are difficult to store. Cement does not have a long life. Enough bricks to satisfy the demands of a busy month occupy a vast amount of storage space, as well as a substantial amount of idle capital. Yet manufacturers with fluctuating demands for their product have only three alternatives: to produce at a fairly steady level, building up stocks in periods of low demand; or to enlarge capacity so that they can quickly expand supply in response to demand, yet keep working well below capacity in times of low demand; or to fail to meet demand in boom periods. In the building materials industries the first of these solutions is impracticable for reasons we have already indicated. The second is very expensive and could be justified only if higher prices were obtained throughout the year. The third is what usually happens. In places where house building is done mainly with easily available timber, simple sun-baked bricks, or similar materials, all of this is obviously less important. But if large house-building programmes are contemplated the first steps must be to ensure that there are adequate supplies of materials and skills.

The capacity of the house-building industry clearly sets an upper limit to the total amount of work that can be done at any time. It is an industry that is not easily isolated, for some workers move freely between house-building jobs and other building or construction jobs. Road making will compete with house building for cement and other building materials. At all times, house building has to compete with other activities for skills and materials, as well as for finance.

This means that these other activities can affect the rate of supply of new houses, and consequently house prices and rents.

Within the housing sector there is a similar interaction. A large-scale public-sector housing programme may absorb so much of the locally available labour, or locally made bricks, that private house building can proceed only if wages are raised in order to entice labour from the public sector or from afar, or if bricks are obtained at a greater transport cost. In a similar way a great deal of private building can create problems for the public sector. In both cases the easing of supply of one kind of house thwarts the increased output of the other kind. Thus, for example, a large public house-building programme may prolong a shortage of privately rented housing, or of new houses for owner occupation. This means that rents in the private sector and house prices will tend to be higher than otherwise for two reasons. The large programme may push up labour and material prices and so cause prices and rents to rise because all building costs are higher, and prolong shortage in the private sector will itself lead to higher market prices. The argument that public-sector rents may be lower, and may even siphon off some of the private sector demand, is valid only if public sector rents are determined by demand and supply, which is certainly not the case in all countries. On the other hand, massive activity in the private sector, while causing a shortage of public-sector housing, would tend to lower private rents and prices through an increase in supply, even though there would be a counter-tendency due to rising costs.

Prices and rents can also be affected when the building industry and the supply of credit are out of phase. If, for example, the supply of loans for house purchase is suddenly increased after a period of shortage and low housing activity, then there will be an increase in the number of prospective purchasers far in excess of the increase that can take place in the supply of new houses during the next several months. Both existing old houses and the trickle of new houses started in less affluent times will be sold at prices reflecting this imbalance between a newly liberated demand and a supply that can be increased only slowly. Higher prices inevitably cause some would-be purchasers to remain, or to become, tenants, and so private-sector rents will tend to rise (if the law allows it) and waiting lists for public-sector housing to lengthen.

Overcrowding

We have already noted that in some towns there is intense overcrowding. In developed countries this tends to exist in certain parts of the inner city, whereas in many towns in developing countries it exists much more widely. Overcrowding is affected by matters considered later, but we may conveniently make a few points now.

In the inner cities of developed countries there are four different sets of residents living in seriously overcrowded conditions. Some are residents dependent upon people who work in or close to the town centre, sometimes during hours when public transport is infrequent, and who consider that living further from the town centre would present them with unacceptable travel problems and so, ultimately, with an inability to keep their jobs. High land values mean that the accommodation that is in a suitable location is expensive, and, legally or otherwise, occupiers share their dwellings for economic reasons. We consider this matter further in Chapter 10.

Another set of people living in overcrowded conditions in the same area are those who have lost their jobs, possibly through the closure (or migration) of the firm that employed them. As long as they remain where they are, they face the problem of high rents to be paid out of low incomes.

Two other sets of people contribute to the problem. There are the grown-up children of residents of the area, who may decide to continue to live there when they marry. Finally, there are those who have migrated into the area, often without having a job. They may do so because of the locational, ethnic or social characteristics of the area, or because it is the part of the city in which it is possible to obtain accommodation (shared though it may be) at a price lower than that charged for what is available elsewhere. There may, of course, be other reasons for their choice, possibly depending partly on one or both of these factors.

In all of these cases the nature of the existing housing structure will matter. Some can be used more easily than others for multiple occupation, which often begins with people renting rooms or small flats for use by one or two people, and then allowing others to stay with them, not always with the knowledge of the landlord. This is much easier in a large old house of the kind frequently found near town centres than in the smaller more modern houses where, apart from anything else, neighbours may be more likely to notice the extent of overcrowding and to bring it to the attention of any official who may have powers to deal with it. Intervention of this kind by neighbours is, of course, rare when the whole area is occupied by people whose social values deviate from those proclaimed by most of the urban society, and this can encourage the growth of pockets of overcrowding.

Thus, in these developed cities, overcrowding tends to be near the town centre, partly because of various demands to live in proximity to the centre where, as it happens, rents are high, and partly because that is where buildings that lend themselves to this phenomenon are most likely to be found. Once it has started it will tend to expand, providing a supply of overcrowded but comparatively low-priced accommodation.

Finally, we turn to the case of the developing countries. Here the phenomena we have already noted in relation to the inner city may exist, but the problem is even more that of absorbing a vast expansion of population due both to natural increase and to migration from the rural areas. The basic cause is that people are arriving in the town faster than houses are being built. The analysis of rented and owner-occupied housing that we have presented in this chapter remains valid, with the proviso that empty houses are almost non-existent, and that while in some cases the landlord will receive rent directly from every occupier, in other cases he will let to only one person, who will sub-let or make other sharing arrangements, perhaps in a way that brings profit to himself and/or to the landlord.

The rural-urban migrant moves mainly in order to improve his lot. During the nineteenth century the developing countries of western Europe witnessed a similar phenomenon, for similar reasons, but the scale was much smaller. No sizeable town then grew as rapidly as the major cities of developing countries are growing today. It is also true, of course, that in those days medical science and transport technology were less able to cope with the consequences of over-dense population: but even today they can do so only if they are provided with an opportunity – which may not be the case especially when shanty towns, and even official urban extensions, are erected without the provision of sewage disposal or suitable means of access. The economic, social and other problems associated with modern urban migration in developing countries are of a scale and quality without precedent: but the basic cause is unchanged. The migrant expects to improve his lot.

This chapter is not the place in which to examine the consequences of this migration. We may, however, suggest that when migration is out of phase with the provision of services, it may bring problems for existing residents and the municipal authorities. Where housing is built privately there will be a tendency for private developers to take advantage of the high rents and prices arising out of the shortage and to provide more houses. Partly in an attempt to cope with the problem as they see it, the municipal authorities will tend to do the same. Unfortunately, this can be a case of supply creating its own demand, for the very act of providing more accommodation may attract additional migrants. In some cases they will hope for some of the new accommodation, and in others they will argue that since their relatives have been able to decant some of their lodgers or extended-household members into new places they can now accommodate another wave of migrants. The total stimulus to migration thus engendered may be sufficient to make the housing shortage worse than it was before. In terms of Figure 5.1, a rightward shift of the supply curve S3, assumed to very very steep, brings about a rightward shift of the Curve D3, in a way that may cause A3 to rise rather than to fall.

[In some cases D3 could seem to pass over D2. This is a point that we must consider more fully. If the demand curve D3 lies, in whole or in part, to the right of D2, the meaning is that the number of people demanding low-grade housing at a stated rent exceeds the number demanding medium grade housing at that price. The apparent perversity of this result stems from the fact that the curves are 'real' only in the vicinities of their intersections with the relevant supply curves. The part of D2 that crosses S3 is so far from the existing reality of demand and supply that it is best forgotten. So is the part of D3 that crosses S2. What matters is that A3 remains below A2.]

In this chapter we have looked mainly at certain aspects of the economies of various sets of people who are associated in one way or another with urban housing. We have considered how the behaviour of one set may affect another, and noted not only certain interdependencies between housing markets but also certain relationships with other aspects of the economy. The most important matter that we have not considered is the whole set of spatial relationships, which may have economic causes and consequences. Until these have been analysed, the conclusions reached in this chapter are necessarily tentative or incomplete: but they will enable us to discuss the parts played by landlords, tenants and others in the competition for locations in a more informed way than would otherwise be possible.

6

Retailing and warehousing

In many towns retailing and warehousing occupy more space than any other activity apart from housing. The shopping trip will in some towns generate as much traffic as the journey to work. Thus in terms of land use and transport, retailing and associated activity form an essential part of the study of towns.

We begin with some comment on the emergence of retailing and wholesaling. Then we consider certain economic aspects of the behaviour of shopkeepers, wholesalers, owners of shop property, shopworkers and customers. Finally we take a more overall view. The spatial aspects are considered in later chapters. As in Chapter 5, we use the set approach where appropriate, but our purpose is to give a background and context for later analysis rather than to demonstrate here the importance of sets.

The emergence of retailing and wholesaling

Except in very primitive economies, very few residents of a town make an appreciable fraction of their purchases directly from the manufacturer or grower. Quite apart from the problems that many producers would have if they had also to be retailers, the task facing the customer, of having to visit the manufacturer of every item (or several shops each selling the products of only one firm), would be so obviously inconvenient and inefficient that some kind of middle-man, offering to the public goods from several different sources, would soon arise.

The links between the retailer, who sells directly to the public, and the manufacturer, or grower, vary not only between countries but also to some extent between different towns within a country. Broadly speaking, the more developed countries have more complicated links, while within a country the organization of these links is likely to be different in big towns than that in small towns.

In small agrarian villages in developing countries there may be virtually no retailing other than purchases directly from local growers and visiting traders. Any other wants must remain unsatisfied until a trader arrives or a trip is made to a larger town.

In slightly larger settlements some simple shops may arise, sometimes through the initiative of a visiting trader or, more usually, because a resident of the village sees that by making journeys to a retail centre and anticipating the purchase needs of others he can make some profit, and perhaps a livelihood. The shop is unlikely to stock anything that is not within the standard purchasing pattern of the villagers, and in order to achieve a volume of business sufficient to provide a livelihood it is likely to be developed into a very small-scale general store rather than a specialist shop. The owner will obtain his purchases where he can, possibly direct from the manufacturer but in most cases from another intermediate source, as we shall shortly see. In even larger settlements the local demand for goods may be big enough to support specialist shops, a clothes shop, or a shop selling various kinds of cloth for the housewife to make her own clothes, may arise. So may a butcher's shop, possibly developing out of the sale of home-produced carcasses supplemented by purchases from local farms or a larger supplier of meat. Eventually there may even be competition between specialists, with several shops all specializing in the same broad category of goods.

Some of these shops, or stalls, will emerge where part of the custom is done with other shopkeepers, and especially with shopkeepers from smaller settlements round about. These will tend to arise most frequently in places big enough for specialist shops to arise, and the emergence of the wholesaler is frequently through an extension of the activities of one of these, with the specialist shop selling at lower prices to other shop-keepers who are prepared to buy enough. Frequently these wholesalers will take up space in a recognized market area alongside pure retailers who may to some extent buy from them and to some extent compete with them, in so far as they are still also retailers. Often there is a tendency for retailers of a particular specialism to cluster together, partly to be close to the wholesaler, partly on the principle that if location is a factor in profit it is better to be next door to an existing business in a good location than isolated in a bad one, and partly because, as this practice develops, different sectors of a market area acquire their own characteristics and reputations. A stall selling spices in an eastern market would do little trade if surrounded by clothes shops – for how could it attract custom away from the part of the market where twenty spice stalls exist, and which is known to all as the place to go for spices?

In almost all of these cases, the shopkeeper, or stall holder, still collects his own merchandise. In some towns small manufacturing establishments will arise within the retail area, with sales to neighbouring retailers and, usually, a willingness to retail directly to the public; but in most cases the retailer is some distance from the manufacturer, as is the wholesaler.

The wholesaler and distributor

The wholesaler fulfils for the retailer much the same function as the retailer fulfils for the public, except that he is more likely to extend credit as normal practice. The distributor is essentially a wholesaler but he derives importance from a privilege. Some manufacturers find it simpler to deal with only a small number of firms who purchase their goods and then sell them to wholesalers or directly to the public. This is especially the case if there are foreign markets, when a single firm can become sole distributors of a range of imported products. Other manufacturers act as their own distributors, and in some cases insist on selling only to retailers. In other cases they insist on selling only to wholesalers or other large purchasers. We must consider this a little further.

Both manufacturers and distributors may apply restrictions to supply. One of the most common is to refuse orders of a total cost that is less than some specified sum. This means that amongst retailers only department stores, chain stores, and specialist shops with large sales of the articles concerned are likely to place orders. If the manufacturer or distributor is willing to accept orders from wholesalers, other retailers may obtain some supplies indirectly. The reason for the restriction is partly to avoid the trouble of dealing with small orders, and partly to pursue indirectly a policy of selecting retail outlets.

It is this second form of restriction that is less fully appreciated outside the retailing industry. Some manufacturers and distributors like to choose the shops what will be allowed to sell their goods. Usually the reason for this policy is that a good stockist of their product should carry the whole range, and that this involves not only a sizeable investment in stock but also a willingness to stock some of the more slowly moving items of the range. A retailer is more likely to do this if he knows that no other local shop is selling any of that product: but if he loses his monopoly sales position then he is likely to stock only the fast selling items. On the other hand, some manufacturers and distributors carry the policy to an extent that cannot be defended along these lines, refusing to supply anything at all to a retailer who is judged to be too close to another retailer who purchases some items from them but makes no attempt to purchase others. The shopkeeper, and especially the small shopkeeper, is often unable to stock items demanded by his customers.

Wholesalers fall into two categories. Some operate on a cash-and-carry basis. Essentially they are shops, where the retailer calls, looks at the goods, makes his choice, pays for them and takes them away. There is a tendency for such wholesalers to cluster, and to be dependent upon traders within convenient travel distance.

Other wholesalers deliver goods in their own vans, or by public freight transport, in response to orders received from shopkeepers. Usually they do so before receipt of payment and may allow several weeks credit. They obtain orders by sending out catalogues and employing agents or representatives who visit shops and obtain orders from retailers, usually on a commission basis.

Like retailers, wholesalers make their profit by selling goods for more than they pay for them. They have accommodation and staff costs, and are as vulnerable to the consequences of mistaken buying as are retailers. Most of their other problems are also very similar to those of retailers, even though they may differ in detail, and we shall say little more about them here.

The retailer

We consider first the independent shopkeeper with a single shop. His first prerequisite is a stock of goods. In some cases he will have to pay for these when he gets them, while in other cases he may obtain them on credit. If he is a small retailer he may try to make use of cash-and-carry warehouses where he can usually buy in smaller quantity, and at slightly lower prices, than if he deals with other wholesalers. But in that case he is unlikely to obtain trade credit, and therefore has to pay for the goods before he can sell them. He consequently needs an initial capital which he may have to borrow, and on which interest will have to be paid. The rate of interest may not be fixed and may be outside the retailer's control. Larger retailers are also likely to have a similar problem of stock financing. Even though they may obtain all stock on credit, and sell much of it before they have to pay for it, some items will usually be 'slow movers' and not recover their cost for some time.

Stock also requires space. In some shops virtually the whole of the stock may be on show, but in others an appreciable part of the floor space may be used for storage, especially if the shop buys in considerable bulk (which may be the only way of obtaining some items). The space occupied in this way may represent a considerable cost to the retailer. Another cost associated with stockholding arises out of the depreciation of items held in stock, especially if they are perishable or seasonal and subject to changes of fashion.

Just as stock requires space, so does selling; and this brings us to the retailer's second need – premises. His locational requirements are considered in Chapter 8, but here we may note that rent and local taxes associated with the premises usually form a large part of his costs. There are, of course, some central-area shopkeepers who own their premises, but where new shopping centres and precincts are built it is usual for all of the shops to be tenanted, just as are most other central-area shops.

Most shopkeepers who rent premises in a shopping centre have a lease of tenancy and a rental agreement. In some cases the rent may be fixed for the duration of the lease, but in developed countries a more common arrangement in recent decades has been for the rental agreement to specify that the rent will be reviewed every five years, or every seven years, during the life of the lease. The agreement may set limits to the review, or it may give the landlord freedom to set the new rent at any level that he wishes, subject, usually, to some arbitration procedure in the event of strong protest from the tenant. The shopkeeper is legally obliged to pay the rent, subject to reviews, throughout the life of the lease. If he decides to close his shop he is still obliged to pay rent unless he can find some new tenant who will take over his obligations to the landlord.

Thus a prospective tenant-shopkeeper has to consider not only whether he can sell enough, at a sufficient margin of gross profit, to be able to cover his costs, but also whether his revenue is likely to grow sufficiently to cover rent increases that are likely to arise on fixed dates. If he has doubts about this he has to consider whether he is likely to have difficulty in off-loading the tenancy on to somebody else.

Apart from the rent, the shopkeeper has other costs of which some are not under his control, especially in a small shop. There will be local taxes, subject usually to annual review, and possibly comparable in magnitude with the shop rent. Fuel charges are only partly under his control, especially if the law prescribes a minimum temperature below which he is not allowed to employ staff. Insurance payments may also be partly obligatory. Some of these costs also exist in developing countries.

Broadly speaking, once the shopkeeper has selected his premises the costs just mentioned are fixed, at ruling prices, independently of the volume of sales (unless local taxes include some kind of sales or income tax). Two other costs depend to some extent on the level of sales or of planned sales. These are labour costs and the costs associated with the holding of stock. We must now look at these and consider to what extent the shopkeeper can control them. We shall then look at revenue.

The shopkeeper has several tasks to perform, either by himself or with assistance. He has to sell to his customers, to deal with their complaints, and possibly to accept special orders and to provide advice. He also has to guard his stock against shoplifting. These two sales-floor tasks will at times require greater help than at other times, and if too few staff are employed sales may be lost (through the customer's reluctance to wait or a lack of positive selling), or shoplifting may increase. What the shopkeeper has to try to consider is whether the marginal cost of an extra member of staff is less than the marginal addition to profit arising out of increased sales and reduced shoplifting: but to estimate this is far from easy.

Apart from these tasks of selling and stock protection, the shopkeeper has a variety of tasks that must precede selling. He has to meet sales representatives, inspect catalogues and visit exhibitions and warehouses prior to placing orders for the merchandise that he hopes to sell. This has then to be collected or received and unpacked, checked for shortages and damage, priced (in a way that will be discussed later) and put on display or suitably arranged in a stockroom.

Finally, the shopkeeper has to keep accounts, and in some countries to prepare weekly wage and tax-deduction cards, and generally to keep all the records, and to make all the returns, that the law may require.

These tasks of buying, controlling stock, and keeping records will often depend more on the number of suppliers, and the number of different items sold, than on the volume of sales. A shop selling only two or three items all supplied to it by one firm would have problems that would be trivial compared with those of another shop, having the same weekly turnover, but selling a thousand different items from the same two or three suppliers; while the shop selling a thousand items obtained from a hundred suppliers would have the additional tasks of dealing with more sales representatives, corresponding with more firms, checking more invoices, keeping more accounts, and so on. This means that a complicated shop needs more 'back-up' staff than a simple shop, and therefore needs to make more gross profit in order to pay the higher wage bill.

While the shopkeeper determines how many staff he will employ, subject to his impression of his needs, he may have little say in what he will pay them. Quite apart from possibly having to compete with other shops and other forms of employer in the local labour market, there may be minimum wage rates for shopworkers and associated conditions of employment laid down by law. At times the real choice facing the small shopkeeper will be the simple one of either changing the whole character of the shop, (probably by simplifying it or by stocking only the popular fast-moving items) or doing more work himself (probably in the evenings and at weekends, keeping the accounts and unpacking and pricing deliveries). This may be because what he needs is a part-time assistant and he cannot find a suitable one, or because he needs to reduce labour costs without reducing sales.

The other cost that depends on the levels of sales and of planned sales is the cost of holding stock, which has already been mentioned.

We now turn to the shopkeeper's revenue. Clearly it depends on the quality and range of stock, its display and advertisement, his location, his selling methods, staff and quality of service, his competitors and his pricing policy. This last requires special consideration by us.

First we must note that there may be restrictions on the prices charged by the retailer. The main remaining forms of constraint on prices are competition and the desire to survive. No shopkeeper can expect to sell much merchandise at a much higher price than that charged by neighbouring shopkeepers who may happen to sell the same product. If he can, he may deliberately try to sell some items for less than other shops charge, but here, too, there is a limit, for while lower prices may attract custom and increase the volume of sales, there may also be a rise in costs due to this increase in volume.

Pricing policy is rarely a matter for the individual retailer acting alone to determine. Under pressure from competing retailers, wholesalers or producers may (legally or otherwise) create difficulties for a retailer who sells at very low prices. In some cases (as in the sale of books in the United Kingdom) the law may specify a minimum price, while in some countries many (or even all) of the prices may be fixed by the government. There may also be laws that limit the price increases that a shopkeeper may introduce. Even in the absence of such constraints, the shopkeeper has to charge in a way that depends to some extent on his own purchasing costs.

Yet within these bounds, there remains in most cases some flexibility. The usual practice is for a retailer to add a percentage 'mark-up' to his purchasing price, and (subject to the points just made) the choice of mark-up is left to him. He will try to choose it so that his profit is as high as possible, believing that low prices may attract more custom, yet provide less profit on each item. His problem is to strike a balance.

In branches of retailing where the mark-up is fairly high, a moderate price reduction may be justified if it leads to only a small increase in the volume of business. For example, if the normal retail price is double the wholesale price (representing a mark-up of 100 per cent), then a reduction of 10 per cent in retail prices will increase the retailer's profit provided that the volume of his sales increases by at least 25 per cent. As the mark-up falls, the necessary increase in sales if profits are to be maintained will rise. If the mark-up is 50 per cent then a reduction of 10 per cent in retail prices will be justified only if the volume of sales increases by well over 40 per cent; while if the mark-up is only 20 per cent the volume of sales would need to increase by almost 170 per cent – approaching a trebling – in order to keep profits unchanged. This assumes that such sales could be achieved without involving higher labour and other costs, which may well not be so.

The brief account just given of certain problems facing mainly the independent shopkeeper who rents premises needs only little modification for other kinds of shopkeeper; but the modification, though easily described, may have important consequences.

Retail chains benefit from many economies of scale. Bulk buying will often ensure favourable terms and in some cases will break through restrictive practices on the part of suppliers. Stockholding can be reduced, with one shop borrowing stock from another if it cannot satisfy a customer from its own resources. Much of the paperwork can be centralized, and the size of the operation enables various control policies to be implemented more efficiently. In emergency, staff can be moved from shop to shop, and in general a better quality of assistant can be attracted by better career prospects. The group resources enable a shop in a town where there is a local price war to operate at a loss if necessary, perhaps for long enough to defeat the opposition. Advertising and other promotional activities become a more viable proposition than they may be for the single shop.

Department stores may be single stores or parts of chains. Even when single they may cooperate with others in their buying. The extent to which they share the benefits seen by retail chains depends partly on the extent to which they are themselves chains and partly quite simply on their size. Where they differ from other kinds of shops is in their use of space and of clerical and other administrative services, and in their ability to manipulate staff.

If, for example, the menswear department is not making much profit considering the amount of floor space that it occupies, the management can fairly easily allow some other department to take over part of the space, with the aim of increasing the total profit of the store. Similarly, if the toy department is capable of earning more profit than any other at Christmas time, provided it has enough space, the management can consider allowing it to have its seasonal expansion at the expense of departments whose Christmas sales are comparatively low.

Concentrated accounting and other clerical services, including perhaps those of a computer, are obviously more likely to be practicable and economic in a large enterprise. The other benefit of size is that while staff are normally attached to particular departments it is possible to switch staff from one department to another when emergency or other needs arise. By making greater use of this facility the store can sometimes 'manage' with fewer staff, and so the room for economy on wages is greater, provided that the staff are prepared to cooperate.

We still have to deal with various other kinds of shopkeeper, including the corner shopkeeper – the man (or woman) whose shop and home are combined, and who can involve members of the family in the shop activities. The problems facing him are much the same as those facing any other small shopkeeper, except for the flexibility in labour that arises out of his living on the premises, and the fact that he may very well own the property and so be protected from increases in rent. On the other hand, the total hours worked by him and his family may be very great.

Finally, we may note the existence in developed countries of open-air and covered markets, where stallholders of various kinds sell their wares under circumstances that are not typical of other retailing. The market stalls are usually comparatively flimsy structures and may be erected and dismantled every day. The stallholder brings his ware to the stall and has no deliveries by firms or wholesalers. The space is normally rented and, in a covered market, certain costs such as heating are likely to be shared. In the covered market there is no vehicular traffic and no inclement weather problem, while even in the open air market traffic is usually absent. The basic problems of pricing and costs are very similar to those already described for the small tenant-shopkeeper, but the costs and mechanics of stock purchase are different.

One very important, and surprisingly frequently forgotten, fact must now be made. Independently of all else, a shop-keeper's profits do not rise and fall in simple proportion to his sales. Especially in the more complicated arrangements that exist in developed countries, the various costs that we have described may be virtually insensitive to any but very sizeable variations in the level of activity. Rent, wage costs and other items have to be deducted from the gross profit before net profit is made. Broadly speaking, gross profit will be a more or less fixed percentage of sales but costs are likely to be fairly steady or, in inflationary times, to be rising. If sales fall by, say, ten per cent, and cause a ten per cent fall in gross profits, then if costs are not falling this may be quite enough to turn a net profit into a net loss.

The reference to inflation needs a little elaboration. It affects shopkeepers in several ways. Wages and other costs rise, but for a given volume of trade, so do turnover and gross profit. Whether gross profit rises as much as costs depends on specific detail of a kind that cannot now be considered. We must, however, consider certain points about increased purchasing costs and increased selling prices.

The first is that if a retailer is in the habit of having to pay for a delivery of stock when only some of it has been sold, then rising prices may mean that in order to replenish stock a retailer has to pay out sums of money that rise faster than his available cash does. If interest rates are also rising, as they tend to be in periods of high inflation, then to maintain the same level of stock he has also to pay higher interest on this rising debt.

Operating in the opposite direction is the opportunity to raise the prices of existing stock, thereby making a capital appreciation. In practice this may be limited by law, or by the knowledge that competing shops have not yet had new deliveries and consequently are selling at old prices. The shopkeeper has then to decide whether to sell new, more expensive, stock at increased prices or to wait until his competitors are in the same position. Finally, if he is selling a wide range of related items, like saucepans of different sizes and colours, he has to consider the compatibility· of prices for items out of new deliveries and items already in stock. On balance the opportunity to increase prices of existing stock will in almost all cases result in a net gain, but whether it is sufficient to offset the adverse effects of inflation is a question to which there is no general answer.

Shop property owners

We have yet to consider the provision of the shop premises themselves. In some cases a shopkeeper (or a retail firm) will take the initiative in converting or building premises, but in developed countries this is normally the case only for very small shops of the 'corner shop' type or very large ones, such as premises for a department store. Nowadays the building of new shops is mainly for renting, and undertaken for profit. The mechanics of the operation vary not only from country to country but also from town to town and from time to time. The essential points however are common. The developer, be it an individual, a private firm, a municipal authority, the state, or any other organization, has to have a site, or an option on a site, and the opinion that if this site is used for retailing he will obtain a good return on his costs. While the prospective shopkeeper has to form expectations of sales, costs and profit, the prospective developer has to assess his development costs and form expectations of the shopkeepers' expectations. The time between the decision to start work on building a shop, a group of shops or even a whole shopping precinct, and the actual signature of contracts of tenancy may be several years, and so the developer has to form expectations some years ahead of the shopkeeper. We shall have more to say about this when we consider financial aspects of urban development.

Shop workers

Three aspects of labour supply need to be considered by us. The first is the matter of accessibility. Normally shops will be located where there is good access by customers; and this implies good access by shop workers provided that they have comparable means of transport. In areas where a large part of the custom depends on car-borne customers the public transport system may not be very good over the whole of the customer catchment area, especially at the times when shop staff need to travel. This will effectively reduce the area from which shop staff are drawn, unless they have cars (which is unlikely for many of them). In some cases, such as those of small market towns in country areas, this can mean that it is very difficult to obtain shop staff. The usual answer is to offer higher wages, or to offer working hours adapted to the needs of whoever is willing to work. In either case the shopkeeper is likely to incur costs, and the customers to have these or some inconvenience passed on to them.

Wages and working hours are our two other subjects of concern. Apart from the normal relationship of wages and hours to supply and demand, there may be constraints imposed by national or municipal government or by labour organizations. In some cases enforceable minimum wage rates may exceed those at which labour would be available locally, and act as a deterrent to the expansion (or continued existence) of shops providing a larger number of less well paid jobs. Legislation may also mean either that certain kinds of shops are not allowed to open at certain times, or that they can open only by incurring high marginal labour costs. Such legislation protects shop workers from the threat of dismissal if they are unwilling to work long or unpopular hours, but may also prevent shopkeepers from providing a service at the time when customers would find it most convenient. It may also tend to concentrate the timing of the work trips of shop workers, possibly into the hours when other work trips are concentrated for other reasons.

Usually shop workers have low pay and work some hours when most other people are not working, and the points we have just made are viewed differently by them. Some of them, unable to afford cars, are faced with having to travel long distances which effectively lengthen their working day or to live in poor quality accommodation nearer to the town centre, because better accommodation would cost them more than they can afford. In large towns this is particularly likely to be the case.

Customers

We have already touched upon a number of customer requirements. Ideally most customers probably seek good access to a wide range of goods, readily available from stock, easily examined, offered at competitive prices, and being sold by staff who can answer all their questions, provide abundant guarantees, and be on duty at all times convenient to the customer. Most of these requirements could be met only at the expense of the shopkeepers' profits, and it is doubtful whether they could all be met at the same time. The interaction between customers demands and shopkeepers responses has been considered to some extent earlier in the chapter, and will appear again in the next section, as well as in later chapters.

There are, however, a few more general points to make. Shops are not the only places of expenditure for customers. At any moment the money available for spending in certain kinds of shops is often a residual that acts as a severe constraint. After seeing to rent and other obligatory or contractual payments, many households have to consider carefully the allocation of their remaining income between food, clothes and other items. Anything that increases obligatory expenses, such as increases in local taxes, rents or travel expenses is likely to reduce expenditure in shops. An increase in expenses for low-paid workers may so reduce their spending in non-food shops that in areas where wages are low many of these shops will be forced to close, leaving the local population with poor choice in slightly more prosperous times.

Some other aspects of relationships between income and the provision of shops are considered elsewhere, especially in Chapter 8.

The interaction of sets

The above comments on the behaviour of sets of wholesalers, shopkeepers, property owners, shopworkers and customers have all involved some reference to the behaviour of other sets.

Later in the book there will be further comment on this. We must, however, deal with certain matters here.

We begin by representing the set of people who are customers of shops in a certain town by the space C in Figure 6.1. Some of these will also be shopkeepers in that town, but there will be other owners of shop-businesses in the town who are not customers. The set of shopkeepers is represented by S. We can assume that all people who work in the shops, be they also shopkeepers or employees, spend some money in the shops and so are customers. We denote the set of shopworkers by L (for labour). The wholesalers (W) may or may not also be customers, depending largely on whether the town's shopkeepers buy from local warehouses or go further afield (as they may be forced to do). To simplify we assume that no wholesaler is a shopkeeper or a shopworker.

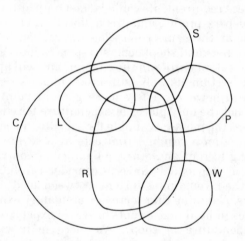

Figure 6.1

The property owners may be the shopkeepers themselves, customers who own property and rent it, and non-customers. They are represented by P.

Not all of the customers are likely to be residents of the town, and this may also be true of some of the workers. We may suppose that the set of residents is, however, a sub-set of the set of customers, and show this by drawing R.

There are, of course, other sets and sub-sets that we could consider, but the six sets depicted in Figure 6.1, along with the sub-sets defined by their intersections and unions, are sufficient for our present analysis.

Each of these sets has to consider its balance of payments. We have already remarked (in Chapter 4) on how the municipal council, acting on behalf of the residents R, may impose a tax on shopkeepers S, who attempt to restore their balance of payments by charging more to their customers C. If some of these customers are dependent upon the profits of their wholesaling businesses for their income, they may react both to the increases in prices charged to C, and perhaps in increases of local taxes on wholesaling W, by raising their prices to shopkeepers S, thus adding another round to inflation. Similar point can be made about the ways in which property owners may react to rising prices by raising rents, and workers by seeking higher wages.

We must also note that those parts of the sets S, P and W lying outside C contain people who will be receiving money directly or indirectly from the set of customers C but not directly re-spending it in local shops. They may, of course, in some other way pass some of the money back to the customers, possibly as wages. Perhaps the 'ideal' arrangement would be for S, P and W to be entirely contained within C (or even within R) even though W would clearly need to purchase from non-members of C.

If we look at matters from the viewpoint of members of R, the residents of the town in which the shops are located, it is clearly in their interests that the sub-set CR, of non-resident customers, should be large, as then it will be possible for the shopkeepers to pass on to its non-resident customers a larger local tax that will provide amenities for the residents. It will also make viable a larger and better shopping centre, and provide more jobs, of which some may go to residents. It is also in the interests of residents if they can ensure that as many members of S, P and W as possible belong to their own set, so that profits earned by them remain within the set and stand a greater chance of being spent internally. We refer further to this in Chapter 9.

It follows that residents should actively seek to extend the catchment area of their shopping centre, the local establishment of wholesalers, and the local ownership of shop property. On the other hand it is possible that in doing so they may generate traffic problems that they do not welcome.

7

Urban transport

Introduction

Sometimes we forget that not very long ago there was no mechanized transport, and that in some towns even now there is little. In the absence of cars, buses and trains people walk longer distances or travel on a horse or some other animal. Goods are carried by men, women or animals, possibly with the help of carts. Even with this primitive unmechanized transport towns may become very large. The population of inner London had passed a million well before the city had a railway line and by 1851, three years before the first underground railway was sanctioned, it was approaching two and a half million. But large towns with primitive transport are congested, not with cars but with people. It was, indeed, for this reason, and in an awareness of the improvements that cheap mechanized transport could bring, that in 1861 it was enacted by the British Parliament that certain London railways should run 'workmen's trains' at a cheap fare. Urban transport was recognized as a service that enabled people to live away from their work; and mechanized transport enabled them to live further away.

This view of transport is easily generalized. Basically, transport enables activities that occur in different places to combine sequentially, through the movement of people or goods. Men may eat their breakfast in one place, earn their money in another, and spend it in yet another. What they make in one place may be carried to another place to be combined with something made yet elsewhere by other men. In industrial and commercial terms, a cheap and speedy transport system facilitates specialization and reduces the need to carry stocks; but it also facilitates the separation of different kinds of land use (which may or may not be desirable) and the dispersal of population (which will have other economic and social conse-

100

quences). Producing nothing that is wanted for its own sake, transport acts as a catalyst to urban economic and social activity. If we extend the definition to embrace the transport of energy, the concept of the catalyst becomes even more apparent, as the efforts of one set of men in one place, producing electricity, enable a man to perform some task in his own home, with the help of a power-tool made elsewhere by others. His great grandfather would have needed to employ a craftsman who would have travelled to him, probably on foot. Improved transport has facilitated the combination in one place of energy expended by various people in other places. It may be argued that in this example the facility of combination is due to electricity: but it is the carriage of that electricity from the power-station to the user that is the essential point.

Yet transport requires effort and incurs costs. Some of these costs are borne by those who provide or use the transport, but other costs (called 'externalities') are inflicted on people who do not use it. Noise, fumes, and other undesirable consequences of mechanized travel impinge upon many, and in some cases to such an extent that those who experience them are willing to pay money to have them reduced.

Moreover, transport requires a transitory occupation of space, as well as a permanent allocation of space for roads or railways. A short stretch of road can be occupied by only one car at a time, and a particular car may be prevented from occupying it because another is there. Every traveller is thus likely from time to time to interfere with other travellers, possibly in a way that imposes a cost upon them, in that it makes their journeys slower, or more wasteful of fuel.

Finally, we may observe that transport requires investment in tracks and vehicles, their maintenance, the purchase of fuel and, in some cases, the employment of labour. It also involves the traveller in the expenditure of time. Various economic and social problems arise out of these investments, operating and using costs.

We can identify several different sets of people associated with urban transport, and most of us will belong to several of the sets. Few people are always pedestrians, or never passengers in vehicles driven by others. Where transport services are provided by public authorities those who pay taxes and are affected by matters of profit and loss will tend to look upon transport in commercial terms, almost as a private bus operator may, even though the fact that these taxpayers will also be users of, or potential users of, or competitors with the public service may affect their final judgement. In short, different sets of people will be affected in different ways but, as in other realms, views will be influenced by the membership of many sets. We now consider certain aspects of urban transport from the viewpoints of various 'pure' sets of people, before attempting to explore some interactions of these views.

Public passenger transport

Urban transport can conveniently be divided into human transport and freight transport. We consider first the former. This will include passenger rail services, buses, taxis and private cars and bicycles. (In some towns passenger travel by boat will also be important.) We will refer to passenger rail and bus services and to taxis as public passenger transport, not in the sense that the services are owned by or provided by any public authority but in the sense that every member of the public has the right to use any particular service and vehicle, not necessarily as he would like to use it but within the same constraints as those imposed on other users. The motor car, not used as a taxi, is the main form of what we will call private passenger transport (even though the 'passenger' may be the driver).

Public passenger-transport services may be owned by private enterprises, or by the municipality or the state, possibly acting through some public corporation. The purely private enterprise is rare, since the means of transport normally consists of a vehicle and a track, and although many buses and taxis are privately owned, few of them operate exclusively on privately owned roads. The easiest example of a purely private public transport service is a privately owned railway: and there are many fewer of these than there were.

We begin by looking at public passenger transport from the viewpoint of the operator. This will vary from one kind of enterprise to another. Perhaps the one that most easily leads us to the central problems is that of the private firm operating a public bus company. Like all private firms, it will attempt to make a profit, and if it long fails to make a profit it will go out of business.

A private bus company will normally have one or more garages and maintenance depots, administrative offices and a fleet of vehicles. It is this last that is most easily varied in size by the operator, who can buy more buses or sell some that he has. If he is attempting to make as much profit as he can then he will try to use his investment in buildings, machinery and vehicles in a way that brings in most money after paying out the wages and other costs associated with using it. This has important implications for the ways in which he uses his buses. An idle bus is a cost. It is earning no money, but is occupying space and, by becoming older, tending to lose its re-sale value. To use that bus will add to costs, as labour and fuel will be needed, but it may bring in revenue. If the revenue is entirely at the expense of lower revenue at some other time then obviously it is uneconomical to run the bus. On the other hand, if running the bus adds to total revenue by more than the (marginal) cost of running it then the operator gains. Here we must emphasize the word 'total'. The operator may not only obtain revenue by providing an additional bus route, or running an extra bus on an existing service, but also increase his revenue on trips that already exist without incurring appreciable extra costs on these. Whether he does obtain sufficient revenue to cover his marginal costs will obviously depend on wage-rates, fuel and other costs, and passenger demand at prevailing fares. This last will be affected by several factors some of which we will consider later.

A bus operator who examines the marginal costs and revenues associated with every bus-run that he provides may decide that, even when the addition to his total revenue is defined widely, as above, there are some trips which do not pay. In this case, he will be able to increase his profit by eliminating the trip. That will mean an idle bus, and he may consider that there is no profitable alternative use for it during the time at which it was previously engaged on a loss-making trip. If he can rearrange his services, schedules and allocation of buses to them he may be able to lengthen the time of idleness to a complete day without loss of revenue; and in that case he will be able to increase his reserve fleet or to sell a bus. There is no point in holding unnecessary surplus capacity. But in most towns the story is complicated by the way in which demand for buses varies during the day. The profit-maximizing operator may well feel that it pays him to keep one or more buses that will be used for only a few peak hours a day, because he can take sufficient money during those few hours to cover his costs. He would use these buses during off-peak hours only if the consequent addition to total revenue exceeded the marginal costs of operating them. Revenue is a function of price, and the argument that we have just presented is incomplete until prices have been made explicit. It is possible, for example, that the demand for transport is so great during peak hours that the operator can most increase his profit not by running extra buses but by putting up his fares during those hours. This may result in some passengers travelling earlier or later, when fares are lower, thereby increasing his revenue in the off-peak periods. On the other hand, this may be quite impossible for many of the passengers who will react to the higher fares by seeking an alternative form of transport. Moreover, for some people the journey in one direction may be in the peak period while the return journey is off-peak. These people will be affected by such factors as the existence of cheap return fares, the timing of off-peak periods, the problems of using two different transport modes, and so on. What the operator has to do is to find that distribution of services during the day, and that fare-structure, that will allow him to max-imize his profits. There may be constraints on the fares, service routes and service frequencies, such as those imposed by any authorities that have the legal right to allow or to disallow the running of a public bus service. Other constraints may arise out of competition, passenger reaction, and so on.

Very similar points apply to the operation of any privately owned railway (or other fixed-track) public-transport system, except that in this case there is less flexibility in the choice of routes and the selection of alighting points. There is also a different cost structure, since the abandonment of certain services can mean savings in the maintenance of track and, possibly, in various operational services, such as signalling. Similarly, the opening of new routes is likely to involve considerable investment in track.

Privately owned taxi services normally provide the remain-ing alternative to one's own transport. Taxi fares are usually fixed by local law as part of an arrangement between taxi owners and the municipality that allows them to operate. The taxi driver uses his skill and judgement in deciding where to drive or to be while seeking passengers, and decides for himself (or has decided for him by his employer) how many hours to work (subject to any legal constraint). If the fares are not enough to provide him with the income that he requires he will probably go out of business. Here arises an interesting exam-ple of the membership of a set being available only at a fee because of legislation limiting membership.

If the municipality restricts the number of taxis licensed to operate in a town, and operating a taxi appears to be profit-able, then normally there will be people who will want to take over the licence of some existing taxi owner. How this is done depends on local customs and laws, but effectively there is an inducement to an existing owner to retire from the business and to pass his licence on to somebody else who pays him for it. This may be done by direct arrangement between the owner and the new taxi operator or, perhaps, through agents (who may or may not be officials, and may or may not be operating legally). Frequently it is done through the sale of the taxicab, and the price reflects not only the worth of the vehicle but an agreed sum that is in exchange for the right to ply for hire. Clearly, if the operation of a taxi is highly profitable, an existing taxi owner can acquire a useful sum of money by selling that right to somebody else – who will expect to recover out of fares at least a reasonable interest on the purchase price. The purchaser may also expect to be able to sell out at a profit in some years to come.

It is this that makes taxi drivers tend to resist any growth in their numbers. If the number of licences grows then not only will the frequency with which a cab is hired tend to fall (thereby making the service less profitable) but also the supply of licences available to would-be operators will rise (thereby tending to reduce the profit that can be made by selling out).

Although we have been considering privately owned public transport services we have not been able to avoid reference to the public authorities, either as imposing constraints on the activities of bus operators or as limiting the total number of taxi operators. This public intervention is normally under-taken on the argument that it helps to ensure a safe and adequate service. It is argued that if anybody could be a taxi driver it would be difficult to enforce safety regulations or to prevent rogues of one kind or another from operating. The rewards to the better and more honest drivers would fall, and eventually the standard of service would decline. A similar argument applies to buses, but here the number of operators may be limited very severely, and bus companies forced to operate some services that run at a loss, in return for the privilege of running other profitable services. Urban tramway and railway services have been similarly constrained, and in some cases judged to be so profitable to their owners that municipalities have extorted considerable 'favours' in return for the permission to build or to operate them. Here the argument changes, for effectively the operator is buying his monopoly powers from the municipality. It means that, in return for a right to operate a transport service at a profit, with no, or restricted, competition, the operator pays back some of his profits in a way that enables local non-transport services to be maintained on a lower local tax revenue.

Now we turn to a different aspect of public intervention – that of municipal ownership of public transport. There are, of course, many variations of this, but the essential point we have to consider is that the ownership is vested in some public authority, answerable, ultimately, to the electorate which expects it to run a transport service of high quality, preferably at low prices, and preferably making neither profit nor loss. If it makes a profit then it finds it difficult to resist pressures for running additional (loss-making) services or reducing fares. If it makes a loss then, unless there is an agreed policy to subsidize the service out of local or national taxes, it is expected to eliminate it pretty quickly. Moreover, there will be some services that run at a loss but which a public authority will feel obliged to maintain as a matter of political expediency or social policy. In short, the economic problem facing the municipal operator is usually not one of choosing services and fares in a way that will maximize profits, but one of choosing them in such a way that they will provide the 'best' service subject to making neither profit nor loss beyond narrow acceptable limits. Here 'best' may be defined in a very vague way, or precisely in terms of passengers carried, lengths of bus queues, geographical scatter of bus stops, numbers of complaints received or almost anything else that is capable of being measured and defended as an indicator of quality. The solution to the economic problem depends on the precise specification of that problem; and that includes a precise statement of what the decision maker seeks to achieve.

Two aspects of subsidy need to be considered here. One is the implied subsidy that usually arises because of the variation in demand for public transport over the day. The other is the deliberate, explicit subsidy of a loss-making operation out of tax revenue.

The former appears to arise when buses run almost empty at three o'clock in the afternoon and are crammed to capacity two hours later. If the same fares are charged, surely the cost of running the early afternoon bus cannot be recouped from the few fares collected? It is argued that if that is so, then the off-peak passenger is being subsidized out of the profits made from peak-hour passengers.

But what is the cost of the early afternoon trip? The total number of buses owned by the municipality will be determined by the number needed to provide the peak hour service. If the early afternoon trip were eliminated the authority would not be able to sell a bus. It would use less fuel, and its maintenance costs would be lower. Probably its labour bill would also be reduced, but perhaps not by as much as the hourly wage-rate, since the wages expected by a driver who worked only in peak hours would probably have to be at a higher hourly rate than one who worked slightly longer hours. In any case, the marginal costs of afternoon services have to be calculated in the knowledge that the number of buses and the general overheads of the undertaking are determined essentially by the level of peak-hour provision. If the fares taken in the afternoon exceed these marginal costs, as they often do, then in an operation that is intended to balance its budget, the 'profit' made in the off-peak period goes towards the costs of running the peak-hour service. It helps to pay for buses and overheads that would not be needed if the peak-hour demands did not exist. If, on the other hand, even these marginal costs are not matched by fares, the more commonly held contention that the off-peak service runs at a loss is true.

It could be argued that this argument implies that off-peak passengers may be subsidizing on-peak passengers, or possibly the reverse. In a narrow accounting sense this may be true, but, as we shall see later, there may be costs and benefits arising out of either the peak-hour or the non-peak services, or both, for people who do not use these. A balanced judgement on who subsidizes whom will have to take account of this.

The other form of subsidy is when some service that runs at a loss is kept going by a grant paid out of taxes. Here the beneficiaries obviously include the passengers, while the 'losers' are the tax payers. If the subsidy comes out of local taxes these taxpayers may include people who live many miles away, as we have seen in Chapter 4, but local residents will certainly be amongst them. A fuller discussion involves consideration of how different the incidence of taxes would be if the subsidy did not exist. It would also involve the cost and benefits to non-users.

Privately owned cars

The remaining form of passenger transport that we have to consider is privately owned cars intended principally for use by their owners. In some countries this statement is wrong in an important way, since often firms provide cars for use by their

employees. The importance of this emerges in cost-benefit
calculations, and until we deal with these we can think of the
cars as being owned by some member of the driver's family.

Privately owned cars provide the most flexible form of
transport. The immediately obvious costs to the user are the
cost of the car and its maintenance, petrol costs and any taxes
that have to be paid. Most people driving cars probably do not
consider the total cost, although the marginal cost of a trip to a
car owner may become important. In a country where, because
of taxes or any other reason, petrol is expensive one major
element of marginal cost is immediately apparent, and the
high price acts as a deterrent to car use, especially if alternative cheaper transport is available. In other countries, where
petrol may be cheaper but where there is a high tax on cars,
the purchase of a car is inhibited, but once a person owns a car
he is likely to use it frequently because of the low marginal
cost. Those who own older vehicles may also be disinclined to
scrap them.

The marginal cost of a trip may be affected by other things
than fuel prices. These may include parking charges, tolls, and
other monetary costs, and a variety of non-monetary costs
including, especially, the time that the trip takes. How this
will be valued is a matter we consider later. The point for now
is that if for any reason the marginal cost of a trip rises there
will be a tendency for the number of trips made to fall (unless
the trip is essential and the costs of alternative forms of
transport rise comparably). In some cases the number of trips
made by an individual will fall so much, because of high
marginal cost, that he will reconsider the total cost of car-
ownership, and decide that he is making such little use of his
car that the average cost of a trip is excessive. He is then likely
to sell his car. This may have consequences for many people, as
we see below.

Freight traffic

Before we can consider these consequences we must look at
freight traffic, for in most towns the roads, and sometimes the
railways, have to carry goods as well as people, and the flow of
one will interfere with the flow of the other.

Urban freight traffic is normally of four kinds. There is
through traffic, with no essential stop in the town. There is
also traffic carrying goods to destinations in the town from
places outside it. Another form of long-distance traffic carries

goods from places in the town to places further afield. Finally, there is short-distance traffic between points within the town. Many of the economic problems associated with these forms of traffic arise out of congestion and social costs, and will be considered later in the chapter. Here we look briefly at a different economic problem – the problem that faces the person (or firm) with goods to carry.

This is basically the problem of choosing whether to buy a goods vehicle, to hire one, or to send the goods by public carrier. The answer will depend principally on the amount of carrying to be done and the amount that has to be delivered to, or collected from, geographically close points. A firm having a hundred parcels a day to deliver to a hundred different towns will use a public carrier who will also be delivering other parcels in these towns. If the firm has to deliver a hundred parcels a day in a specified town it may well be cheaper to own a van and to employ a full-time driver. If the problem is to deliver a hundred parcels in one town every Thursday it may be cheaper to hire a van.

The analysis of marginal costs is not quite the same as it is for private cars, since in many cases an increase in costs can be passed on to the purchaser of the goods. Moreover, while the car owner considers costs in the context of alternatives, the firm with goods to carry may have no realistic alternative, because of the nature of the goods, the need to have control over delivery times, or some other technical problem.

Public costs

So far we have touched upon certain economic aspects of the operation, ownership and use of different forms of transport. Two of the important points not yet considered are the costs of providing and managing roads, and the related matter of traffic congestion. While more is said about both matters later, certain aspects of these problems are best considered here.

The operators of urban rail systems can fairly easily identify the costs of providing, maintaining and managing their track, even though the marginal cost associated with a particular stretch of track may be more difficult to determine. When we turn to road traffic there is, unfortunately, a much more complicated problem. Buses, private cars and delivery vehicles all use common roads and traffic controls, even though some roads will be used by only one form of traffic. The attribution of costs to different sectors of traffic is virtually impossible.

In most towns the roads are provided, maintained and managed by the municipal authority, but there are important exceptions to this. In some cases roads may have to be provided, and possibly maintained, by the developers of a housing or industrial estate, or by the occupiers of property on it. There may or may not be some contribution to the cost from the municipality. In the latter case there may or may not be restrictions on the use of the roads by the general public.

Another important exception is that some urban roads may be provided or maintained partly or wholly by the national government, rather than by the municipality. The point to note now, however, is that, except in the case of the privately provided roads, the costs have to be met out of the municipal (or national) revenue from taxes. We also have to take account of the costs of controlling the traffic, notably through the use of signs, signals and traffic police.

Road-vehicle operators and users may contribute towards meeting these costs in several different ways. There may be taxes on the purchase of vehicles, on their ownership or use, on the right to drive, on fuel, on fares, on the use of a specified road, and on parking. In some towns (or even some countries) the total paid in taxes of these kinds may far exceed the costs of providing, maintaining and operating the roads. In that case one or more of these forms of transport operator or user is more than covering the costs of his own activity and is contributing to the general revenue. In the reverse case, the ordinary taxpayer (local or national) is to some extent subsidizing the road-user. Before looking at this more closely we should note that in either case one form of road-user may be paying 'more than his share' of costs while another form of road-user pays less.

Apart from the costs we have mentioned there are social costs. Road traffic creates dust. It generates fumes and noise. It adds to risks of injury, and impairs pedestrian mobility. It may also be unsightly. In all of these ways it makes life less pleasant for one person or another, and imposes some kind of cost upon them. These costs, imposed on people who are not directly party to the action that causes them, are called 'externalities'. There are also the benefits of mobility, possibly speedy, convenient and comfortable. Whether any specific set of people is a net beneficiary from the system of traffic and taxes has to be determined by taking all of these factors into account; and since hardly anybody experiences the traffic system in only one way this becomes very complicated. On the other hand, we can sometimes more easily consider two slightly different questions. The first is whether membership of a specific set makes one more or less of a net beneficiary than previously. For example, if we ask whether car owners are net beneficiaries we have to consider that most car owners are likely also to be pedestrians, occasional bus passengers, recipients of goods carried by road freight, and so on. But we can also ask whether an individual who owns a car would be more or less of a net beneficiary if he sold it. A different question is how the whole set of car owners would be affected if they all sold their cars. If only one person does so he is able to use existing bus services at existing fares. If all car owners do it the whole system of public transport will have to be re-organized. Whether car owners would then be better off or worse off, and how non-car owners would be affected, would depend on the details of the reorganization.

While questions about whether membership of a specific set is beneficial or not in terms of the transport and taxation system may at times be difficult to answer, it may be easier to answer a second kind of question which is whether some action increases or decreases the extent to which a set is a net beneficiary? Clearly, for example, an increase in petrol tax or in car-parking charges will affect car owners adversely, and more than it will affect passengers in diesel-propelled buses. In short, the marginal consequences of changes in the system may well be easier to determine than the overall relative or absolute positions of different sets.

Congestion

We now turn to some economic aspects of congestion. This arises when the vehicular demand for the occupation of road space exceeds the capacity of that space.

When vehicles move quickly they need more distance between them, for the sake of safety, than when they move slowly. Since this distance increases rapidly with the speed, the number of vehicles that can safely pass a certain point on a single lane road in a minute is limited. For example, an average size car about 14 feet long travelling at 70 mph will need to be separated from the car in front by about 22 car lengths – a distance of 315 feet. This speed is equivalent to a speed of just under 103 feet per second, and so if cars are travelling at 70 mph they cannot safely pass a selected point at more than one in every three seconds. To be more precise about it, since we have also to take account of the length of the car, the time between car fronts passing a point must be at least (315 + 14) ÷ 103 seconds = 3.19 seconds, and so about 18.8 cars a minute can pass.

If we now consider a speed of 50 mph, for which the safe separation distance is 175 feet, the same kind of arithmetic produces a maximum safe flow of about 23.3 cars a minute. More can pass safely at this slower speed.

Such is the effect of this safety factor that at 30 mph as many as 29.7 cars a minute can pass the point, and at 20 mph about 32.6 cars. But at 10 mph the number that can safely pass has fallen to 30.3 cars, while at 5 mph it is under 22 cars a minute. At these very low speeds the validity of the formula fails, but the final limit is clearly set by the length of the car. If the cars are bumper to bumper and moving at only 2 mph, the number that could pass in one minute would be given by the number of cars that would occupy a length of 176 feet, which would be fewer than 13 cars. In other words, there is some speed (which is around 17 mph) which allows the maximum number of cars to pass in safety. If the number of cars whose drivers want to pass the point concerned in any minute exceeds the number corresponding to this speed then there are likely to be accidents or disappointments.

The temptation to join a flow of traffic that is proceeding at 17 mph may be great if the alternative is to walk to a bus stop and then to join a queue. The driver who succumbs to this temptation is causing the safe speed of that flow to decline, and at this speed the result is a reduction in the number of vehicles that can pass. He is, therefore, adversely affecting other drivers, causing them to take longer over their journey and so to lose time and probably to use up more petrol, which increases the total emission of petrol fumes. In short, by causing the demand to occupy the space around that point to exceed the number that can safely occupy it in a given time, he is creating congestion.

To the economist the remedy is obvious. One must either increase the capability of that space to accommodate vehicles, or reduce the demand to occupy it. The former may be done by reducing the lengths of vehicles, discouraging or prohibiting the use of large vehicles, or making their safe separation distances less by introducing different braking or bumper devices. There is clearly a limit to what can be done in this direction. Another way of accommodating more vehicles is to extend the space, by widening the road. This cannot always be done, and in any case involves costs.

Before turning to ways of reducing demand we should look a little more closely at these costs. When a road is widened there will normally be the costs of acquiring land and using labour and materials. These costs are normally paid by the local or national taxpayer. A second category of costs are the social costs associated with bringing traffic noise and vibration closer to certain houses, and so on, but in some cases the social benefits to the same people of the removal of the noise and other pollution associated with the congestion will exceed these costs. There are also temporary costs of disruption and construction. Roadworks cause the already noticeable congestion to become even worse, and some drivers choose alternative routes, adding perhaps to congestion and social costs in other places. The construction activity creates local noise and disturbance. Sometimes the heaven of a widened road is achieved only after a period of hell.

While the incidence of many of these costs may, in many cases, be fairly easily determined, the identity of the beneficiaries is less easily seen. Some road widening will simply enable a stream of vehicles to reach another point of congestion more quickly, and there to make it worse. In that case those who drive past both points may obtain no benefit at all, until that second congestion is eased – and possibly a third and fourth.

The other way of tackling the congestion is to reduce demand. Once again, there are several ways of doing it. The main ones are those that alter the timing of the trip (so that peak-hour traffic is diverted to off-peak periods), or the origin or destination of the trip (so that it becomes a trip on some other road), or encourage the use of an alternative route, or encourage the sharing of vehicles, possibly by using buses rather than cars.

Changes of these kinds can often be achieved by the use of some discriminating form of taxation. The municipality could impose (or ask the national government to impose) heavier taxes on journeys made at a certain time of day, on the uses of certain locations by heavy-traffic generators, the uses of certain roads, or the use of certain kinds of vehicles. Various technical and administrative devices that make the imposition and collection of such taxes possible already exist, even though some of them are costly.

The principal argument that has been put forward for not using some form of road pricing is that it would tend to result in wealthy people continuing to use the point of congestion (now less congested) while less wealthy people would be forced to adopt some less congenial route, time or mode of travel. It can, of course, be counter-argued that if any wage or salary structure is to have any meaning then, after taxation has done its redistribution, people should be allowed to spend as they wish; and if they can buy a taxi trip instead of a bus trip, or a first-class train seat instead of a second-class one, why should they not be allowed to buy the use of a congested piece of road that cannot possibly be used by all who want to use it? After all, the revenue from those wealthy users may exceed the cost of maintenance and so be available for the provision of some benefit to other people. Is that not better than either allowing the congestion to continue, or banning all car traffic from the road, or spending public money on easing (or shifting) the congestion? The answer is likely to be decided more on political and ethical than on economic grounds.

Another objection to road pricing is that it may price out or 'unfairly' tax some people for whom the use of those roads is not only essential but even desirable from a wider social point of view. If this is recognized by the granting of exemptions then possibilities of abuse have also to be recognized.

A less common comment on road pricing is that the people whom it will most affect are those who cannot reclaim their motoring costs from their employers, or set them against tax. A driver who can reclaim all his costs from his employer will be undeterred by the tax, even though he may have instructions to try to avoid it. What is more to the point is that the employer will be able to set these costs against profit, and so pay less tax. Thus part of the revenue from pricing roads is, in effect, derived from the exchequer to whom taxes on profits are paid. In some countries this implies a transfer from the national to the local exchequer, and so road pricing helps the municipality to obtain funds from the national taxpayer.

Another part of the tax paid by the employer may be passed on as higher charges to customers and clients, wherever they may be. If they live far afield, the municipality is, in effect, also receiving money from quite distant non-residents. It also does so, of course, if there is a large tourist, shopping, commuting, or other non-resident element in the traffic.

Returning to the impact of the tax on users, we see that those most affected in an obvious way are the private car drivers who may use their cars for shopping, pleasure or commuting. If the tax operates only in peak hours then probably most of those feeling it would be commuters; but even here, those commuters who can, one way or another, claim back some of their costs would suffer less.

Taxes can also be used to discourage generators of heavy traffic from using certain locations, but if these do not already exist, then their introduction will have to be gradual, aimed at effecting a long-term change, unless there is to be a possibly undesirable disruption of urban activity. This is a matter to which we return.

While taxes can be used to reduce congestion, controls are more common. These may restrict access or divert traffic, with economic consequences that we shall shortly consider. An even more common form of control (often exercized in association with a tax) is concerned with parking. This is an aspect of congestion that we have not yet considered.

Car parking can add to congestion in four ways. On-street parking effectively narrows the highway, and causes further interference with flow when cars move into or out of the parked position. Off-street car parks may act as local foci for traffic and generate congestion on local access roads. The existence of parking facilities in any area where there is an excessive demand for them will encourage people to search for them, and to add to congestion by driving around. Finally, any parking facility anywhere may encourage (or fail to discourage) traffic on some access route, possibly to the point of congestion.

The usual controls are to prohibit parking on certain stretches of street, to limit it to specified hours on other stretches, and to charge for the use of certain parking spaces. In all of these ways, the authorities attempt to reduce congestion, and probably they usually succeed. But what other consequences are there?

Congestion arises either because people need (or find it preferable, notwithstanding the congestion) to pass along a certain stretch of street as part of a journey, or because people wish to stop their car, lorry or van, as close as possible to some specified place. Measures that make either of these actions more difficult or expensive will affect the vehicle driver, but they may also affect the economies of various sets of people associated with the routes and stopping places sought by the drivers. If, for example, some of the traders of a certain street depend on motor-borne passing trade, they will suffer if this traffic is forced or encouraged to use some other route, or if it is not allowed to stop. It is not unknown for pedestrianization schemes to be put into reverse because of the adverse impact on shop sales, and double yellow lines have foreshadowed the closure of many shops. Traffic and the right of drivers to stop for trading purposes have to be viewed as essential parts of the urban system, and severe restraint aimed more at keeping the traffic moving than at allowing it to stop may, as we shall later see in more detail, do great harm to the economies of residents, shopkeepers and property owners. We consider this again in Chapter 13.

Against this background two aspects of urban traffic need further consideration. One is the contribution of freight traffic to congestion. The other is the relationship between congestion and modal split – the way in which people distribute their travel between different modes of transport.

In one sense, through freight traffic is best kept out of towns, partly because it occupies road space that is sought by drivers with business to do in the town, partly because it tends to be carried in heavy lorries that cause delays at awkward junctions, and partly because it imposes unnecessary noise, fumes and vibration on people in the town. But its exclusion can often be achieved only at a substantial cost, since there may be no alternative route sufficiently attractive to the driver.

This brings us to an important point that is all too often ignored. The driver will normally drive through a town if that is quicker than driving around it. One-way systems and route severance can help to achieve this, although they may add appreciably to problems of purely internal traffic, and even perhaps to the total volume of traffic movement as a consequence. Another device is the prohibition (often difficult to enforce) of through traffic. Imposing selective charges on through traffic would be very difficult.

The remaining hope of those who seek to divert through traffic must be in the provision of a fast and attractive bypass, underpass, or overpass. Their construction can be very costly, and it is surprising that there is not more emphasis placed on making them attractive to long-distance drivers, such as by providing suitable cafes and other facilities along them, so that they are more likely to be used. Whether the cost of providing and maintaining them is more than balanced by the geographical relocation of environmental effects, and the speeding up of other traffic that becomes possible is a question to which there is no general answer.

Freight traffic with one or more trip-ends in the town creates a different problem. While there may be some scope for shunting it into off-peak periods, or even into hours when the roads are very lightly used, this often can be done only by imposing considerable costs on the generators or receivers of the goods. Some part of these might be passed on to the exchequer or to the general public in increased charges. A serious disincentive to this kind of solution is that it may make the pursuit of certain activities in a town so much more difficult or costly than in other towns that establishments move out. In some cases this may be regretted by few; but in other cases it could be manifestly undesirable. In general, non-through freight traffic is as vital to a town as are its shops and factories, which cannot function without it.

Once this is realized, congestion becomes recognized as a different kind of problem than that which is seen by many car users, for it implies that if road space has to be rationed in some way, the carriage of freight should have priority over those car users who use their cars primarily for convenience, provided that this priority is not carried so far that it causes shops to lose their customers, offices their clients, and both of them their workers. As has so often been said, those who drive their cars to work and leave them parked for the whole day are villains in two senses. They are occupying parking space that would otherwise be available for those for whom, in the last resort, they work – the customer and the client – and thereby tending to drive away the source of their own incomes. They are also tending to drive at about the same time of day, adding to peak-hour congestion.

These, the peak-hour commuters, are the people whose decision to change mode of travel, using buses and trains rather than cars, would have widest social benefits. A single bus can replace scores of cars, and few acts could reduce congestion as much as a large translation of car drivers into bus passengers, especially during peak hours. As many car drivers live a long way from bus routes, this would be most likely to happen if there were many well distributed car parks in the outer areas with frequent bus services to the more congested areas. Even then, some flexibility would be needed if the car driver was to be persuaded, rather than forced, into this bi-modal approach to a journey. Cheap (or 'free') bus travel, the ability to alight at a point not too remote from one's destination, and equal ease of return, are all part of the necessary inducement that lowers the cost to the driver of abandoning his car. If enough people do so, many gain, as all the externalities of car usage are reduced. These social costs apart, it could be that the savings in the time of municipal workers and in costs of road schemes and traffic control would more than compensate for any loss made by the bus operator.

An alternative approach is to coerce car drivers into this form of behaviour by restricting access to, and parking in, the congested areas.

In this chapter we have looked at only some of the economic aspects of traffic. Even so we have been forced to consider matters of land-use and the economies of various activities not immediately connected with traffic. We have paid little attention to location. These and other matters will be considered further, in a more integrated way, in later chapters.

8

The locational requirements of urban activities

In considering some of the economic aspects of housing, retailing and transport we have paid little attention to location. We have more or less ignored the facts that different activities can be more easily or profitably carried out in one place than in another and that the private and public consequences of an activity will depend on its location.

Neither the causes nor the consequences of the location of an activity will be purely economic, and if we attempt to ignore the impurity we will risk the loss of realism. In the analysis that follows we will try to reduce this risk by keeping the non-economic factors well in mind, even though we emphasize those that are economic.

We will consider in this chapter the locational requirements of those associated with various urban activities. Then we consider (in two subsequent chapters) some of the public and private investment decisions that are involved in enabling an activity to be conducted at a specified location. This brings us to the question of how the rival claims for locations are settled, first in a free market and then when there are various degrees of public intervention.

Location decisions

In every town, almost every piece of land is used as it is because of one or more decisions. Certain natural features (such as rivers) may define certain land uses, but wherever there are roads, buildings, hedges, parklands, dancing, rowing or any other human activity, human decisions have interacted to locate that artefact or activity in that place. Possibly, if the decision had been taken at a different time, if different people had been party to it, or had been of greater or lesser influence, the location might have been different. In fact, the decision

119

would have been different, and it is this that we must emphasize.

Views about the desirability of locations for activities, and of
activities for locations, may be held by many people, including
not only those who are likely to engage in the activity or to
visit the location. Activities in one location may affect people
in other locations, and these people may well have views about
them. Other people, neither participating nor affected, may
hold views based on principles, attitudes towards 'freedom',
'pollution' or some other concept, or some kind of attachment
to, or hostility towards, some of those more immediately
involved. In this chapter we are concerned mainly with the
locational requirements of those who wish to engage, in one
way or another, in one of the major urban activities. Although
we shall touch upon views held by others, the emphasis is upon
these requirements as generators of demands for the occupation of various locations. How these demands are satisfied,
or rejected, will be considered in later chapters.

Retailing

We consider first the locational requirements of retailing. We
do this first because it is retailing and its peculiar requirements that do most to determine and to characterize the
land-use pattern of a town. This will become clearer as we
proceed, but even here we may note that often it was the
concentration of other activities around the market place that
gave rise to towns, and while there are some residential
settlements located around purely industrial complexes, these
settlements are not described as towns until they have been
vested with retailing and other services.

Several sets of people are involved. The decisions to build
shops, and to do so at specified locations, will have been made
by developers (of one kind or another), in the knowledge or
expectation of decisions made or about to be made by shopkeepers, customers and others, including those who may be in
a position to forbid development. Whether, when and where
shops are built will be influenced by all of these people, whose
actions may affect land use (and other matters) in ways that
they neither expect nor intend, and who will not always have
the same ideas about where the shops should be.

The customer will normally consider three attributes of a
shop location. He seeks accessibility, preferring being able to
get to shops easily and quickly to having a difficult or lengthy

journey. He also seeks variety, so that he can purchase different commodities on the same trip. Finally he seeks comparisons, in the sense that he likes opportunities to compare qualities and prices.

The last two of these considerations means that a customer welcomes some concentration of shops or stalls selling similar items, preferably along with a wide variety. The traditional eastern market, and the provincial town centre in developed countries, both provide this blend of variety and comparison, even though the smaller towns may not have as much variety as the larger ones.

The first requirement, of accessibility, is difficult to define precisely unless one is content with some arbitrary definition. It clearly tends to decrease as distance increases, and will depend upon the individual's access to different modes of transport. Road congestion, car-parking problems, over-crowded pedestrian routes, long waits for buses, and many other nuisances or deterrents may all reduce the ease of access to shops. So may high transport costs. In an extreme case, if the shopping journey cannot be afforded, the shops are inaccessible, not for physical but for economic reasons. These may be purely financial, but if people place a value on their time then they may look upon the cost of their journey as the sum of the monetary cost and the value they attach to the time that it takes them.

Generally speaking, the more highly a person values his time, the less does he relish spending time travelling to the shops or moving between them. This means that accessibility and variety become relatively more important than opportunities for comparison. In affluent communities the small shopping centre located close to a residential area, offering variety but not an opportunity to compare qualities and prices, is more likely to survive than in a poor area, not simply because rich people may spend more but also because they are less likely to spend an hour in order to save a pound. In some countries where there is high unemployment and very low incomes quite sizeable settlements may have no shops at all, simply because the time taken to travel to the central market where prices can be compared is no deterrent to the trip; and if there were a few local shops the very limited nature of the opportunity to compare prices in them would not be sufficient to persuade the local population to forgo the trip to the market.

While we have emphasized the importance of variety and comparisons it would be wrong to suppose that no other factor is important. Those relating to car-parking and public-transport facilities are best thought of as related to accessibility, even though they may be essentially part of the shopping-centre design. Also part of the design may be such factors as protection from the rain, wind, sun or snow, the general appearance of the place, and the existence of related amenities such as toilets, cafes and cinemas. On the other hand many of these may arise as the result of commercial or municipal decisions taken independently of the original design decisions. In one way or another all of these will affect the power of a shopping centre to attract customers, as well as the qualities of the shops themselves. It is, however, the importance attached to variety and comparisons that immediately affect land-use, for they point to a clustering of shops at the wish of customers. No shopkeeper can ignore the wishes of his customers, even though he may attempt to change them. The shopkeeper's view of location is influenced mainly by consideration of the relative profitabilities of different sites, and these depend to a large extent on the views of his customers. While factors other than location affect both his costs and his takings, he knows that rent, possibly local taxes, and the level of sales can all be highly dependent upon it. His ideal location is one that is very accessible to a large number of potential customers, located close to other shops whose customers may become his, or on a route along which such potential customers may be expected to walk, yet having a low rent and low local taxes. He will also want easy access for his delivery of stock and his employees.

Rarely does he find his ideal. Just as some cinemas have more people seeking seats in the back row than there are seats, so more shopkeepers may seek certain locations than those locations can accommodate, and this usually means that while the locations may still be ideal in most respects they will (in effect) have gone to the highest bidders (or selected tenants) at high rents. This is a matter we consider more fully later.

A location that involves the shopkeeper in a high rent will mean that the shop will have to have a high value of sales, simply to make enough gross profit to pay the costs of location. This may entail employing a large number of staff, and this, in turn, affects the size of the shop and so, once more, the rent. If either the profit mark-up or the probable sales per employee are high then small shop units can produce higher profits and enable high rents to be paid. This is one reason why a town centre is likely to have more jewellers than pet-shops, and why a town-centre jeweller may occupy a smaller shop than a town-centre hardware store.

But shopkeepers do not often build shops. They normally purchase or rent shop premises that already exist, and while some of these may have been built long ago by individual shopkeepers, it is likely that most of them will have been erected by a developer who has been influenced by expectations of profit. In some cases they may have been provided partly or entirely by the municipality, possibly with an eye to providing a facility for the neighbouring residents with profit as a secondary (or even non-existent) consideration. This development decision rests on very many factors, and is considered more fully in Chapter 9. The point to notice here is that while the developer will consider whether to build, in which town to build, whether to build shops or some other kind of building, and precisely where to build, he will make all of these decisions on the basis of his knowledge and expectation of many factors, including the views of prospective shopkeepers about the suitability of that location for themselves, at rents that will be attractive to the developer.

Briefly, the shopkeeper with a shop in a place where sufficient customers do not exist will be in a wrong location. The developer who puts a shop in such a location is unlikely to let it. Shops are built and occupied in locations where custom is expected. But the customer is not quite sovereign: the developer may have reasons for not providing shops just where the customers want them, as we shall shortly see.

In recent years there has been the important development of a different concept in shopping, where one firm acquires a large site (usually on the edge of the town, where land tends to be cheaper and site acquisition is easier) and provides a single multi-commodity store with a large car park. This provides accessibility and variety. Price and quality comparison is achieved by advertising, which tends to reduce this as a factor in determining location. In some cases these edge of town sites may be occupied by more than one retailer, thus affording the traditional form of comparison, but here there is either a developer in the sense we have already described or one of the retailers as acting as developer.

Wholesaling

Wholesalers need a warehouse, where goods may be received, stored and displayed, and from which they may be despatched.

They also need an office. Frequently the same building provides both, especially if a large number of the customers collect their own goods, when access to the accounts department may be important. At times, however, almost all of the despatches may be in transport owned or organized by the wholesaler, who obtains orders through his agents and representatives and is rarely visited by customers. In this case, separation of the warehouse and office is more common.

The wholesaler who is frequently visited will tend to seek a location by considering that his customers, too, want accessibility, variety and comparison. For this reason, cash-and-carry warehouses tend to cluster, but there is less attention to display. The shopkeeper is concerned with buying what he thinks he can sell in his own shop, and is less influenced by the appearance of the warehouse and the quality of display inside it, than by the goods on offer. Consequently the warehouses tend to occupy property where rents are comparatively low, considering their accessibility. Car and van parking is very important to them. Partly for this reason, and almost as an exact parallel to the edge-of-town store, there have recently arisen large edge-of-town multi-line warehouses, offering accessibility and variety but no direct price and quality comparison facilities.

The wholesaler who is not often visited has different criteria. High amongst these are his own accessibility to his suppliers and to delivery routes. If he is a direct importer he will wish to be reasonably close to a port, to a good road to it, or to a railway goods depot. But there are reasons that may determine his choice of town quite as much as his decision about where to locate within a town. Unless there are many customers to whom deliveries have to be made within the town, and comparatively few elsewhere, the best location may well be in some small village where there is a disused chapel or cinema, for which the demand is so low that he can obtain a great deal of space at a low cost.

Offices

It is convenient to divide offices into several different categories. Some are principally the accounts and correspondence end of a totally different kind of business. Many shops or factories will have a small room set aside for this purpose, and the essential locational requirement is that the office is part of or very close to the main building. We shall say little more about these, but when we do refer to them we shall speak of 'small restricted offices'. In some cases businesses will require larger offices, often occupying different sites. For example, a retail grocery chain is likely to have a small office in every branch shop, but also to have a headquarters office. A very large firm may find it convenient to divide some of its centralized administrative functions between several offices differently located, but essentially these are still restricted offices, serving one firm, and having little direct contact with the public. It is useful to separate them from the small restricted offices, and we do so by referring to them as 'large restricted offices'. Another example is the administrative office of an education authority. Access is restricted to those connected with the business of the authority.

A very different kind of office is conveniently called 'the client office'. This is an office to which members of the public call as clients of, for example, the solicitors and accountants who occupy them. They do so in order to seek the services of those who work in the offices. We must note that some offices have as their clients not so much members of the general public as other offices. We shall refer to these as 'professional client offices'.

Finally we shall speak of 'counter-offices', where the public may go in order to conduct some transaction for services over the counter, such as banks, post offices, insurance and building society offices, and offices where cash payments of local taxes may be made.

It will be noticed that we have classified offices according to the kind of involvement that they may have with the public. The reason is obvious. There is no point in a client office being perched on top of a mountain (unless the services provided from it are highly specialist). Equally there is little case for locating a restricted office in the middle of a shopping precinct, unless the business of that office is essentially connected with the precinct. There are, of course, other ways of classifying offices, but if we are concerned with locational requirements this classification provides a useful basis.

Unfortunately many offices straddle the classification. We say 'unfortunately' not because this straddling invalidates our approach, but because it has led to location decisions that in many cases are both wrong for the office occupier and harmful to other users of the town. If we consider the requirements of an insurance office, for example, we can see that in one sense it is a counter office. On the other hand many of its functions will be those of a restricted office. This dual function is often unavoidable, especially in a small office, but in larger offices it exists to an unnecessary degree.

A counter office needs to be accessible to the public, but a restricted office does not. While most members of the public will conduct most of their insurance business by correspondence or through brokers, some will at times wish to call at an office in order to discuss some aspect of their insurance. As long as there is a counter, or set of interview rooms, suitably staffed by persons with access to records and, if necessary, experts by telephone or closed-circuit visual-data transmission, the public's reasonable requirements of access are satisfied. It also enables the offices to compete with each other in attracting custom and funds (which is why, like estate agents, they tend to congregate). Frequently, however, an insurance company will occupy a large office in some central location, where it conducts 90 per cent of its work by telephone or post, and only a very small fraction of the employees meet members of the public. In short, most of the employees are doing just what they could be doing if the office were many miles out of the town, servicing and fed by a counter office.

A very similar point can be made about banks, building societies and other institutions. It can also be made about municipal and government offices, as we shall shortly see.

The big argument for a central location for these offices is concerned with staff. It is argued that it is easier to obtain suitable staff if the office is centrally located. In some towns this may be true, but in others it is very doubtful. Most towns have some sectoral element in their residential patterns, with some areas more likely to contain or to be close to the homes of professional and office workers than others. If this is so, then provided that there is a suitable public transport system, there are areas where large restricted offices could be located without staff problems, except perhaps for one thing. Many office workers like being able to visit shops during the lunch-break, or to get out of the office into a cafe or bar. An isolated large restricted office might not provide these opportunities for its employees, and so, despite its good access for them, not be very attractive to job-hunters. In other words, the large restricted office need not be in a central location, but it is likely to have fewer labour problems if it is where the staff can enjoy some urban amenities, out of the office, at lunch-time. Many suburbs of larger towns provide these amenities and some of them have attracted large restricted offices. Unfortunately those responsible for location decisions have too often failed to look afresh at the locations of their offices, and to consider whether a separation of counter and restricted functions, and therefore perhaps of locations, is possible. Even when it is possible, it may not be economic for the firm to divide its office in this way. But if central area rents are high enough compared with suburban or rural rents then the costs of communications and some inconvenience may well be lower than the saving in rent. Wage rates may also be lower, as staff will in many cases have lower travelling costs.

In some towns municipal offices are the prime examples of this failure. As with insurance companies, the proportion of town-hall employees who meet the public is small. Most of the business could be conducted equally well if the public never called: but people need to be able to make payments by cash, and to discuss matters relating to housing, public cleansing, schools, building and planning, social services and other matters, depending on the powers and duties of the municipal authority. To suggest that these discussions can proceed usefully only if all of the employees who are involved in these matters have desks in the same building is clearly nonsensical. This implies that there is a counter function and a restricted function; and while the former needs locations based on accessibility to the public, the latter does not. Moreover, accessibility may be increased by having a limited number of counter offices in the suburbs as well as in the town centre, so that people may conduct their personal business more conveniently. If these counter offices had good communications with the large municipal restricted office, to which the public could go if necessary, there would be little justification for a great centralized accumulation of municipal employees.

Before we leave the question of counter offices and restricted offices we should note that we have been talking about locational requirements, rather than locational demands, and arguing that many offices are located where they may not need to be. We have gone further, and suggested that in certain rent structures the office occupiers are incurring unnecessary costs by being where they are. All of this is concerned with the costs to the office occupier, but if there are unnecessary demands for the occupation of central area offices then there are associated social costs, for this unnecessary demand unnecessarily generates traffic and unnecessarily tends to drive up office rents that will have to be paid by others for whom a central location is more essential.

We have still to consider client offices. A typical client office may be thought of as being that of a solicitor. In a large town a solicitor setting up a new practice will choose his location partly with an eye on the kind of business and client that he wants to attract. If he wishes to be, for example, essentially concerned with such matters as house-purchase, minor criminal offences, divorce and family matters he may look around for a residential area that is ill-served in these respects, and consider opening his office there. In this case he will tend to be attracted by any other offices of a kind that may generate custom, such as an estate agent's office. On the other hand, if he is seeking to establish himself essentially as a criminal lawyer he may either look for an area with a high crime rate or seek a central position, possibly close to the law courts so that he can quickly move between the court and his office, thus wasting as little time as possible between court appearances and consultations. This may also help him by bringing him closer to the offices of other lawyers with whom he may have to work in court cases. If his ambition is to establish a commercial practice, rarely appearing in court but handling property and business transactions he will try to locate close to the kind of commercial office that is likely to bring him business or to be involved in it. This is also the area where businessmen are likely to call for other purposes, and where they will find it convenient to have a lawyer. A commercial lawyer will therefore tend to seek a location where there are banks, financiers, property companies, accountants, and others who will to some extent be his clients or have him as a client. In short, his practice will have a professional client-office element. So will a stock-broker, who will also need to locate close to a stock exchange.

This last point, like that concerning the law court, is important. Certain institutional buildings will attract certain kinds of offices, which will tend to attract others, either because of professional links or because their occupiers consider that people seeking professional services but having no established adviser will tend to go to the area where advisers abound and choose between competing brass plates. Hospitals will attract offices (if such a term may be used in this context) occupied as consulting rooms by specialist doctors. Theatres may attract lawyers, accountants and agents specializing in professional services for actors. All of this emphasizes that the location of a client office depends very much on the kind of service that it is intended to provide, as well as on catchment areas, clusters of other offices and professional links.

An important element in the location of professional client offices is the need to have 'face-to-face contact' with clients and others. Another is the need to be able to get documents quickly from one office to another. Yet a third is the value of being able to meet potential clients while out of the office for lunch, or to learn useful news in casual conversations. While there are undoubted advantages in clustering for professional client offices, possibly around some institution or other related building, the location may be unduly influenced by this. A large professional client office will eventually tend to develop a restricted office element, and in some cases this could profitably be relocated, especially if rents are rising faster than the costs of modern communication systems.

Two other points must be made about the occupier's view of office locations. Whatever we may say about where offices of certain kinds need to be, or should most profitably be, the fact is that many of them are where they are because that is where they were. When they were established the surrounding areas were different, communication possibilities were less developed, road access was easier, and the business being carried out was on a different scale and possibly of a different nature. Over time there has been gradual change, and now that location clearly has its disadvantages. On the other hand, moving would involve many costs, and would probably mean losing some business in the short run at least. In the judgement of the decision-makers the choice is between staying and moving, as a division of functions between two locations has either never been considered or been rejected. It is not an easy choice to make. And because it is not easy it is often postponed, and so made by default.

The other factor affecting locations is prestige. Some firms of professional people will seek certain locations because of the address, which may help to attract clients and may help to impress those with whom there are likely to be business dealings.

Finally we must turn to the office-developer, who builds new offices. We have more to say about him later but, as with retailing, we may note that normally he is guided by his expectation of being able to develop in locations where prospective tenants want accommodation. On the other hand he has a greater chance of influencing location than he has with shops, because if he provides attractively designed offices with good parking and access facilities at profitable but not excessive rents he can often persuade restricted offices to move out of expensive congested areas into his new premises. But if he is providing for counter offices or professional client offices (or to some extent other client offices) then he has to pay much more attention to localized demand.

Other non-residential uses

While shops and offices are the main non-residential claimants upon specific locations in a town, there are others whose claims may be important. Industrial users have locations which may become important in terms of their effects, but in most cases the locational requirements of industry do not point as inexorably to specified places as do those of shops and offices. Access to transport for raw materials and finished product and to a labour force are the main prerequisites; and these will be affected by the locations of railway stations, docks, roads, canals, rivers and airports. Much more likely to affect the locations of urban industry are planning controls and public attitudes towards noise, waste disposal, traffic generation and other externalities: but these reflect the constraints imposed by public intervention rather than the locational requirements of the industries.

The locations of churches, mosques and other religious buildings are often historical, and in themselves have affected the traditional locations of markets and other activities. In changing towns the dependence of these buildings on accessibility to worshippers is manifested by their closure in areas of declining population, although tourist elements often delay or prevent this.

While hospitals were once widely spread and small, changes in medical and nursing techniques have tended to favour the provision of larger centralized hospitals, away from the bustle (and high land values) of city centre locations, along with smaller more scattered clinics. School locations tend to be determined by the existence of areas of catchment population.

One can go on in this way, identifying the locational requirements of cafes, cinemas, libraries, football stadiums and other land uses, but doing so adds little to our understanding of the general problem, partly because none of these uses demands a great deal of land, and partly because the concepts of accessibility, competition and public need between them contain most of the explanation of requirements, as opposed to constraints.

Residential uses

Very few towns do not have houses as their main claimant upon land. The present pattern will usually have emerged over a long period, and in many countries it will have been constrained (especially in recent decades) by laws and controls. The question facing us now is how people seek to determine and to express their preferences for different locations within a town.

Most people seek access to some located land-users. These may be unique, such as a specific church, a close friend, a specified factory or the only university. Alternatively they may be duplicated, so that people are satisfied by being close to shops and to a school, rather than to specified shops and a named school. The package of accessibilities, and the weights attached to them, will vary from person to person, but normally access to the place of work, or to workplaces, to shops, perhaps to schools, and to good roads or public transport facilities will play an important part in determining locational preferences.

Four other factors must be mentioned. Different people will have different ideas about the kind of social and natural environment in which they wish to live; and few will be completely indifferent to both. Since at least one member of most households will have to travel to work, the implications of residential location for the journey to work will matter. There are also considerations of housing costs, which will vary from one part of a town to another. Finally, the size, age and quality of house will matter, and this often depends upon location. While redevelopment has meant that in some towns there is a great deal of new housing fairly close to the centre, most towns have grown and changed by outward extension, and the newer houses are to be found mainly on the less densely developed fringes. There are, of course, exceptions to this, as we shall shortly see. Frequently most of the houses close to a town centre are old, and often very small.

How people combine considerations of accessibilities of various kinds, environment, costs and housing size and quality into a location decision, in the context of decisions being made by other land-users is the subject of our remaining chapters.

9

Obsolescence, decay and development

In discussing the locational requirements of various land uses we referred to the developer as the person who provides buildings of various kinds. In providing them he produces changes in the physical fabric of a town. We also remarked upon changing needs of occupiers of property. In this chapter we consider these processes of change more systematically.

There have been many attempts to explain or to describe urban land-use patterns. Frequently these have been based on ideas of growing and conflicting demands for the occupation of land for various purposes around some small settlement that has been a focus for growth. While these attempts have often been valuable, some of them have lacked realism or usefulness by failing to acknowledge the importance of those local features and chance events that so often shape the development of a town. Instead of trying to present a theory of urban land-use that takes these matters into account, we are going to consider the role of economic factors in contributing to changes in, or the maintenance of, the existing land-use pattern of a town. What now causes towns to change? How important are economic factors in generating these changes? What are the economic consequences of urban change? These are the questions for us to consider. In considering them we shall use the ideas that we have presented in our previous chapters.

Assumptions

Urban change may be manifested in many ways, and in choosing to begin by concentrating upon changes in land-use we are not intending to imply that this is the most important or, necessarily, the most obvious. It is simply because it is most convenient that our analysis starts in this way.

A piece of land will have its broad category of use determined when a decision is made about whether to build upon it, and, if so, what to build. In order to examine this decision we must first look at certain points about the ownership of land and the power of representatives of the community to influence or to make decisions about land use.

We have already seen, in Chapter 5, that there may be many different forms of landownership and tenure. Here, in order to establish the essence of our theory, we shall simplify by deeming the owner of a piece of land to be the person or other legal entity endowed with the legal right to build upon it, and to demolish buildings upon it, subject only to any constraints that are exercised on behalf of the community, to any agreements that he may have accepted at the time of purchase of the land from its former owner, and to any agreements that he may have with any occupiers of the land.

The decision to demolish or to build may be initiated by the community, by the occupier of the land or by the owner. For the time being we will assume that the community does not become involved in any way, either in initiating or in controlling any development. We will assume that all land is privately owned, and that only owners or occupiers are involved in the decisions we now consider. Later we will modify these assumptions.

A piece of land may be occupied by its owner or by somebody else. If the occupier is not the owner then either he has little or no security and can be forced to surrender his occupation at short notice, or he has some agreement (which we will call a 'lease') that gives him the right to occupy the land until a specified date. If the owner wishes to demolish a building whose occupier still has the right to occupy it for several years then either he must wait for these years to pass, when the lease expires, or he must obtain the consent of the occupier. One way of doing this is to buy it. We shall consider this more fully shortly. The point now is that when he obtains the occupier's consent to demolish a building, or to change the use of a piece of land, it is very likely to be at the expiry of a lease, or through an agreement that in effect produces the accelerated expiry of a lease.

We can, therefore, assume without serious departure from realism that when an owner initiates a change he does so at the expiry of a lease of occupation. But the initiative may come from the occupier. In this case he will need the owner's consent. This may be obtained by the owner agreeing to a termination of the existing lease on condition that the occupier takes a lease on the new building on terms that are acceptable to the owner. In other cases it is simply by agreement but this is not often the case except where the change is trivial.

We now make two assumptions of a different kind, not about the content of the decision but about the decision itself. We assume that when the owner makes a decision on his own initiative, or by agreement with the occupier, then the owner considers that at that time he has chosen a course of action that is, in his judgement, probably not inferior to any other. We also assume that if the occupier takes the initiative and proceeds on terms agreed with the owner, then both the owner and the occupier consider that (after taking account of any transaction or agreement between them) there is probably no better course of action.

These two very similar assumptions need to be amplified. We are not assuming that either the owner or the occupier acts as a rational man. Nor are we assuming that anybody has perfect information or that all people have identical information about certain things. We are assuming simply that the owner and (if he is involved) the occupier, each with the information that he has and cares to consider, and each using whatever decision processes he does, and defining 'best' in his own private way, initiates (or agrees to) a change when he considers that to be the best thing to do – or, at least, when he considers that nothing else is better.

No landowner is likely to subject the use to which he puts his land to decision every day. If he has granted a lease to an occupier he may have little realistic opportunity to reconsider its use for many years: but even if he occupies it himself there can be at least two reasons for not reconsidering an earlier decision. He may well feel that he has better things to do with his time and mental energy than perpetually ponder the fate of a piece of land, especially if there seem to be no new facts to be taken into account. Even if new facts do emerge, he may be unable to take advantage of them because he has embarked on certain actions in the expectation that his last decision will remain effective for some time. Consequently there is a tendency for land-use decisions to respond only slowly to new circumstances, although, of course, there are many exceptions to this, and individual decisions may respond quickly to events, or even anticipate them.

Obsolescence

There will come a time, however, when the expiry of a lease, an approach from the occupier, some new circumstances or some other factor may present the owner with an encouragement to reconsider the land-use in the knowledge that he can initiate (or agree to) a change without excessive constraint by legal agreements or his own activities. Taking account of those things that at the time appear to him to be important, he decides whether to lease the land as it is, or to change its use, or to sell it. In the last case the new owner decides whether or not to make changes, and his decision (including his decision to purchase) may be influenced by his views about the chances of acquiring neighbouring sites in a way that will permit a large-scale redevelopment. For the time being we put aside this consideration, and look simply at the decision about a single piece of land.

Even when the decision is to leave the land as it is, there will still have to be other decisions (taken actively or by default) about whether to spend money on whatever buildings may already be upon it. Thus, putting aside the decisions that result simply in a transfer of ownership, when decision time is reached one of the following decisions will be made:

1 to do nothing to the land or its buildings,
2 to spend money improving, repairing or maintaining the existing buildings,
3 to redevelop the site for the same land-use but possibly more intensively,
4 to redevelop the site for a different land-use.

Decisions 1 and 2 may be made more by default than by active processes.

In making these decisions the landowners will usually be influenced to some extent at least by the rent that they obtain, and expect to obtain, from any tenant-occupiers. If they occupy the property themselves then, as owners, they should consider whether it is best still to occupy it; for perhaps if they moved out they could let it (changed or not) to somebody else at more rent than they would have to pay for the occupation of an equally suitable property elsewhere. In any case, as occupiers of the building they would be influenced by the suitability of that building in that place to their needs.

It is this question of suitability that lies at the heart of the whole matter. A firm or person wishing to engage in any activity needs a place in which to do so. He will select that place from those that are known to him to be available. We may suppose that when he decides to occupy some place he considers that, taking account of suitability for his purpose and the rent that he has to pay, there is no better place than the one for which he opts, even though there may be others as good. This means that, in his opinion, there were no equally suitable places at a lower rent, no more suitable places at the same rent, no places amongst the more expensive whose additional suitability justified the additional rent, and none so much cheaper that the saving outweighed their lesser suitability.

But as time goes on things change. The property that he occupies may become, in his opinion, no longer the most suitable of the buildings available to him. This can happen in many ways. Perhaps the building itself has deteriorated. Perhaps the social image of the area has changed in a way that he considers to affect his business or his prestige adversely. Possibly car-parking or pedestrian access has become more difficult. Alternatively, there may be changes elsewhere that cause other places now to be more suitable than the place that he occupies. Yet another possibility is that his requirements have changed, as when the household size alters, or a business grows, or requires the use of a new kind of machinery, or is required by some new law to occupy premises of a certain standard. In short, because of either a change in the suitability of that place, or a change in the suitability of some other place, or a change in his own requirements, that place is no longer the best place for him to occupy. Another factor that can lead to this is simply a change in rent levels, with the occupied place becoming more expensive than at least equally suitable other places.

When the occupier decides, for whatever reason, that his continued occupation of a building is no longer his best policy we will say that that building is subject to *tenant obsolescence*. We must note that this is an attribute of the occupation of a specific building by a specific tenant. Some other person, wishing to do exactly the same thing, but with different ideas, tastes or information, might occupy the building and feel that it was undoubtedly his best option.

Just as there is little point in the owner of a piece of land constantly reassessing its use, so there is little in a tenant reviewing continuously the relative merits of different locations. If he has a tenancy agreement then a move may be extremely expensive, unless he can find some other person to take over the tenancy. On the other hand, when any stipulated period of tenancy ends, not only may he be free to move without penalty, but also the owner of the property is likely to be reviewing its future.

This is one of the occasions when changes in rent may arise. One of the questions that the owner may ask is whether his best option is to leave the land and building more or less as it is, but to seek a different rent for it. If he decides that this is so then we will say that there is rental obsolescence. If there happen to be several people willing to occupy it at the previously charged rent, then it is likely that some of them will be willing to offer even more. If the land owner is astute, and if there are not too many more or less equally desirable buildings to let, he will probably be able to let his building at a considerably higher rent. In this case we say that there is *upward rental obsolescence*. On the other hand, if nobody is willing to rent the building at its current rent, then he may hope to find a tenant by offering it at a lower rent – which will still be a more lucrative option than keeping it empty. We call this a state of *downward rental obsolescence*.

We have suggested that an owner may feel that he should leave the land-use and building unaltered, but spend money on repairs or improvements. This means that to leave the building in its present condition is no longer the best thing to do. We refer to this as *condition obsolescence*. It corresponds to decision 2 above.

Corresponding to decisions 3 and 4 is the discovery that the continued occupation of the site by the existing building is not the optimal use of the owner's resources. The best thing to do is to demolish the building and then to erect another one or to put the cleared site to some other use. We call this *building obsolescence*.

Decision 1 implies that decay is about to win. All buildings except, perhaps, the very new ones require some degree of maintenance, lest they become increasingly damaged by their users, vandals, wind, rain, frost, sunshine or atmospheric pollution. If decision 1 is taken then there is no expenditure to combat these forces of decay. Briefly, when a building's owner has decided that decision 1 is in his best interests we say that the building is *decaying*, even if no sign of actual physical decay is yet apparent.

There are clearly important links between these various concepts. As an example we may consider a case in which car-parking restrictions lead to a loss of business for a tenant shopkeeper. He decides that he is no longer in the best place. There is tenant obsolescence and eventually an empty shop. The owner may decide that he cannot get another tenant without reducing the rent, and that to do this is his best option. In that event tenant obsolescence will have led to downward rental obsolescence. If this is severe it may lead to a decision to spend nothing on the property, and so to decay.

Another possibility is that, despite the parking restrictions certain kinds of shopkeepers are very eager to occupy the vacated property. The owner feels that he can get a higher rent. But it may not be simply a case of upward rental obsolescence because it could be that an even higher income could be obtained through redevelopment – the case of building obsolescence.

The first form of obsolescence discussed by us is identified by a decision made by the tenant (or, more precisely, by the occupier). The other forms so far described are identified by decisions made by the owner. Here we relax one of our assumptions and allow the community to intervene, for public decisions may lead to a different form of obsolescence. Even if the community owns no land or buildings, the fact remains that the ways in which land and buildings are used will impinge upon people who are neither their owners nor their occupiers. In some cases those who are adversely affected may persuade others that the continued use of a certain piece of land (or building) in a certain way is no longer in the best interests of the community. Once the community or its accepted representatives have decided that this is so then *community obsolescence* arises. Whether this has any effect on the building or land-use depends on what action, if any, is taken as a result of the decision.

Community obsolescence can lead to decay. It is worth while to consider this a little further. A simple example is when the municipal council decides that it disapproves of the present use of a piece of land, and the councillors (or their officers) agree privately to try to end that use. One way of doing so might be to create a refuse dump next to it, or to initiate some very protracted roadworks that so restrict access, and create so much disturbance, that the land becomes a bad location for its present use. In such a case, downward rental obsolescence would probably begin, and this might lead to decay. With the onset of decay the market value of the land and the property would be low, and if the law allowed it to do so the municipality would then perhaps be able to acquire the land for its own use at a low price.

This unscrupulous kind of activity is a less common cause of decay than the publication of some long-term planning ideas. These, decided upon by a small set of officers and elected representatives, and not necessarily finally settled, so affect the outlook and expectations of property owners, existing and prospective occupiers, and speculators of various kinds, that many of the buildings slowly become empty or ill maintained. People seek new locations while they can, and refuse to spend money on properties that may soon be knocked down, and in any case are unlikely to be let or sold because of the uncertainty of their future. Here, too, is a device that can be used unscrupulously to transfer land into public ownership, paying some of the property owners less than they would have obtained if the plan had been more specific or more speedily implemented.

A common instance of community obsolescence leading to decay is when it produces a *functional obsolescence* on neighbouring sites. For example, a community decision to move a bus station may mean that a neighbouring site is no longer a good place to have a cafe. This functional obsolescence may lead to downward rental obsolescence, and then to decay. New shopping precincts may similarly affect older shopping streets.

Generally, if community obsolescence coincides with decay the scene is set for redevelopment, although, of course, this may occur under other circumstances. If community obsolescence has led to a downward rental obsolescence then it may be possible to forestall decay by buying the property, albeit at a higher price than might later be possible. Sometimes, however, a property may decay before there has been any explicit manifestation of a 'community' view on the use of the site. Far-seeing councillors or officers may recognize that in a few years' time there is likely to be some worth-while public use for it, but there is no certainty of this. In such a case there may at times be an argument for the municipality attempting to buy the property in order to prevent some differently thinking private person from buying it, attempting to develop or to renovate it, and so perhaps causing its value to rise. In short, decay almost always arising out of a decline in the demand to occupy an existing building, and possibly accelerated by public actions of a more positive kind, serves the public purpose of facilitating the public acquisition of land at a low price. Whether other circumstances allow this acquisition to take place, and allow the municipality to take advantage of it, are different matters.

We should notice that both the timing and the type of obsolescence depend upon many factors. For example, in periods of great building activity there may be a large increase in the number of leases of new tenancies. Many of these are likely to be for identical periods, and so in, say 21 years (or some other period prescribed by the fashionable length of a lease) large numbers of owners and occupiers will be faced with decision-making problems. The nature of these problems will to some extent depend on the rental provisions of the lease and the changes in building costs over the period of tenancy. If costs have risen appreciably and the lease has been for many years at a fixed rent then in later years maintenance may well have become impossibly expensive, and so decay may have set in. Towards the end of the lease owners will be wondering whether to raise the rent, simultaneously spending money on improving the building, or to redevelop it. The occupier will wonder whether he should look for an alternative location at a lower rent than the landlord may shortly demand from him if he is to renew the lease. But if the lease has a rent-review clause in it, enabling the owner to raise the rent at (say) five-year intervals during the tenancy, then decay will be less likely and the occupier will already be paying a rent that is more realistic in contemporary terms. The contrasts between opportunities before and after the termination of the lease for owner and for occupier will be less pronounced than if the rent had been held at its initial level.

We have said sufficient to indicate that in a country where long-term tenancies are common, the timing of the opportunity to redevelop on a large scale may be determined by the history of building activity; and the incentive to do so will be influenced by the conditions of tenancies. But we still have to consider how the foregoing analysis has to be modified if all land is owned by the community.

Clearly the answer will depend on the detailed laws of land-use and property that apply, but generally certain points will be valid. In every town some sites will be in greater demand for certain uses than will other sites. If the land is owned by the municipality or some other public body then, as land-owner, it will tend to keep in mind that it can turn this pattern of demand to financial advantage by renting every site to the highest bidder. More precisely, and this is not quite the same thing, it will try to let land in such a way that the total rental income is maximized, or that the total of rent and site-based taxes is maximized.

On the other hand, the land-owning authority will also take account of other factors, including ideas that it may have about what is socially desirable, or in conformity with its own views (or the views of other public bodies) on town layout. This means that in renting land with the purpose of income-maximization in mind it will be constrained to some extent by other considerations. If this is carefully considered it will be seen that, if the land-owning authority is at all motivated by income maximization, then in effect it will behave like any private landowner who is subjected to land-use controls determined by the same considerations. The one qualification to be made to this remark is that the authority behaves like a large private land-owner, whose views about the optimum use of a site will be coloured by the ownership of other sites.

It follows from this that, even when land is publicly owned, the owner will review from time to time the optimum use of sites, and be guided by essentially the same concepts of obsolescence as those we have just described.

The remaining important possibility is when the public authority owning the land is completely uninfluenced by rental income. In that case it will probably have its own strongly held views about the suitability of different sites for different purposes, and seek to achieve these. But even then the demand for occupation of the sites has to be considered. To examine this case in detail would take up more space than is warranted in this book, but it seems likely that a modified form of our obsolescence approach would be applicable.

We now consider how development is actually achieved. The developer needs money and access to building resources. How he obtains these is the subject to which we must now turn.

Development finance

We have argued that development takes place at the initiative of, or with the consent of, the owner. Strictly speaking this is true, but in some cases a person will have become owner in order to develop. Different people will have different views about the potentials of different sites and buildings. Moreover, some people will feel that for financial or other reasons they are unable to take advantage of the potential that they see. This means that frequently an existing owner will consider that the best thing that he can do with a building is to leave it as it is, while a prospective owner will feel that, provided that he can acquire it for a reasonable sum of money, then he would best redevelop it. In such a case the possibility of a sale arises, with the existing owner expecting a sum that compensates him for his loss of rental income, and probably seeking more, while the prospective owner will be unwilling to pay so much that his total costs, including those of redevelopment, are too hiigh when compared with the rental income that he expects to receive. There is usually room for bargaining.

The basic approach that we have adopted is unaltered by the sale and purchase of properties, because sale and purchase do not in themselves change the buildings, even though they often alter the likelihood of a change. It remains true that the owner, now the new owner, does what he considers to be best.

On the other hand, sale and purchase become a very important part of large-scale redevelopment. If a private developer considers that a large building or complex of buildings could profitably be erected in a particular location, and learns that at present there are several different landowners each owning some part of it, then he is faced with the task of trying to acquire all of the separate sites, so that they can be assembled into one large site. Usually he will try to do this unobtrusively, buying each site as cheaply as he can, and trying to conceal his ultimate intentions, and his ownership of neighbouring sites, from the seller, lest the seller raise his price. This is a process that may take decades rather than years, and during it buildings may be let on short-term leases, and have little money spent on them, or even be left empty. In either case there is likely to be decay, for it is rarely advantageous to the owner to maintain them. Eventually, possibly by offering extremely high prices, and possibly by beginning redevelopment before he has acquired all of the sites (and so contributing to a functional or other tenant obsolescence for existing occupiers) he completes his site assembly.

Another device open to the developer is to acquire as much of a site as possible, and then to interest the municipal authority in some development scheme on that land. If the municipality has the power to acquire land compulsorily then it may obtain the rest of the site, and either sell it to the developer or enter into some partnership with the developer, and agree to some other business deal. In some cases this has involved the provision of various public amenities by the developer. Sometimes, of course, the developer is the municipality, who finds its easier to acquire a large site, or parts of it, in this way than to use its powers of compulsory acquisition.

Throughout this process of site assembly, the developer is interested not in the building that he buys but in the site on which it stands. That site has a value for him, because he considers that if he uses it in a certain way he can obtain a good financial return. This is a subject that we consider in more detail in our next chapter, but we need to be a little more specific about it here. Suppose that if a developer spends £100,000 erecting a new building on one site then he expects to be able to let it for £15,000 per annum, while if he erects an identical building at the same cost on another site he expects to be able to let it for £40,000 per annum. Clearly the second site is more valuable to him than the first one is; and he would estimate that value in a way that reflects the difference in annual income of £25,000. What exactly this would be would depend on a variety of factors, including taxation provisions, the costs of raising any purchase money, and so on. In other words, the site would have different values for different developers, and even at different times for the same developer.

When the owner of a site, or a prospective owner, contemplates a development scheme he may have easy access to sufficient money, and in that case he will simply have to consider whether the scheme is the best way of using the money. In particular he will keep in mind that if he has to borrow the money he will need an income (annually or eventually) exceeding his borrowing costs, while if it is his own money he will need an income exceeding what he could get by lending that money to a bank or some other secure borrower.

A more frequent and interesting case is when the developer does not have easy access to money. In other words, one way or another he has to persuade some institution to lend it to him. This means that while the developer has to consider the development to be 'best', the institution will also have to consider that the development is good enough to warrant its support, and that the developer himself passes their tests. This can mean that some of the more speculative ideas, firmly believed in by the developers, cannot proceed because the institutions providing finance judge their prospects, and their claims upon support when viewed against other claimants, less favourably; or because the developer is not regarded favour-

ably. Thus, institutional reactions mean that there is likely to
be a wider comparison between essentially competing projects
for financial support than would arise if the developers had
easier access to funds, disposable at their own discretion.

Development and income flows

The detail of the involvement of institutions, sometimes in a
tripartite agreement involving themselves, the developer and
the municipality, varies considerably. Frequently the arrangement means that some part of the rental income passes
to them, increasing as rents increase. It may also mean that
eventually the ownership of the site and property does so.
These institutional details, which are very important, vary
from country to country. From our point of view the interesting
and somewhat neglected fact is that the involvement of institutions in redevelopment has been yet another factor changing
the composition of the sets involved in the decisions and in
their consequences.

   This can best be appreciated if we contrast two towns – one
in which small-scale local property owners finance their own
small developments, possibly with some simple borrowing
from a bank, and the other in which there are large developments by property companies entering into deals with institutions and the municipality. In the former case there are
likely to be more owner-occupiers of shops than in the latter,
but this is not the most important point, as can be seen from
Figure 9.1 below. This is similar to Figure 6.1 but we use it to
make a slightly different point. In Figure A there are important overlaps between membership of the sets of shopkeepers S,
shop owners P, customers C and residents R. In Figure B,
corresponding to the institutional case, there are noticeable
differences – fewer shopkeepers are residents, fewer are owners, and fewer owners are residents. It is also true that fewer
shopkeepers or owners are customers. In many cases the
fractions of the sets S and P lying outside C and R will be very
much larger than is indicated here. While the involvement of
property companies and institutions in ownership explains the
shift of the set P away from C and R (unless the institution
happens to have a very high local ownership, as might happen
in the case of a small local pension fund), it does not explain
the outward shift of the set S. As we will recall from Chapter 6,
where large-scale shopping developments take place there is a
likelihood that the shops will be rented by multiples rather

than by private local shopkeepers. This means that unless many residents or customers are shareholders in these firms the shift will occur.

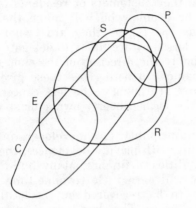

Figure 9.1A

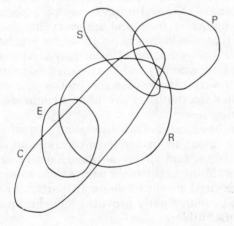

Figure 9.1B

If we now translate this into flows of income we see that in the case shown by Figure B a large part of the profit made by the shopkeeper, and a large part of the rent paid by him to the property owner, will end up in the pockets of people who are neither residents nor customers – yet it is from customers that this money comes. Between them, the multiples and the developers drain money out of the economy of the customers.

Some of it goes back as wages, but much of it is a permanent leakage from the circular flow of incomes.

Yet another aspect of this changing composition of the sets is that, be they customers or residents or neither, they are likely to be people who will make their decisions in a different way. So far as they are owners by virtue of being shareholders they are likely to delegate their decisions to others, probably the directors of the shop companies and property companies. In both cases these directors (or other decision makers) are going to be less concerned with local matters than the local property owner or shopkeeper would be.

When the municipality is a developer, in its own right or in partnership with private developers, there are slightly different possibilities of finance. Many buildings erected by a municipality will earn little revenue, and their cost will probably have to be recovered out of local taxes over a period of many years. This has been discussed in Chapter 4. In some cases, however, the municipality is involved with private developers in promoting lucrative schemes. In these cases their share of rental income may be expected to exceed their repayments of loan and interest charges. Thus part of the rent that would otherwise go to non-residents becomes available for the reduction of local taxes. As we have seen, this benefits all who pay local taxes, and consequently some of it goes towards increasing the profits of companies and so the national tax that they pay: but the commercial landlords may be paying less.

While we have concentrated on that part of development that is most apparent in our town centres and certain other places, we have said little in this chapter about housing development. Many of the main points were raised in Chapter 5, but some need attention here. In particular we have to refer again to municipally provided housing and to the speculative housebuilder.

Older houses soon tend to suffer from some form of obsolescence and, especially if they are rented and subject to controls, this is likely to lead either directly to redevelopment or to decay and then perhaps to redevelopment. In an expanding town many of the older houses are likely to occupy sites whose owners could find more profitable uses for them. Sometimes, too, the continued occupation of these sites by housing has led to community obsolescence. In all, the forces for change are great. On the other hand there may be many social, political or legal obstacles preventing the owner or the community from doing what seems best in economic or land-use terms.

Depending on many factors, not least the existence of any legally enforceable constraints, owners or occupiers of some houses may convert part of them to some other use, such as a shop, and slowly adapt the building to changing circumstances. In such cases the original use may eventually disappear, but a building designed as a house rarely makes a satisfactory shop, and sooner or later the case for complete redevelopment is likely to emerge, as further adaptation becomes more difficult.

These pressures for the replacement of old houses on certain sites by other land-uses imply a need for the provision of new houses somewhere else. Demographic forces may add to this need. There will also be need to replace old housing simply because it is now sub-standard, and in some cases this can be in the same place.

But wherever the new housing is built, questions of costs and returns arise. Unless the municipality is able to acquire land that has a high commercial price at a low cost it is likely to build its new houses on cheaper sites. There may be strong political or social reasons for not doing so, and these may be sufficient to persuade the municipality to incur high land-purchase costs, even though this may mean charging uneconomic rents. This is something that the speculative builder can rarely do, which means that he is much more likely to try to build houses where land is cheap. The principal exception to this is when he may build more expensive houses or flats on costly sites and hope to let them or to sell them to wealthier people who may place a high value on living in a specified area, such as a town centre.

A question of some importance is whether under certain circumstances it makes better sense to spend money rehabilitating a house, or a number of houses, instead of demolishing and building anew. Various mathematical decision formulae for answering this question have been proposed. The essential point is that if money is spent now on building some new houses, those houses can be expected to provide a certain standard of shelter over a number of years, and, by using certain assumptions and discounting techniques (such as those described in Chapter 12), we can put a present value on this shelter. If the same sum of money is spent, instead, improving a greater number of existing houses then these will provide higher-standard shelter than they would otherwise do, or last longer. Thus the future stream of shelter is altered, and a value can be put on this. The rule for choosing between 'new-build' and 'rehabilitation' is then to compare these values to see which mode of expenditure gives the higher present value.

Unfortunately, this kind of decision-rule, once put forward by myself, ignores an important aspect of the question – namely, the identities of those who pay now, those who will pay in the future, and those who will have to repay in the future loans now being obtained. This kind of question is considered in Chapter 13.

Development and utilities

Finally, in considering development, we must say a word about the provision of water, electricity, gas, sewage, roads and the other services and infra-structure that have to be provided. We will refer to them briefly as 'public utilities' or simply 'utilities'.

In many developing countries towns may expand in the complete absence of these utilities. Where this happens there is likely to be not only a low standard of living but also disease. Many authorities argue, with some empirical justification, that the cheapest way of raising health standards in these countries is to provide stand-pipes (rather than wells) and to improve the facilities for sewage disposal. As towns become more developed (socially and economically, as well as physically) there is a greater demand for piped water in every building, and piped sewage disposal. There is also an increased demand for properly surfaced roads, partly for convenience but also, again, for health reasons. Unmade tracks are much more likely to accumulate decaying waste. While the local provision of roads, water and sewage disposal may be entirely at the cost of the developer, there have to be connections to a wider system, and here central costs are incurred.

Some idea of the problems can be gained if we look at water provision. The existing reservoirs and main pipes may be sufficient to provide for the existing houses, factories and other users, but if a thousand new houses are to be built on the edge of the town two questions arise. Do the reservoirs have enough water to meet the extra demand? Are the main pipes to that part of the town large enough to carry this extra quantity? There may be similar questions about filter arrangements, pumping and other matters. If the answers to all of these questions are affirmative, and the development proceeds, then anybody who is making any profit out of it is doing so because the water authority has invested in capacity greater than its present needs. The cost of this is probably borne by the national taxpayer, the local taxpayer, or consumers of water. It has been argued that the developer should be expected to pay the authority for the privilege of connecting his local pipes to the main piped water supply, so that the costs of providing water to the new houses will fall less upon others. If this were done there would be widespread consequences. The developer would tend to pass this charge on as prices or rents for the houses. Any part not passed on, and thereby reducing his profit, would possibly result in his paying less tax. It would also make the provision of houses a less attractive activity and might reduce the supply of them, thereby once more affecting prices or rents. The price and rent effects would affect the whole local housing market. Thus the imposition of this kind of water-services charge on the developer would tend to spread costs fairly widely, even though their principal impact would probably be upon the occupiers of the new houses. In times of inflation this would give rise to some of the arguments we have already considered in Chapter 5.

We must remember in this context that there is no difference in costs to a water authority between providing for public sector houses and for private houses. This means that a municipal housing authority would, in principle, be faced with the same duty of paying a contribution to the cost of providing the water facilities. If it chose to cover it out of local taxes there would be questions about the local taxpayer subsidizing the provision of water for municipal tenants but not for private sector occupiers.

The argument could go on, but enough has been said to indicate that it is complicated and far-reaching. While we have developed it in terms of water supply, it applies in its essentials to other utilities.

Two further points must be made. One is that the provision of utilities affects the value of a site. If a developer knows that there is no water supply to a site, and that the water authority will provide it only if he pays the costs of a lengthy supply pipe, then he will consider that developing that site will be less profitable to him than it would have been otherwise. This means that he will offer less for it to its present owner. It has been argued that as development is possible only after services have been provided then the whole of the additional income arising to the owner as a result of the development should be credited to the provision of these services. This is an un-balanced approach, since it is also true that the provision of services and no building does not allow the owner to reap much rent. A more balanced argument might be that the additional income arises from various inputs, of which the provision of services is one, and that the income might be attributed to these inputs in proportion to their costs. Even in this case, however, if the providers of services attempted to recoup their proportion of the revenue a result could be the kind of chain reaction on prices, taxes and other matters that we considered a few paragraphs ago.

The remaining point concerns threshholds. Again we can illustrate it by considering water supply. A time will come in the expansion of a town, or in its changing use of water, where existing reservoirs or filter stations cannot cope with further increases in demand. To provide a new reservoir will cost a very large amount of money, but once this has been done there will be surplus capacity able to meet expected demands for some years to come. In other words, water demands can grow without requiring further major investment until a certain threshhold is reached. When that happens it requires a major investment, which not only enables the demand to be met but also shifts the threshhold. In any programme of urban growth, or growing utilization of services, these investment thresh-holds have to be kept in mind.

We should note that this concept of threshholds is relevant to the argument just considered about charging for connection to an existing system. If an existing reservoir copes exactly with the demands from 100,000 houses, but the presence of another 10,000 requires further provision, should a small new reservoir be built, and then perhaps another small one a few years later, and so on, or should the water authority take advantage of the fact that a reservoir for 40,000 houses costs less than four reservoirs each for 10,000? If it does take advantage of this then three sets of water consumers seem to be involved: the original 100,000 households, the next in-crement of 10,000, on whose behalf the new reservoir is built, and those who later come along and enjoy some of its capacity. As time passes some of these households disappear and others arise. There is also movement between houses. Who is subsi-dizing whom, and who should subsidize whom, become compli-cated questions.

10

Land rents, values, prices and use

In the large literature on land values and prices a major common confusion arises out of a failure to recognize that value is an attribute of an entity and of a valuer, simultaneously. It is usual for something to have several different values at the same moment, even though only one of these may be publicized. This is a point that we shortly develop in a way that allows us to relate some of these values of land to the price paid for land in a specified kind of transaction. We also consider how different sets of people place different values on variously located plots of land; and how the price paid for a piece of land affects various sets. We will not here be entering into the political and philosophical attempts to ascribe or to apportion value to any particular factors, but will concentrate on describing how land-use and land prices are determined in a free market. In the next chapter we consider the reasons for public intervention, and examine the consequences of intervention of various kinds.

Urban land rents (non-housing)

We must emphasize that we are concerned with land devoted to urban uses. On the fringe of a town there may be a conflict between urban use and some other use, and we shall shortly have to consider this, but for the time being we consider that urban land is occupied solely for the pursuit of some activity contained within a building, or some activity closely associated with buildings (including movement between them) or with some other use (such as recreation) intended primarily for the residents of the town. The land may be publicly or privately owned.

The occupiers of urban land will normally pay rent to the owners or, if they are owner-occupiers, save themselves from having to pay rent to others. If the land carries buildings then it may be difficult to determine how the rent should be apportioned between the building and the land; and a similar point applies to the contribution due to the services with which the land has been endowed. These are matters that are probably more pertinent to a discussion of value rather than rent, and which we therefore defer. The point is that the occupier rents a building in a specific location, and pays a rent for the right to occupy that building.

Another complication arises out of land used for public buildings. While it is easy to estimate the rent that a municipality would have to pay for its offices, if it did not own them, or the rental income that it forgoes by occupying them rather than selling them, there are difficulties in establishing a rent for a school, a church or some other non-commercial building. A similar point may be made about a public park. In both cases the special non-commercial nature of the land-use, and the fact that no rent is actually paid, combine to make our simple rental approach invalid. This, too, is a matter whose discussion we defer. We restrict our present analysis to buildings that are used for some purpose that commonly involves a payment of rent, even though in special cases that rent may not be paid.

We argued in the last chapter that a tenant will consider the rent that he has to pay if he occupies a building and take it into account in choosing between the opportunities that confront him. The essential point here was that certain activities are more likely to flourish in some locations than in others. This means that incomes, net of expenditures on matters other than rent, are expected to be higher in some locations than in others; and so shopkeepers and certain kinds of office firms will tend to seek these locations, and be prepared, if necessary, to pay higher rents for them. At the end of a lease they will consider whether to try to retain the tenancy (probably at a new rent) or whether to move. Obviously the rent that a tenant is prepared to pay will depend on his estimate of the 'earning power' of that building for his purpose. This is a matter discussed by us in Chapters 6 and 8 where we pointed out that in order to pay a high rent a shopkeeper might have to do so much business that he would need to employ more staff. In other words, the 'earning power' of the tenancy would have to be assessed after taking account of all operating costs, including any that arise out of its occupation. The crucial question must be, 'If I occupy building X rather than building Y, will my surplus of income over expenditure be so much higher that it will justify my paying the higher rent?'

While the concept of marginalism is useful, it has to be treated with more caution than sometimes appears in mathematical treatments of the subject. There are three major reasons for this. One is that not all tenancies and rent agreements are reviewable at any one moment, which is another way of expressing the fact that most such agreements are reviewable only at widely separated specified moments. The second is that the tenant has to form his own expectation of marginal income, which will differ from tenant to tenant, and may not be right. He will also have to form some expectation of the consequences of any rent reviews that may occur during his period of tenancy, when he may not have the right to opt out. Finally, it is not quite a question of marginal income exceeding marginal expenditure inclusive of rent, for the question as we have worded it asks whether net income will 'be so much higher that it will justify my paying the higher rent'. The tenant himself has to feel justified, and he is unlikely to feel so if his expected income is only slightly better than the increase in rent, unless he is very confident of his expectation. Most tenants are not. There is, therefore, a variable amount by which expected income has to exceed expenditure before the tenant is ready to move. Many factors, such as frequent changes in local or national tax rates, changes in wage levels, and other items that appear as expenditures and are effectively outside the tenant's control, influence this amount, and the more unpredictable these become the greater is the uncertainty that he must attach to his estimates. This means that he seeks a greater margin of safety.

We now consider how these reactions of tenants are manifested in an existing town. We are not concerned with attempting to explain the existing pattern of land use, which in any case has almost certainly evolved not only in accordance with broadly stated principles of spatial and locational demands, but also in response to important local factors, not least the timing of certain key developments, that are likely to be taken adequately into account in no general theory. Instead we take the existing land-use pattern as a starting point, and consider how it affects and may be affected by tenants attitudes towards rents.

Since we start with an existing pattern we have to take account of the existing concentrations of different types of land-users. Why these concentrations are exactly where they are, rather than a few hundred yards, or a few miles, away is a matter for local historians and geographers. That they are concentrations is due to the fact that certain activities benefit from proximity to other activities, or to other performers of the same activity, as we saw in Chapter 8. In particular we will note the presence of a shopping and office centre, sometimes with a specialist office area containing very few shops, or with a specialist shop area in which even the upper floors are devoted to retailing rather than to offices. The different detailed spatial requirements of shops and offices, with their consequent outbidding of each other for sites, will be partly responsible: but so will individual development decisions that will often have had an element of accident in them. Be that as it may, the fact remains that the basic pattern exists, shaping the central area of the town, and the lesser sub-centres that may be scattered around it, serving mainly local suburban needs. There may also be certain streets – often streets leading to the centre – with shops or offices along them, in contrast to their hinterland of housing.

A prospective shopkeeper or office tenant seeking accommodation will normally have two possibilities to consider. He may look at vacant property. He may also approach existing tenants and offer to buy their tenancy rights. This latter action is, in fact, what he may be doing when he enquires about vacant property, for although it is vacant there may still be a tenant with the legal obligation to pay the rent who has decided that it is better to do so and to leave the place unoccupied than to incur wage and other costs in keeping it open for a meagre return. (This is frequently the case when a new development has encouraged occupiers to move out of their older properties into new locations which turn out to be less profitable than they expected.) In other cases the existing tenant agrees to surrender his tenancy rights and obligations in return for some payment from the new tenant. There may also be cases where the property owner secures a higher rent by cancelling the existing agreement in return for the right to re-let the property on a new basis. Thus in some cases the new tenancy provides the property owner with a higher income than previously (in that the property is now let, or let at an increased rent) while in other cases it leaves him unaffected until the time for a contractual rent review arrives. In this case, however, the withdrawing tenant, knowing that neighbouring properties are hard to obtain, or are commanding higher rents than the one he agreed to pay some years ago, will try to extract a payment that the new tenant can rightly regard as part of his rent. In other words, the rent that the new tenant has to pay, either entirely to the landlord or partly to him and partly as a premium to the retiring tenant, will tend to reflect the current pressures of demand and supply. If tenancies are scarce and the few empty (or available) premises are sought by many then rents will be pushed upwards. If there are several empty shops or offices the story may be different, for while some owners of unlet premises, and some legally responsible tenants of unoccupied premises, will be inclined to let at rather low rents, preferring these to none at all, others will prefer to leave their properties unlet in the hope of obtaining a higher rent later. But there comes a time when unfulfilled hopes weaken, and offers of lower rent are accepted. In short, be there few or many empty properties, except in a very finely balanced state, either upward or downward rental obsolescence is very likely to be present. And any factors that affect either the demands for tenancies or the supply of unoccupied premises will be reflected in the consequent rental charges.

We have already indicated how rental obsolescence may lead to decay and/or to development. This is a matter of action (or inaction) by the owner altering the supply of available accommodation, partly in response to demand but also in reaction to the ways in which other owners may be altering it. Redevelopment, while increasing the supply of some kinds of premises, will often reduce the supply of others, and possibly do so in a way that drives up the rents of what remains. In the short run it creates disturbance, which will sometimes cause customers and clients to change their habits, and so affect the profits of tenants, possibly in a permanent way. When it is completed it often means that yet another new pattern of habits arises, and in anticipation of this some existing tenants will move to the new premises.

In all cases, be there redevelopment or changes of tenancy of existing buildings, the owner is normally likely to let the property to the tenant who will pay the highest rent. We have already seen that this may affect the type of shop, with some premises more likely to be occupied by a jeweller than a hardware store. It also means that there is a strong tendency for the privately owned shop, or the unusual shop, to disappear, as the ability to pay the rent depends more and more on the ability to benefit from the economies of mass-retailing, and the inclination to risk having wrong expectations of that ability rests increasingly on whether there are other outlets whose profits can support a temporary loss on one or two sites.

A similar tale is true of office clients. The accountant, the dentist, the piano teacher and the insurance broker are all people who place some importance of being accessible to the public, and on having their windows or name plates noticed by those who pass by. But their income rarely allows them to pay the rents for their premises that other clients will offer. If they acquire a clientele derived largely from central area businesses and their employees they may feel that they must stay where they are, and they probably raise their fees in order to pay higher rents. But others will move to less expensive premises, possibly, at first to a back room on a top floor rather than a front room on a first floor, but often to a totally different location that may have advantages for car parking but where new business will depend on only local passers-by and on reputation.

We have concentrated on offices and shops. The rents of land for warehousing and industry are similarly determined, although the nature of the requirements may play a very much more obvious role in determining the location, and land let for industrial purposes may be let on a very long lease because the movement of industrial plant is often extremely difficult. Matters of ownership and public control are also much more important factors in these cases.

Land values

Before considering land devoted to housing we relate land rents to values. We have argued that in the absence of controls or prohibitions locations will tend to acquire the tenants who pay the highest rents. In Chapter 9 we indicated that increasing rents, manifesting upward rental obsolescence, might presage building obsolescence, either because the owner considered that a building devoted to a different land-use would be even more profitable, or because he wished to provide a new building, with more floor space and amenities, devoted to the same use, and earning even higher income. In short, provided that regulations allow it, if a certain kind of land-user will pay higher rent for the occupation of that land than will any other land-user, the land is likely to acquire that use, and possibly to do so intensively.

As we shall shortly discuss further, the clustering of land-users of a similar kind, the precise location of activities, and the nature and timing of redevelopment are all closely related. Now, however, the important point to establish is that the rent obtained by the building owner reflects the profitability of the most profitable use of the site, but possibly only after a substantial time lag. If he has lately redeveloped, and done so in the right way, then the rental income is likely to be the highest that can be extracted from any user of that site for any permitted purpose. If there is a long lease, or some other limitation on the land-use, he tries to obtain the highest rent he can subject to these restrictions; and when the opportunity to redevelop arises he considers whether to do so, but that may be many years away. If the demand for a tenancy is low, and downward rental obsolescence occurs, then (as we have seen) the process of decay may begin. The rent obtained may be one determined several years previously, and not adjustable for some years to come. It reflects what seemed to be most profitable at the time of the rent agreement.

Frequently, redevelopment takes place after land has been sold to a new owner. This raises questions about the price at which it changes hands, and so to questions about land values. As we have already indicated in our discussion of rents, the question is complicated by the fact that urban land usually carries associated buildings and services. Normally some allowance for this can be made by considering what it would cost to provide the building and services on that site if they were not there, or by determining what it will cost to remove them and to make the site usable for some other building or purpose. This second cost is sometimes so high that the site value becomes very low. On the other hand, many purchasers and sellers simply look upon a transaction as involving one entity, a building in a location, rather than two entities, a building and a site.

Another difficulty arises from the fact that local or other laws may prevent a site from being used for certain purposes. This means that the price has to be determined in the context of existing permitted uses. If, however, there is reason to believe that other uses may become permitted then some purchasers, or the existing owner, may be inclined to make some allowance for this possibility when settling on a price to be paid for its ownership.

The 'price' of which we have been talking is related to, and often the same as, the 'market value'. We shall use this term to mean the highest price offered by a purchaser who is aware of prices being paid for, and asked for, other pieces of land in the vicinity (or elsewhere if approximately equally suitable for the same purpose) at a time when the availability of the land is known widely. The highest price will often be the actual selling price, but sometimes a purchaser may be ignorant of local prices and ill-advisedly pay more than he would have done if he had been better informed. In this case the selling price is higher than the market value. At other times a land owner will sell without widely advertising his willingness to do so, and too eagerly accept an offer lower than he would have obtained if he had sounded out the market. Here the selling price is below the market value.

If the owner of some land receives an offer for it he will not necessarily agree to sell. Even if he knows that the offer is the highest offer that he is likely to get in the next year or two, and that it compares well with prices recently paid for similar sites, he may still consider that he puts a higher value on the land than this market value. Whether he does this will depend on many factors, including his own financial circumstances. If he badly needs cash he is more likely to sell than if he has no cash problems. He may consider that the market value of the land is likely to increase in a few years time, and that then he could sell the site for more than the amount of its present market value augmented by interest. This view may be based on his private knowledge, his judgement or his hopes. It may or may not be right. What matters is that the current owner has added a personal speculative value to the current market value, in order to determine the value that he puts on the land.

Speculative value may arise in other ways. A prospective purchaser may offer more than the current market value (and thereby increase it) because he expects later to be able to sell the land at a profit, or to be allowed to develop it in some way that is not at present permitted. In both cases he is gambling on being able to derive a higher income from the land than is currently possible. If others disagree with him they will not value the ownership of the land as highly as he does.

This brings us up against the question of whether a value can be 'wrong', and, if so, what we mean by 'the right value' of a piece of land. What we have to remember is that, when it is bought by a private purchaser, urban land is bought not because of any agricultural or mining possibilities, but because of its location relative to other land which is being used, or is expected to be used, in certain ways. The purchaser considers that, because of this location, he will be able either to rent the land to somebody in a way that will bring him an income that provides a good return on the capital sum he has paid for it (and for any buildings that he puts upon it) or to sell the land (as it is or possibly with some development) at a good profit. Here are questions not of fact but of expectations. They may have expectations that have associated dates, so that after that date we can say without doubt that they have been fulfilled or were wrong. But often there is no terminal date. The purchaser expects eventually to obtain an income that will, in retrospect, justify his decision to purchase at that price, and while he may often consider that so far his decision has not been shown to be right, he will also consider that it has not been shown to be wrong.

The rightness or wrongness of a value that has recently been placed upon an asset can be regarded only as an expression of opinion about whether the expectations that have given rise to that value are likely to be fulfilled. More historically, we can ask whether the expectations were fulfilled, and (as with the assessment of forecasts made long ago) it is easier to reach agreement about such a question than it is to assess the chances of somebody's current expectations being fulfilled. If we could all make 'correct' valuations, buying and selling would become very difficult. Normally the price paid for a property is somewhat less than the purchaser's valuation and somewhat more than the seller's. Equality of valuations would turn oil into glue.

It is not only the purchaser and seller who have to value a piece of land. If the purchase is being made with borrowed money then the lender will also consider the value. He may well take a different view from that of the borrowing purchaser, arguing that it is not his policy to hold land for speculative purposes, and that what he has to consider is whether, if the borrower defaults, he can recover his loan by selling the land (and property) quickly.

This involvement of lenders, who are often insurance companies or other institutions, sometimes acts as an important factor in the spatial pattern of land values. Their views on whether a site and property are likely to have a high enough value in the event of a forced sale are likely to be coloured by experience rather than by hope. They will lend more readily for purchases and developments in areas where there is strong evidence of rising values; and in this way, by making it easier for purchasers to borrow money, will tend to increase demand for sites in these areas, and so to help to bring about the rising values that they seek. In some cases, too, the institutions will become involved as sole or joint owners.

Land for housing

It is convenient if we temporarily abstract from reality and consider all housing to be rented. Immediately we see that in the absence of controls there are some parts of a town where there is likely to be very little housing, simply because the rents that landowners will be able to get from shop, office or other tenants far exceed what can be obtained for houses or flats. But we still have to explain how rents of otherwise more or less identical houses will vary with location, and why certain types of houses are more likely to be built in certain places.

The essential difference between the occupation of a house and of a business premise, as far as rent and value are concerned, is that while the business occupier tends to choose the location that will allow him, in his judgement, to maximize his profits, the occupier of a house has other considerations in mind. Normally, they are more difficult to define, much more likely to vary between occupiers, and probably they are less likely to be fully appreciated by those who make the decisions.

Amongst the factors that a householder may consider to be important in his choice of a house are some that are essentially concerned with the house itself, rather than with its location. We may call these 'accommodation factors'. They include such things as size, design, amenities and so on. There are also 'environmental factors', such as the view, noise, pollution, the appearance of neighbouring property, the apparent behaviour of neighbours, residential density, and so on. Both of these factors will tend to be functions of location. Another factor that, as we shall see, may also depend on location, is the size of the plot of land occupied by the house and its garden.

Some householders seeking accommodation will specify fairly precisely what they require in accommodation factors, environmental factors and plot size. In most cases this will still present a choice of houses in different locations and at different rents.

The choice between them is made by considering, amongst other things, the accessibility of the locations to different places, or to different activities, in which the householder is interested. Access to the place (or places) of work of members of the household, to transport facilities, to shops, to schools (or to a specific school) and to other places that may be as specific as a particular church or as unspecific as 'the countryside' will matter. Between them, and in a highly personal way, these define the 'accessibility factor'.

While there may well be other factors involved in the decision, these four factors probably contain the main items that a householder considers in determining whether a particular rent is 'worth it'. But the accessibility factor enters into the consideration in a special way, because associated with it are travel costs, which include expenditure of both money and time. A location that is 'too far from work' may be one that involves payments of travel expenses that are too high, or one that implies the expenditure of too much time travelling between work and home.

What 'too high' or 'too much' will be will depend on many factors, not least the household income. Poor people will want to live close to their work, so that their income net of travel costs is as high as possible – but only if the rents are suitable. There is little doubt that some people act with the intention of minimizing their total expenditure on housing and travel. But others, who can afford to do so, may attach more importance to environmental or other factors. We consider these matters more fully shortly, but even here a further word about rents is necessary.

The behavioural tendencies just indicated will affect people's views about how much rent they should pay for a house in a specified location. Another factor affecting this decision is how much they can afford to pay. We could imagine that in an existing town all people would state how much money they would be prepared to pay in order to live in this empty house or that, taking account of the points we have just made. The house owners would also decide the rents that they are prepared to accept. Many people would not be interested in a particular empty house because it would be unacceptable to them on environmental, accommodation, accessibility or plot-size considerations, or not sufficiently better than their existing house to justify the upheaval of moving unless there was a significant reduction in rent. Others would express no interest because they would expect an acceptable rent to be beyond their means. At the end of the day, some of the houses are let to the highest bidder and some remain unlet. If they are left unlet for long then there is probably a downward rental obsolescence and a tendency to decay, which may accelerate redevelopment, partly because the market value of the site may be high if a different land use, or a greater intensification of the existing use, is permitted. Similarly, if there is great competition for the tenancies of certain kinds of houses, or houses in certain places, their rents will tend to rise. Knowledge of this may encourage accommodation owners to consider demolition and rebuilding more intensively in the same place (if it is the locality that attracts competition) or to replace houses of one kind by houses of another kind. This latter may be done by subdivision of a large house into flats, by combining two or more adjacent houses into one, by extending or modifying a house, or by demolition and replacement. In all cases it is the expectation of a sufficiently higher rental that initiates the change.

Thus, even in the absence of housebuilding on new sites, the nature of the housing stock can be expected to change in response to the revealed preferences of prospective tenants, including those existing tenants who may contemplate moving.

We may approach a more realistic analysis if we now consider that some of the houses are owned by their occupiers, rather than rented. We will also suppose that these owner-occupiers are interested only in selling their houses, to other owner-occupiers, when they move. They do not let their houses for rent.

People who have decided to seek a house for purchase will be guided by more or less the same considerations as tenants, except that such matters as the state of repair, and probable ease of resale, will also be considered. Owner-occupied houses that are on the market in a highly desirable location will have a high price compared with similar houses elsewhere; and if certain kinds of houses are scarce relative to the demand for them then they, too, will fetch higher prices than might be expected by comparison with other kinds of houses in the same locality.

Thus, broadly speaking, the spatial pattern of house prices will tend to be similar to that of house rents, although the similarity will often be obscured by the fact that in some localities all of the houses will be to rent, or all of them for sale, and that it may be impossible to rent or buy certain kinds of house anywhere.

When we allow the housing stock to be altered by new housebuilding, we introduce some complications, as now the decision by the house occupier has to be preceded by a decision by the house builder, who may not be the same person. We also have to consider the land owner, and it is convenient to start with him.

Except where there has been municipal intervention (which we consider later) almost all new house-building takes place on undeveloped land. This may be part of a large garden belonging to another house, or it may be agricultural land on the edge of the town. In either case, the owner may decide to build houses upon it, or to sell it to a developer for that purpose. He will expect some return from it, either as a rent or as a sale price, high enough at least to compensate him for any environmental or agricultural loss. Normally he will try to make this return as high as possible, and whether it comes directly from those who will occupy the houses, or indirectly from them via a developer, he will try to do this by considering both the kind and the number of houses that are to be built on the land. The land owner can do little to alter the accessibility of his land to jobs, shops and schools, unless he is developing in a fairly large way and providing these amenities himself – and he may do so – but he can do a great deal to attract occupiers by paying attention to the accommodation factor, the environmental factor, and the plot size. In most cases it is easier to do this if forty or fifty houses are being built than if it is only four or five; and the chance of being able to build that number on a single site will always be greater on the edge of a town than by 'in-filling'. Frequently, when an edge-of-town site is developed in an attractive way, and the houses are rented or sold at high prices, the developer will seek to acquire neighbouring land, not only so that he can develop it in the same profitable way, but also because he considers that if it is developed attractively it will preserve, and even enhance, the attractiveness of what he has already built. The same reasoning will cause him to discourage those who may wish to build less attractive housing nearby. Equally, he will not be eager to develop housing that he hopes to sell to people who will pay a high price for the right environment close to housing that provides what they would consider to be a bad environment. Thus, considerations of these factors tend to result in certain parts of the town edge being fairly widely developed to similar standards.

We should note here that sometimes this attempt to preserve the standards of an area may encourage a house-builder to acquire a large tract of land (if the law allows) on which he will build suitable houses from time to time, as demand seems to warrant, for many years. A pure profit motive may lead to similar behaviour resulting in large tracts of land being owned by builders who have no intention of using them for several years. An important reason for this is that the house-builder must have land on which to build, and by having a stock of land the builder is helping to ensure his own activity in the future. Since this land is purchased some years ahead of its use, and in a less pressured way than it would be if the builder had little land left, there is less panic-buying and it is possible that the builder will be able to provide houses on it and to sell them at a price which, though providing a useful profit on the land, is less than he would have been inclined to seek if he had bought the land more recently. Whether he does so depends, of course, on other factors.

The spatial pattern of land values

The spatial pattern of land rents and market values is determined by the interplay of demands of various kinds. It is possible to translate the above ideas and those that follow into mathematics and, by making various assumptions about the signs and relative magnitudes of different parameters, to reproduce a spatial pattern of rents similar to that existing in certain kinds of towns. Unfortunately, models of this kind rarely take account of such things as an unwillingness on the part of many people to keep moving, the fact that at any one moment most properties are not on the market, and the complexity of factors involved in the house-location decision. Moreover, they are often concerned with attempts to reproduce some kind of equilibrium which is mathematically convenient but a little unrealistic. Towns are not in equilibrium, and land and property values change unevenly, sometimes unexpectedly, and sometimes in some places even explosively.

Instead of embarking on a model of this kind we may usefully consider the identity and behaviour of some of the sets of people who are involved.

First let us note the following:

1 People with low incomes will normally want to spend less on rent and less on travel than will richer people.
2 People who consider that time spent travelling is time partly wasted will try to reduce their travel time.
3 Broadly speaking, the monetary cost and the time cost of a trip by the same mode are highly correlated.

4 Broadly speaking, the faster modes of transport are the more expensive, except where special tracks are reserved for certain modes.
5 Wealthy people will be inclined to value their time, the environmental factor, plot size and the accommodation factor more than poor people value them.
6 Shops and offices cluster and can provide the landowner with a higher income than he is likely to derive from housing on the same site.
7 Shopping and office centres are centres of employment and of facilities to which people seek access. Often they are very close to each other. In what follows we consider them to form jointly 'the town centre'.
8 In most towns there are also jobs and various facilities at other places.

We consider now four different kinds of town-centre worker. The first is the early morning worker, symbolized by the female office cleaner whose husband may be an equally symbolic street-cleaning vehicle driver. They are on low pay and want their total expenditure on travel and rent to be as low as possible. Beautiful houses, large gardens and fine views are dreams that do not affect their decisions. Within walking distance of their places of work there is some poor quality housing, built long ago to old housing standards. Few attaching importance to the accommodation factor or to the environmental factor would live in it if they could afford better accommodation. This means that, despite its closeness to the town centre, this old, poor quality housing will not command a high rent. Even if there are only half as many such houses as there are early morning town-centre-worker households, so that competition for them is high, the incomes of the people who are potential tenants will set an upper limit to the rent that they will pay. Only low-paid workers with early morning central-area jobs will want to live there; and their low incomes cause their demand to fall quickly to zero if rents become too high.

This is, of course, a simplification. Some of these houses may well be sought by others who are prepared to accept, or may even enjoy, the environment that so many abhor, and some of these people may offer higher rents. There will also be others living in these houses whose work hours are more normal: but they, too, will tend to be the low paid, or others who will accept low standards (such as some immigrants from less developed

countries or parts of the same country). The more there are of
these, the higher the rents may become, and in that case many
of the early-morning workers may become unable to pay them.

Even in the simplified case there will be three sets of people
closely affected. Those who fail to find a house will have to
travel further. But public transport services will be few and
infrequent in the early hours, and it may be that the location
at which the sum of the rent and monetary travel cost is lowest
is so far away or so inconveniently placed that the worker
refuses to travel so far every day because of the time-cost of
travel. Alternatively, even this lowest-priced alternative
location may absorb too much of his income. In short, some of
the early-morning workers are forced to seek other work,
either nearer to their new location or at a higher wage. This
reduction in supply affects another set of people – the employers of these workers, who eventually are likely to raise
their wages in an attempt to keep them, to arrange special
transport for them from more remote places, or to try to
provide special accommodation for them (such as is frequently
done for hotel workers). The third set of people affected are the
property owners, for if there is a limit to the rents that their
tenants can pay, and they can be fairly easily evicted, there is
building obsolescence, and the land will acquire either superior houses or a new use as shops and offices compete for space
on the fringe of the existing central area. If eviction is difficult,
decay will set in, leading eventually to the closure of the
houses and probably to redevelopment.

In the more realistic case just mentioned the increased rents
available from other sets of tenants will tend to postpone
redevelopment. But they will also aggravate the problems of
the employers.

Next we consider the young shop or office worker. Here there
are two distinct sets of people to keep in mind. Many young
people in these jobs have not made any active residential
location decision: they live where their parents live. Others
have decided for themselves where to live. The former set is
likely to include only people who have transport of their own,
or who have friends or relatives travelling daily by car from
near their home to the town centre, or who live within
reasonable walking distance of the town centre or a public
transport link. This last point is important in that non-car
owners will try to obtain better public-transport services, and
also tend to demand houses on good transport links, thereby
tending to push up their prices. Any improvement in such

links will increase the potential supply of central-area workers and tend to push up land prices elsewhere, partly at the expense of landowners along existing routes.

The other set of young central-area workers are those who have found their own accommodation. For them some of the problems of the early-morning worker are pertinent. But there are three big differences. Public transport services are likely to be better than in the early morning; many of them will be able to live alone; many of them will look upon whatever arrangements they make as temporary, lasting only until their pay rises with age, or until they marry. The better transport widens their choice of locations. Their individual status allows them to occupy single rooms, or to share with others, thereby being able to consider accommodation in any older larger houses that may be available for multiple occupation, whether properly adapted or not. In many towns these will be houses built many decades ago to what were then good standards in a pleasant environment. Today a room or small flat in one of them provides more spacious and conventionally pleasant surroundings than an old, poor quality, central-area house. Thus the combination of better transport and the flexibility that goes with youth tends to focus some attention on this kind of property. When it was constructed the tendency for houses of one kind to cluster, as we noted above, probably existed, and so we may find well defined suburban areas characterized by this kind of house. Often they will have been built when families were larger than now, and servants more abundant. Now they will usually be too large for the owning household, and the temptation to let one or two rooms, or to divide the house structurally becomes strong. If the town is growing there is probably an increasing demand for bed-sitting rooms and flatlets, and as the older larger houses come on to the market there will be bids for them from people who look upon them as sources of income. Their aim will be to convert them completely into multiple occupation, deriving rent from every tenant. If demand is very high then in some cases the large gardens that surround the houses may be used for extensions or new buildings of purpose-built flats.

Once again we have simplified, and in particular we have ignored the demand for this kind of accommodation from other sets of people, including those who may work outside the town centre and students. The essential point however is that, provided there is good public transport during ordinary working hours to the town centre or other large places of employment, the older large houses in pleasant surroundings will attract a demand for small flats, and the income derivable from rents will drive up their values. In some places, and especially if there are good car-parking facilities and pleasant views, their possible conversion into hotels also becomes an important factor in determining their values.

The middle-income grade of central-area workers includes a very wide range of people, and their behaviour patterns will be diverse. Nevertheless, certain points can be made about their broad locational preferences.

Most of them will be interested in neither the old, poor quality house nor the small flat in a larger old house. All of them will be able to pay higher rents than those charged for these kinds of accommodation, and many of them will have cars. Able to pay for something more in keeping with their personal attitudes towards the accommodation and environmental factors, and to plot size, they seek it, with little constraint by the public-transport service. But they are still concerned to some extent with keeping their location costs, of rent and travel, within bounds. Some will prefer to keep the travel component in costs as low as possible, and seek accommodation near to the centre of as high a standard as they can afford. This may generate a demand for the replacement of old, poor quality housing by something better and more expensive. Others will accept considerable travel costs of money and time if these enable them to live in very modern houses, on large plots, in semi-rural surroundings, or near to a good school.

The high-income town-centre workers behave in a similar way, but they are even less constrained. They can outbid other residential users for high quality housing in central-area sites, possibly making it profitable for a land-owner to provide this where otherwise shops or offices might be considered: although this will not be common. They can also afford to buy or to have built larger high-standard houses on large plots of land, which are more likely to exist on the edge of a town and so to enjoy a more attractive landscape. Only if they place a very high value on saving travel time will they be deterred, and in that case some of them may seek town-centre flats as well as edge-of-town houses. The clustering phenomenon already described will operate, and land prices in the edge-of-town area will rise, partly because of the growth of a prestige element in demand, and partly because of the social life that people of higher incomes can enjoy if they live reasonably close together. This, in turn, will affect the traders in any nearby village or attractive shopping centre, and so tend to push up the rents of shops, and the general quality of local services.

We must now pull together these competing claims on land, keeping in mind that while the town centre will be an important element in determining accessibility, there are also other centres of employment and of shopping services, and that access to variously located schools and other amenities will also be important. Indeed, in an uncontrolled town, developers will see opportunities to take advantage of population growth in many ways. While town-centre type specialist shops are unlikely to flourish in the suburbs – unless they are very affluent suburbs – it is very likely that a sub-centre would do well. Owners of old lower-grade shops, or of houses, may find themselves being approached by purchasers who have site assembly in mind, or they may themselves engage in a piecemeal intensification of commercial uses. And once a few new shops or offices are seen to be paying, others will follow suit, cautiously or otherwise. At times their expectations will be wrong, partly because the bandwagon will become over-loaded, and new properties may remain unlet. In miniature the whole saga of the town centre may be here.

Employers, too, will take advantage of the availability of a local workforce. The emergence of spatial patterns of housing will have led to a spatial pattern of social types, one more likely than another to provide the labour that is required in a cardboard-box factory, a radio factory or a large insurance office. If land is available at a reasonable price one of these employers may well be attracted to it, and so do something to make those residential locations even more attractive to those who become locally employed. At the same time they affect travel patterns, and may also begin a fashion. Here is one illustration of a train of slow but predictable causes and effects. A good school may attract certain kinds of house-holders whose children go to it and later form, for example, a supply of well educated young clerical workers who may work in the town centre and other places. An insurance firm, tired of the problems of a central location, relocates in the area, attracted by the labour. Why the school was put there is another matter; and even when it was put there, there was probably nothing to indicate that it would develop a good reputation. But that, long ago, was a prime cause of the much later office development.

Thus we see industrialists seeking locations that are well served by transport and accessible to labour of the right type being influenced by existing road and residential patterns. These will have been affected by the demands for travel and a variety of factors including the locations of schools and other amenities, jobs, shops and services. Many of these will have been located by decision makers of one kind or another with consideration of existing and probable residential patterns in mind. In this perpetual sequence of location and land-use decisions every land owner and occupier seeks to achieve what he then considers to be his best interests, maximizing his expected monetary gain or (and especially in the case of housing) his satisfaction in terms of other factors. Where there is conflict, the market 'sorts it out' with every piece of land being sold to the highest bidder and put to the use that seems at the time to be the most profitable.

There is one important special case, when land is devoted to a non-commercial public use. Parks, churches and schools provide examples. In some cases these will be on privately owned land that is deliberately made available for these uses by the owner despite the probable monetary loss. In other cases the landowner may give it, or sell it at below market value, to the municipality or religious or other authority. But if the municipality has no power to acquire land compulsorily or to control land prices then these non-profitable land uses will exist only where land is cheap, unless there is some kind of charity, philanthropy or high public demand supported by large voluntary subscription or taxation.

Not surprisingly, there are externalities, as people affect others who are not party to their decisions. Location decisions affect the attractiveness of neighbouring locations. They lead to a generation of traffic flows, and perhaps of congestion. They play a part in determining the sources of pollution. But in a town that has no public intervention in land-use and land prices these are externalities that can be controlled only with great difficulty.

11

Public intervention in land use and land values

In the last chapter we considered some questions of land values and land use in a free market. This rarely exists. Almost everywhere the national or local government exercises some control over land values or land use, either directly by using powers of prohibition and consent, and of taxation, or indirectly by affecting transport, housing or some other activity whose location or finances will affect the land market. In this chapter we consider these forms of intervention in more detail.

Some inefficiencies of the private land market

The essential feature of the uncontrolled market in, and use of, land is that the use to which any piece of land is put is finally determined by a very small number of people whose primary motive is their own private gain measured in terms of money or satisfaction. Whether that use of the land adversely affects others is a question that is unlikely to be considered unless it is thought that there will be some undesirable repercussions on the owner or user. Basically, the social costs of land use are ignored, and if the pattern of land use happens to produce social benefits these will be fortuitous, even though the private decision makers may claim that they were intentional. There are, of course, exceptions, when individuals deliberately forgo private gain in order to improve conditions for others. In those cases their philanthropy is intervening in the market.

In almost all towns at least some land is publicly owned. The land occupied by roads is likely to be public, and usually at least some of the public administration buildings, schools and hospitals will belong to a local or national public authority. If neighbouring land has a use determined solely by the free market then roads may have unexpected volumes and types of traffic imposed upon them, and the buildings we have just mentioned may have noisy or obnoxious industry located so close to them that it interferes with their intended use. Thus, in order to facilitate the intended functioning of publicly owned land, some form of control seems to be needed. It may also be necessary in order to prevent a private user from out-bidding the public sector for a piece of land, and so making it too expensive for it to be used in the public interest.

Very similar arguments apply to the impact of development on privately occupied land. Hotels, petrol stations, slaughter houses, factories, car-parks, dance-halls and maggot farms could all arise next to hospitals, schools, houses or each other, with each development determined by the opinion of the site owner about its profitability. Once again there would be a high risk of traffic, noise or some other pollutant interfering with the enjoyment of occupation of a neighbouring site. Once again, some form of control seems to be necessary.

There is, however, another argument for public intervention in land-use, which is born not out of the idea of controlling but out of an attempt to initiate. It has been argued that there are some land-use developments which will clearly bring added satisfaction to the residents of a town but which would never arise if all developments arose out of profit motives. Parks and pleasantly landscaped roads are examples. So are road layouts that may involve apparently 'wasteful' uses of land, or call for the demolition of some existing buildings, but result in less traffic congestion. Briefly, the argument is that land may be used to greater public benefit if its use is planned with that in mind rather than determined by market forces and possible attempts to control these.

Thus the criticisms of the private land market are of two kinds: it generates externalities that impair the efficient use or enjoyment of established public or private uses, and it fails to generate overall coordinated decision making of a kind that can produce a town, or a part of a town, in which living and working will be easier or pleasanter than it would otherwise be. In that sense, it is inefficient.

Forms of intervention

Two broad opportunities to intervene arise. One is in exercising some kind of control over proposed developments emanating from the private sector. The other is in generating public proposals for development.

While the opportunity to intervene is clear, the best means of doing so are very difficult to determine. The common argument is that certain kinds of land use are unsuitable for certain locations because of their externalities, and that therefore they should not be allowed.

This is a logically crude approach, for it rests on the assumptions that land use can be categorized in a way that identifies different kinds of use by their externalities; that these uses will necessarily have those externalities; and that those externalities are so unsuited to certain locations that, regardless of other factors, that land use should not be allowed. In some countries the sweeping nature of this last assumption is recognized and procedures exist for securing permission to develop despite the nature and magnitude of the externalities: but that is the exception. The fact is that the pure approach of development control by land-use category calls all pots black, assumes that there is no way of making them bright silver, and bans them at all costs from certain places.

The economist has to consider the opportunity costs of an action. What is lost by not allowing a car-repair garage to be opened in a certain place, or a cement works from being built where the cement firm considers it would be most profitable to build one? Clearly in both cases there would be adverse effects on many; but may not their prohibition deprive others of benefits? If that is so, we must somehow try to weigh the good against the bad. As we shall see in the next chapter, this is not easy, and simply in terms of expediency, of ease of decision-making and of having rules that can be clearly understood (even if the reasons for them are not), there is an argument for foregoing the exercise and confirming that certain developments will be prohibited regardless of any cost-benefit considerations.

A long-established principle of economics is that when an action imposes a cost on others one may consider the possibility of compensation. If a car-repair garage creates noise and disturbance for those in neighbouring houses, may there not be some way of requiring the garage proprietor to pay residents sufficient money to compensate them? If they are difficult to compensate and require too much money the garage proprietor will seek a different site; but if he can make a profit by providing a repair service there, despite the need to pay compensation, does it not mean that society places a high value on his being there, and that this value exceeds the value put on their suffering by the neighbours? This argument presupposes that all of those who are adversely affected can be identified. In some cases they can be: but in others it may be impossible to do so, and so the offending land-user would pay less in compensation than he should be paying. It also presupposes that some socially acceptable way of settling the compensation issue can be found. In particular, if a hundred neighbours (or others) are equally adversely affected, and ninety-nine of them are content with £1000 compensation each, but the remaining neighbour insists on £1 million, what is to be done? One can always raise questions of this kind, and find administratively acceptable solutions for them. Doing so is a matter for administrators, moralists and politicians rather than economists. So is the problem of choosing whether and how to control development, however the economist may advise them.

The remaining assumptions behind this method of land-use control are that land uses can be categorized according to their externalities, and these will remain unchanged. For example, certain industries generate heavy traffic, noise and smoke. Such industry is undesirable in a residential area. Adopting crude classifications, we will therefore ban all manufacturing industry from certain parts of the town. One consequence of this will be that manufacturing industry of a kind that is not offensive in these ways will be banned. The common defence against this objection is that if one industry is allowed to locate on a site it will be difficult to prevent it from changing its techniques or activities in a way that would become offensive.

This answer itself points to the second objection, which is that by banning industry from a site we are failing to take an opportunity to stimulate innovations of a socially desirable kind. In many industrialized towns in various countries existing industry has been told to reduce, or even to eliminate, certain forms of pollution; and often the industries have found it cheaper to do so than to move to sites where the regulations would not apply. Here, in the case of a land use that has already been determined, is a control over some of the generated consequences of that use. It is a control that has not simply shifted the location of the source of pollution but has absolutely reduced the amount of certain kinds of pollution.

The question that immediately arises is whether, in place of land-use control, there could not be control over that which is, in fact, at the root of all objections to certain uses, namely the consequence of land use. Most forms of interference with neighbours or others can be measured, even if only roughly.

Noise, smoke of various kinds, vibration, traffic, effluent and litter can certainly be measured. One way of controlling development would be to specify that in certain parts of a town no land-user could generate traffic or pollution (widely defined) beyond certain levels, on pain of severe penalties which would increase if violation continued and culminate in eviction from the site and forfeiture or substantial other penalty. In such a case clean inoffensive industry could operate on those sites which were judged to be most profitable, while prospective users who felt unable to comply with the local pollution standards would have an incentive to devise or to use techniques that were less objectionable. Development control would be part of an attempt to reduce pollution rather than to shift it.

The common objections to this form of control are that it would be difficult and costly to devise and to enforce the standards, and to deal with offenders. Whether this is so, whether it would be more expensive than systems already in use, and how these costs compare with the benefits associated with a greater flexibility and freedom for the industrialist to choose an economically attractive site provided that he did not use it offensively are questions that have yet to be answered. Another consequence of this form of control is that by permitting a more diversified pattern of land use it would give greater accessibility to jobs, and would probably tend to reduce the total volume of journey-to-work traffic.

Positive planning

Positive planning as a means of intervention must now be considered. A municipal or other public authority may plan a completely new town, an urban extension, or some change to an existing part of a town. In all three cases the plan provides a broad framework within which action is expected, and in some cases much or all of that action will be specified. But plans cannot be implemented without decisions by people who have the power and the resources to demolish, to build, to enforce, to permit, or to disallow. In many cases the power and resources of the municipality do not enable it to do the first three of these things on a scale as extensive as would be necessary for the implementation of the plan for a large area, and so they fall back on the last two. In other words, the plan has two components: one which the municipality intends to implement on its own initiative by demolishing, building, and forcing others to do so; a second which is simply an indication of what the municipality will or will not allow to happen in various places. Much of what we have already said about development control applies to the latter, but we should keep in mind that some land-use consequences could make the implementation of the plan more difficult. If the plan is couched, in part at least, in terms of permitted standards of generated effects rather than in terms of land use *per se*, the likelihood of this is reduced.

Whether positive planning adds to or detracts from the efficiency of land use depends partly on how that term is defined, and partly on the plan. There is no general answer, and even in a particular case it is a question that is extremely difficult to settle. First, efficiency has to be defined, and some way found of measuring it, or of comparing two instances of it and deciding that in one case it is larger than in another. In practice there are obvious ways of attempting to do this, providing a composite picture of efficiency embracing journey-to-work, noise levels, landscape assessment, and so on. If these components are combined in any way to produce a single figure then there is an implied system of measurement and weighting that raises many questions about measurability and value judgements. Alternatively X may be judged to be definitely more efficient than Y only if it is demonstrably preferable in terms of every component. Many of the problems can be removed in this way: but there will be many cases where this test simply fails to reveal which is the more efficient. That may be acceptable. If 'X is better than Y' on some grounds but not on others, then the issue is known and a judgement can be made – or recognized as impossibly difficult on logical, political or other grounds.

This, however, fails to bring out another great difficulty. Plans are about the future. In judging whether positive planning will lead to a more efficient use of land we must first predict what will happen if the plan is adopted and what will happen if it is not adopted. Moreover, we have to make these predictions for several different moments in the future, and judge for each of these moments which outcome is the more efficient.

It is not surprising that the question has become a focus for assertions of faith rather than empirical investigation. We can, with difficulty and without overcoming all of these objections, attempt to examine concepts of efficiency in towns where there has been a lot of planning and towns where there has not. Doing so might well be illuminating, but it would not answer the important question, which is about the future, with intervention based on present techniques and knowledge.

As with other matters of urban intervention, the economic test is not the only one to be applied. A plan must be judged on various grounds, of which efficiency, however it is defined, is only one. The economist can be of some service if he helps to define it, and to devise ways of taking it into account, in either the evaluation of plans or in their formulation, or both. This is a matter considered further in Chapter 12.

Intervention and land values

There is, however, one aspect of public intervention in the use of land that is not disputed as a fact, but which engenders various responses. Public intervention affects the market price of land. We must now turn to this.

As a general point we may observe that if the supply of anything is reduced while the demand for it is constant or rising then its price is likely to rise. This will be so not only if the supply is reduced beyond the amount demanded at a previously ruling price, but also if choice is reduced. If, for example, there are 1000 sites suitable for occupation by new houses and only 200 house-sites are currently wanted, and then the number of sites is suddenly reduced to 600, the prices at which 200 will be bought will rise, partly because the purchaser has a lower bargaining power, being able to refer to a lesser number of comparable sites, and partly because some people will be bidding for sites in the expectation of using them later on, and the 200 immediate builders will constitute only a portion of the demand. This means that any intervention that reduces the amount of land that can be used for a specified purpose, or in a way that produces specified consequences, is likely to result in the price of other land available for that use or consequences rising. It also means that the price of that land, now with restricted future use, will be less than would otherwise be the case.

The same decisions may also cause land of other uses to increase in value. The assurance that neighbouring land cannot be used for industry will make some land more attractive for housing than it would otherwise have been, and so lead people to offering (and expecting) higher prices for it.

Roads, actual or planned, arising out of public decisions, will affect accessibilities, both by connecting points along the route and, sometimes, by acting as barriers. They may also become sources of noise. In these and other ways they, too, influence the attractiveness of different sites for various purposes and so affect land values.

Thus in towns where there is public intervention in the use of land both the pattern of land-use and the market prices of land are different from what they would otherwise have been; and every public decision permitting, forbidding or ensuring some change of use is likely to affect the values of that land and other land. In saying this we mean that the market value is likely to be affected, and that the values put upon a plot by its owner, occupier and prospective purchaser (which are unlikely all to be equal) may also be affected. It has been argued that since these changes in land values arise out of public decisions taken in the public interest the ensuing rise in market value should go, at least in part, to a public purse. This is an argument based on considerations that are not economic, and we shall not attempt to refute or to support them. We may, however, put them into a wider context of public intervention and changes in values, and consider the economic consequences of some of the methods that have been suggested for ensuring that not all of the gain accrues to the owner.

Public ownership and compulsory purchase

An extreme approach to this problem, which is also put forward as a solution to other problems, is that all urban land (and perhaps non-urban land) should belong to the municipality or some other public body. In that case there would be no land market of the kind that we have described. Land-use and other decisions would still affect the suitability of land for various purposes, and so the rental income that could be derived from it. If the land-owning authority takes advantage of this then the effects of public intervention would be to alter the rents payable by land-users to the authority. In some cases they would rise, while in others they would fall. The impact of this on different sets of people is worth noting. In the first instance occupiers of certain properties would have their rents increased, either in anticipation of or on evidence of increased profit or enjoyment from their tenancies. Conceivably other occupiers would be granted reductions for similar reasons, but probably these would be fewer, or, at least, lesser sums would be involved. Thus the land-owning authority would derive greater income but its tenants would be paying more.

The tenants who pay increased rents may be able to pass on some of this increase in the same way as they pass on local taxes – either in increased charges to customers and clients or as a claim against national taxation. Some of the increased rental income attributable to public intervention would in that case come from those residents of the town, and others, who would be customers, clients or national taxpayers. But probably the tenants themselves would be the net payers of a substantial part of it. So far as this was justified by greater profitability of business use they might nevertheless be no worse off. Yet this increased profitability could well be at the expense of other businesses located elsewhere who would have difficulty in convincingly attributing their decline to the intervention of the planning authority.

This last paragraph applies equally to rental increases that are payable to private landlords. The public ownership of land will in these matters affect nobody other than the former landowner if that authority seeks to maximize its rental income. It may, of course, have wider effects through replacing commercial site assembly by other processes, and so on; but that is not at present our concern. The essential difference for us to note now is that instead of the private landlord getting higher rents, the public landlord does. The gain to the public purse seems to be the total rent received, reduced by the tax that the private landlord no longer pays, and further reduced by the administrative costs associated with public ownership and rent collection. In a country where rents are highly taxed, or public administration expensive, the gain may be very slight. On the other hand, the change in income redistribution could still, according to some lights, be considerable, as no individual would be receiving a large pre-tax income through rental receipts.

Another aspect of this rise in land values is that it is possible, in a free market economy with private ownership of land, for a landowner to find that the market value of his land rises appreciably with the announcement of a public decision, and so he is able to sell the land at a substantial capital gain. That he can do so is because the purchaser expects to derive an income or satisfaction from it that is related to this new market price. Essentially the capital gain represents some fraction (determined by bargaining power) of the present worth of the increase in rent. That public ownership removes the possibility of this gain leads to an argument very similar to that concerning the abolition of private rental incomes.

Public ownership of land could also remove the circumstance under which the municipality may have to pay a high price in order to acquire land for its own purposes. Whether it would do so depends on the financial links within the public system. One could imagine a land authority seeking to maximize its own income even at the expense of the municipality.

In some countries this particular phenomenon is avoided by allowing the municipality to purchase land compulsorily at below the market price. Here the question of who gains and who loses is a very difficult one. Obviously the owner of the land loses in the sense that he has to take for his land less than he could get by selling to somebody else. But that is not the end of the story. If the land is acquired by the municipality for some use other than that which it would otherwise have had then the supply of land for its original use is reduced. One consequence of this is that people seeking land suitable for this use will tend to be paying more for it. Thus current land owners of various kinds may find the market prices of their land rising, to the benefit of themselves and at a cost to would-be purchasers. Even if the land purchased by the municipality is used in the same way as it would otherwise have been used a similar result could follow because public demand would be added to private demand: but in some cases the private sector would revise its interest in land for that use.

A further difficulty in answering this question arises because a decision made by one means has replaced a decision made by another. If land is used in the way that the land market produces, it is used in the way that somebody considers to be most profitable. Moreover this judgement is in most cases confirmed by the views of others who would have used the land for a similar purpose but would have paid less for it. Financial institutions may also have confirmed that opinion. In short, there is a strong opinion that if used in that way the land will help to produce a service that will attract considerable money – a service for which there is a high demand. But land acquired compulsorily by the municipality and put to some other use will not have had that use assessed in this way. Some official or committee, possibly in consultation with others, will have made the decision. Who gains and who loses, and how much these gains and losses might be, is often more a matter of hunch than of careful analysis. And even careful analysis may be inconclusive. We consider this further in the next chapter.

Public ownership or acquisition of land does not shelve the need of a mechanism for determining its use. If that mechanism involves public expenditure, or itself imposes costs on anybody, be they monetary or otherwise, then these factors have to be taken into account in any appraisal of the economic arguments for and against this (or, indeed, some other) form of public intervention.

Taxation and land values

We turn now to a different kind of intervention in the private land-market – the use of taxes. The main possibilities are to tax the recipients of rents from land, the occupiers of land, the owners of land because of what they own, the sellers of land, and to tax the purchaser of land and the inheritance of land. In most towns at least one of these forms of taxation exists. We now consider briefly some of the economic consequences of these taxes, restricting our discussion to urban land.

Tax on rent recipients

First we consider the taxing of recipients of rents from land. This phrase needs some explanation. In many cases the person from whom a tax is collected is not necessarily the person who pays it. Most taxes are in fact taxes on activities, and all who engage in those activities may be affected by them and in one sense or another perhaps contribute to them. When we speak of recipients of rents being taxed we mean that after receiving the rent the recipient has to pay some of it to the tax collector: but who exactly 'suffers' is a question we have yet to determine.

The tax paid is presumably related to the level of the rent. It may also depend on the income or other circumstances of the recipient, and on the location or nature of use of the land. If such a tax is introduced (or increased) then the owner of land derives less net income from his existing tenants at their existing rents. If he offers his land for sale then a prospective purchaser will also view it less favourably than he would otherwise have done. In short, its value falls, even though the precise value put on it by an individual will depend on his tax circumstances. There are likely to be two similar reactions. Owners of unlet land will tend to seek higher gross rents than formerly; and when rent review opportunities arise the owners will tend to raise the rents. In both cases they try to pass some of the tax on to tenant. A third reaction may be a temporary reluctance on the part of landowners to let their land or property, as they prefer to forgo income in the hope that market rents will rise. If they do rise then the market value will also increase.

Any full analysis of the consequences of such a tax must depend on how the proceeds from the tax are used, and how the reduction in net income for the landlord, and probably for the tenant, influences their spending and saving. If, for example, many of the landlords are insurance companies, and these are taxed on their rental incomes, then people whose pensions or insurance bonuses depend on the profits of these companies will in effect be paying part of the tax; and then we need to know how their spending and saving may be affected. Taxes, like other increases in prices or costs, tend to be all pervasive.

Despite this caution, a tax on rents that varies from use to use and place to place has some interesting possibilities. Instead of a rigid land-use control policy one could have a preferred-use policy, with rents from (say) offices taxed at a higher rate than rents from shops in areas where office-building is to be discouraged in favour of shop-building. In other areas office rents might go untaxed. In yet others they might be subsidized. Thus there would be a tendency towards the officially favoured form of development taking place; but if a developer considered that, despite the tax, he could make an attractive profit by providing an office block in an unfavoured place then he would be able to proceed. He would need to charge high rents, in order to cover the tax, and these would be higher than elsewhere. If he lets the building at these rents then it means that in somebody's judgement, that unfavoured location is, despite the tax, the best place in which to be.

This is not the place to develop this possibility any further, but the caution must be re-emphasized. In an exploratory run of a highly simplified version of a central-area system it was found that under certain circumstances a high tax on rents from offices would lead to increased shop rents: and an analysis of the results suggested that this could happen in a real situation if these circumstances existed.

Tax on occupiers

Occupiers of land may be tenants or owner-occupiers. If the former are taxed, the tax may be related to the rent paid or to the area, kind, use, location or some other attribute of the land. In the latter case there may be a tax on some notional rent, or on one of the attributes just indicated. In either case, the cost of occupation rises, and this will tend to reduce the demand for it, or to drive people to finding ways of reducing their tax liability. This will depend on how the tax is levied, but it could result in their seeking smaller units of land, or land in less heavily taxed locations. Thus, although the tax will make the tenant tend to reduce his demand, and to be less willing to pay high rents, it could also cause the demand for certain kinds of land in certain places to increase. In general, however, land-owners will derive lower rents, especially from new agreements, while the tenants will as far as possible pass on their taxes to others, such as customers and clients and, under some tax systems, to other taxpayers. Owner-occupiers may tend to try to let some of the land that at present brings them no income. This will cause a further decline in market rents and in the incomes of other owners, and do something to offset the impact of the tax on tenants able to negotiate new rents. Once again, the effect will be far-reaching.

Here we should mention 'public goods'. These are defined to be goods (or services) such that the amount consumed by one individual is unaffected by the consumption of another individual. Clearly this would not be true of potatoes, for if many individuals trebled their consumption during a specified week then either there would be none left for others or prices would rise and cause some to reduce their demands. But if we consider radio transmissions from a local radio station then if several people suddenly decided to listen at times when they did not normally do so it would leave other listeners unaffected (provided that they all had radios and did not impose noise on each other).

Another example of public good is expenditure on national defence. In towns we can look upon police services, and fire protection and ambulance services as rather impure examples of public goods. We say 'impure' because strictly speaking, while the broad effect of the existence of these services is almost unaffected by the amount of protection enjoyed by one individual or another the fact is that if twenty fires or burglaries arise simultaneously the twenty-first may receive very little attention. It is also true that the services may be more readily available to people in some locations than to people in other locations.

It has been argued that this last point should affect the levels of local taxes, since people living near to fire stations enjoy greater protection than those living further away. This is a doubtful proposition. If people valued closeness to fire stations one would expect to find this reflected in house prices, and in house advertisements: but I have seen no reference to evidence of this. Moreover, it may be argued that noise, by day and night, and the hurried passage of fire vehicles, detract from the enjoyment of a peaceful life. People living close to fire stations may be more disturbed by the public provision of services for others. Finally, if property is insured then possibly it is the insurance company rather than the occupier who gains. This is not to deny that some people may, because of their locations, have better access to certain public goods than do others; but that is not the whole of the story.

Tax on owners

A tax on the ownership of land has to some extent been covered, but it needs some further consideration. An essential point is that the tax cannot alter the amount of land in existence but can alter the amount of urban land in existence, and if the tax applies differently to urban and to rural land it may well do so. By making people less eager to convert rural land on the town edge to the more highly taxed urban land it could restrict the total supply, and so tend to drive up its price. If it applies to all land the tax will cause some people to wish to get rid of, or to reduce, what they own: but it will also cause others to be less eager to buy it. On that score, the market price of urban land should fall, but this does not mean that rents will fall, for the purchaser of land that is let will look upon the tax as a tax on his rental income, and do what he can to pass it on. Instead of market value being related to rent, it becomes related to rent less tax.

Some other reactions must be noted. The owner of land, let or unlet, will try to recover some of the tax by increasing his income from the land. He will be inclined to drive harder bargains when rent reviews arise, and more inclined to try to let land that he has previously withheld from the market. Here are two conflicting responses, and large landowners may well tend to act differently than small ones, knowing that if they let too much of their land they may not be able to extract higher rents from what is already let. The small landlords, usually unable to affect local rent levels, have a simpler problem and will be more inclined to let all that they can. In other words, the consequences of the tax will depend very much on the structure of landownership.

Yet even this structure may be changed. People with little income may feel unable to pay so much land tax. Although, like others, they may feel that one day the tax will change in their favour, there will be a temptation for them to sell. But people and institutions with large incomes or reserves may feel justified in speculating, buying the land despite the tax on it, in the expectation that one day the reduction of the tax, or some other event, will raise its value. Thus one consequence of the tax could be a tendency for landownership to become more concentrated. Of course one possibility is that much of the selling would be to the public sector.

Tax on land sale

Taxes on the sale of land are a little different. If the tax is collected from the seller then he will seek a higher price than he would otherwise do. We may imagine that he is already in receipt of rents, on which he may be taxed, and is prepared to sell the land for what amounts to a certain number of years' rent. To do otherwise would not make sense, from his point of view, unless he is desperately short of cash. If a tax reduces the proceeds of sale he will want his net proceeds to be the same as before. In short, he is unlikely to sell unless the whole of the tax is added to the selling price. Moreover some landowners will decide that they will not sell at all. There may be two reasons. One is that they object on principle to the tax and are determined either to show that it causes land scarcity, or to avoid contributing to it. The other is that they expect the tax to be removed or reduced, and consider it better to wait.

The increased purchase price of land that results means that prospective purchasers will need to reconsider their arithmetic. Some will decide that it is still right for them to buy the land, as even the reduced profit on its operation is acceptable to them. Others will decide to buy but to demand higher rents from those who will occupy it. Yet others will decide not to buy. This reduction in the number of purchasers will tend to depress the pre-tax market price, but it is unlikely to depress it to the extent that the owners' reactions raise it.

Thus the people who in the end pay the tax are likely to be those who purchase the land and any on to whom they can pass it, directly to tenants, or indirectly via tenants. At the same time some land that may be ripe for redevelopment is held back. In particular virgin land (for house-building and other uses) is likely to be held back and to be more expensive, not because of what it is earning in its present use but because of political reasons or an expectation of an easier tax policy.

Tax on land purchase

If the tax is collected from the purchaser, the seller is not likely to lower his estimate of what net proceeds will make sale his best policy. Nevertheless it is possible that before the tax many sellers were getting prices above the minimum at which they were willing to sell. If purchasers are asked to pay the previous market prices plus the whole of the tax then demand is likely to fall unless the purchasers are confident that they can pass the whole of the tax on to others by charging higher rents or reducing other tax liabilities. In most cases they will probably feel that only some part of the tax can be passed on in this way. The net result is likely to be a reduction in the amount of land sold, some reduction in the post-tax income of sellers, and an increase in rents. If purchasers decide to postpone their activities in the hope that the tax will be abolished or reduced, then prices may fall further, with sellers receiving less and rents tending to fall. If sellers withhold supply for a similar reason the reverse is likely to happen. Any tax that is very controversial and consequently of uncertain permanence may have unplanned consequences if it can be avoided by inactivity.

Tax on inheritance

If the recipient of inherited land is taxed he may well have to sell some of it, or may decide to sell all of it. If he is able to pay the tax without doing this he may still be inclined to look upon the tax as a once and for all tax on its ownership and to try to recover it by raising rents. If, however, he is more or less forced to sell some of the land then the consequences depend on whether the municipality or some other public body has the right to purchase it. If it does then this process will lead to the slow acquisition of land by the public sector without immediately affecting the land market. On the other hand, this gradual reduction in privately held land means that those who wish to buy or to build on it have fewer opportunities and so slowly, the prices of privately-held land will tend to rise.

If the forced sale results in the land coming onto the market it will probably go to the highest bidder. The sale price may be lower than it would be if the seller had had more time in which to sell, and so his inheritance will be effectively reduced by more than the tax, to the benefit of the purchaser.

This kind of tax will engender avoidance procedures, and the tax authorities will devise counter-procedures. All of these will have their own further consequences, which can be considered only when more is known about the structure of land owner-ship and inheritance and the general system of taxation.

Conclusion

It is, of course, possible to have various packages of taxes and control policies. There is little point in attempting to list them here, let alone to analyse them, but some important points must be emphasized. First we may note that unless they are very specific (possibly in the way we have suggested) taxes affect land-use patterns in a broad way through influencing the volume of land sales, and levels of rents. For example if a tax is likely to cause rents to rise there will be a greater tendency to seek locations in low-rent areas. This is especially so if the tax results in some increase in rents that is multiplica-tive rather than additive. For example a shopkeeper may consider renting one of two shops of equal size. One in the town centre has an annual rent of £10,000. The other, further from the centre, has a rent of £4000. He decides that in the former location his gross profits before paying rent will be £8000 higher than in the cheaper location. It therefore pays him to rent the more expensive shop. If a tax is imposed in such a way that rents rise by 50 per cent, the difference in rents becomes £9000 instead of £6000, and so exceeds the difference in gross profits. Unless he is able to increase his prices in a way that raises his gross profits it would pay him to move, if the terms of his tenancy allow it. As we have seen, this may be difficult, but in the long run the increased rents will meant that the less profitable kinds of shop are even less likely to have central locations than they would have in pre-tax days. The tax also means higher prices. Thus taxes that may result in increased rents affect both the pattern of uses and the level of prices; and through the price level, the spending power of the residents, which will have further land-use consequences. This is a point that is often forgotten in the political and philosophical ar-guments about land taxes.

Land-use controls of a non-market kind have a very different impact, and can be much more specific and have more predict-able immediate consequences. On the other hand, they suffer

from the logical crudity and other defects that we have
mentioned.

Some form of intervention in the free-market determination
of land use is necessary. Unfortunately a blend of control by
land-use consequences (as described above) with zone or plot-
specific taxes (as described above) has not yet emerged, despite
its apparent advantages.

Two other points must be made. One is that any intervention, of any kind, may have unexpected results; and we need to
improve our knowledge of urban activities and their relationships if we are to reduce the risk of intervention leading
to undesired consequences. The other is that costs of intervention may be much greater than is commonly appreciated. To
illustrate this we may ask, but cannot answer, a simple
question: in a town where permission to erect a simple extension to a house may require up to six copies of four or five
different drawings, to be considered by various officials and
committees, and where that permission may not be finally
granted or withheld until an appeal and a public inquiry are
held possibly even a year after submission, what is the cost of
intervention, who pays it, and how does it compare in magnitude and incidence with the benefit?

We have said that this is a question that we cannot answer.
Our inability to do so is due partly to the fact that we have not
specified enough detail, but even more to the complexity of the
issues involved, and the inevitable uncertainty about who will
eventually be affected by the development or its absence. We
can, however, draw one useful conclusion from this. If we can
somehow reduce the costs of this attempt to obtain permission,
especially in so far as they fall on people who are likely to
derive no benefit, then the answer to our question will still be
unknown, but at least it is more likely to be favourable to the
contention that the procedure is worth while. The identification of the various sets of people involved is an essential part
of attempts to make legislation and control more efficient and
less wasteful of resources.

12

The analysis of costs, benefits and consequences

In preceding chapters we have several times pointed out the need to compare the costs of an intervention in the free market, or some other action, with the benefits that arise from it. This is not a new idea, and many articles and books on the subjects of measuring and evaluating these costs and benefits exist. In this chapter we will not be concerned with summarizing these, or explaining the techniques of measurement and evaluation, but we will explore some of the more fundamental questions that are raised by these techniques and their application. We will also look at another possible technique.

The principles of cost-benefit analysis

The basic idea of cost-benefit analysis is that all of the costs and all of the benefits of a project should be identified and analysed, whether they fall on those directly associated with the project or on others. For example, the construction of a railway between two towns will cost a certain amount of money, and more money will be required in order to operate it. Passengers who use it will derive some benefit, for which they will pay a fare. Some of these will value that benefit at more than the fare that they pay. (In that case they are said to derive a 'consumer's surplus' from the railway.) If some of them previously travelled by road then those who continue to use the road now find their route less congested, and benefit thereby. There may also be less noise and pollution for those living near the road, but more for those living near the railway. Even for people who seldom travel between the towns, the ease of doing so is now greater than formerly. In these and other ways, various sectors of the public experience 'social' costs and benefits which should be taken into account if the decision about whether to construct the railway is supposed to be not simply a commercial decision based on profit and loss.

In an attempt to facilitate this approach to public decision-making a sizeable battery of technique has evolved. One chapter of a book is sufficient neither to summarize it nor to appraise it in detail, but certain points about the techniques, and about the underlying assumptions, may be made.

The most frequently occurring consequences of a public decision that appear in cost-benefit analysis are probably

changes in time spent travelling to and from work or some other activity;

changes in noise and other pollution levels;

changes in the man-made heritage (as when a building or painting is created or destroyed);

changes in the natural heritage ((such as landscape);

changes in accident risks, life expectation and health;

changes in property values;

changes in incomes and wealth; and

changes in opportunities.

In all of these cases the changes may occur for few people or many, and may represent gains for some and losses for others. In some cases they will be related to each other, as when a change in noise levels leads to a change in house values; and then there can be problems of double counting. This, however, is a comparatively minor problem compared with others facing the cost-benefit analyst. Essentially his task is to identify these changes, and the sets of people affected by them; to find ways of measuring them; to predict their levels; and then to find some way of comparing them, usually by attributing financial values to them.

Data problems

When a municipal or other authority is considering an invest-ment or a choice between schemes it is faced with information of three different qualities. There is fairly firm financial information about what it will have to pay in order to carry out the scheme. In some cases this may turn out to be wrong, especially if the scheme involves unusual problems or if it is going to take a long time to complete. Frequently, however, this estimate of the financial costs of the scheme will be accurate to within a few per cent.

Most of the other information is of a very different quality. Estimates of operating costs will depend on estimates of quantities of labour, materials and other items that will be necessary in operating, say, a railway. They will also depend on estimates of wage-rates and prices, which will be very difficult to predict with much confidence for some years ahead. A similar point may be made about estimates of revenue. In short, the authority's financial estimates of costs and revenue associated with the operation of a scheme are not likely to be ones in which we can place much confidence, partly because they involve factors (such as prices and levels of demand) that are not within the control of the authority.

This criticism of the data is not, of course, a criticism of the idea or techniques of cost-benefit analysis. On the other hand a sow's ear does not make a silk purse, however clever the purse-maker may be, and whatever techniques he may have. The fact is that, whether cost-benefit analysis or any other technique is used as an aid for decision-making, so far as it may rest on estimates of operating costs and revenue, the conclusions reached may not be very reliable.

When we turn to the third kind of information this is at the disposal of the authorities we are faced with the same kind of criticism. Information about social costs and benefits in fact poses five problems, and all five of them may involve errors or uncertainties in their answers. We must now look at these.

Identification

First there is the problem of identifying the costs and benefits and allocating them to those who experience them. Normally this requires very careful thought and investigation but can be done fairly completely. On the other hand, major items may be omitted or wrongly included. If, for example, there had been a cost-benefit study of the early London underground railways, it is almost certain that the list of benefits identified in (say) the year 1900 would not have included their use by hundreds of thousands of people as air-raid shelters forty years later. It may be argued that probably hardly anybody in 1900 even anticipated air-raids, and that all that anybody can expect of any evaluative technique is that it makes good use of the data and experience available. To criticize it for lack of perfect foresight is to knock down one's own Aunt Sally. That is true, but at least we should recognize the fact that at this stage there may be errors due to this lack of perfect foresight.

Measurement

The next problem associated with social costs and benefits is that of finding ways of measuring them. We may take noise as an example. We may measure the intensity of noise, and the number of seconds or minutes in each day at which this is at various levels. Is such information what we need in order to measure the dis-benefit of noise? Should we take account of the quality of the noise, of pitch, of discord, of its pattern, of the time of day when it occurs, and so on? If we should, how do we do so? And how do we eventually combine all of these charac-teristics and measurements into something on which we can place a value? Here it may be argued that the right approach is to say that we need to measure only those aspects of noise that affect people, and that we can do surveys to establish this, and to determine how people value them. Audiologists will respond that often people are affected by aspects of noise without knowing it. If we therefore decide to rely on audiologists instead of on mass surveys are we to assume that they agree with each other, and will be of the same opinions in ten years time? In short, however hard we try, measuring a cost or benefit in physical terms is very likely to involve problems of a kind that will eventually lead some of us into accepting a measurement as being the best that we can do under all the circumstances including the resources then at our disposal, and others of us to accepting it later because it has been used by some of us. Once again, this is inevitable, and im-provements in measurement are constantly taking place. Once again, it is a point to be kept in mind.

Prediction

The third problem is that of predicting what these measurements will be, for cost-benefit analysis is concerned with predicted changes resulting in the future from a contem-plated action. How many people will save how many minutes of travel time on the way to work in five years time? How different will it be in six years time? And seven? This is not a book on prediction and any detailed analysis of the state of the art would be out of place in it, but since cost-benefit analysis depends so much upon it we must digress for a moment to make a few observations.

Any statement about the future, other than some of those involving natural phenomena, has an element of uncertainty. This is especially true if a date or time period is associated with the forecast. To say that one day the world's population will be double what it is now is not to make a statement that is bound to be true, even though it may be to make one that has a high probability of being true. To say that by the year 2010 the population will be doubled is to involve a greater risk of being wrong. Even greater risk is attached to the statement that the population will become double its present level during that year.

Yet for purposes of cost-benefit analysis we need not just one prediction about, say, savings of travel time, but a series of predictions for a sequence of consecutive time periods – usually years – over the life of a project, or at least over its first few decades of life. (The reason for this will shortly become clear.) Each of these predictions involves uncertainty. The art of forecasting is to make the best use of existing knowledge in order to make a statement that has as little uncertainty as possible associated with it. If, on the following day, new information exists, or a better forecasting technique appears, then a new forecast should be made, for the old one no longer makes the best use of existing data. This is one reason why cost-benefit evaluations carried out at different times may disagree. Since different people may also have different access to data or techniques it may also help to explain why evaluations conducted by different analysts may disagree.

Unfortunately cost-benefit analysts frequently produce their best forecast and endow it with precision and certainty by failing to state, or properly to estimate, the associated margins of error.

Thus we may find a prediction that in five years time 873,000 people will save between 20 and 24.99 minutes of travel time twice a day on every working day. This is, at best, an incomplete statement. A more properly stated prediction would be that the number of people saving this amount of time will most probably average 873,000 over the year, and that the chances of the average deviating from this by more than (say) 50,000 in either direction are one in twenty.

Evaluation

After the costs and benefits have been predicted they have to be evaluated. Here there are two fundamentally different approaches. Some analysts believe that it is their task to value every cost and benefit. Others believe that their task is to value as far as they can with reasonable confidence, and to report on the existence of costs and benefits that they consider to be pertinent to the decision but which they are unable to evaluate. The danger with the former approach is that the decision-makers will not get a correct impression of the uncertainties attached to the estimated value, or of the assumptions on which the estimate is based, even if these are clearly stated by the analysts. This is at times due to an attitude often to be found amongst decision-makers which we consider more fully later. For the moment we shall simply note that in many cases it is very difficult to place a precise value on a stated social cost or benefit, even when it is of known magnitude, and to be confident that that value is correct.

As an example of the difficulty experienced in evaluating social costs and benefits we may consider attempts to evaluate savings of travel time. There are other subjects, such as landscape, where perhaps the difficulties are usually considered to be greater, and many that are probably easier to evaluate: but few have had such energy and ingenuity devoted to them as 'savings of travel time'.

The usual starting point is that the man who behaves in a rational economic way values his leisure time at his wage-rate. More precisely, he receives a wage for his work and one way or another could add slightly to his income by working longer hours, but he chooses not to do so, because he values the leisure time that he would lose at more than the extra income he would receive. Similarly, he could slightly reduce his hours and get less pay. That he does not do so shows that he would value a slight addition to his leisure time at less than his pay. In other words, he is just at the point of equilibrium where his marginal wage-rate is equal to his marginal valuation of his own leisure time.

If this argument is accepted then it follows that a man with a high marginal income values his leisure time at more than a man on a low income.

We now turn to travel time. This is time that is not spent in the same way as work time, but it is hardly as welcome as leisure time, and so its value is likely to be lower than the marginal wage rate.

Various empirical investigations designed to determine the value put on increasing leisure time by reducing travel time and its relationship to income have taken place. Usually they have taken the form of surveys showing how people who have choice of routes and/or modes of travel that involve different travel times and different monetary costs, have made their choice, and what their views have been about the changes in money and time costs that would persuade them to change route or mode. Most of the results of these surveys have been interpreted as meaning that people value a saving in travel time on the way to or from work at something between a quarter and a third of their marginal wage-rate.

These studies can be criticized on various grounds, many of them because the differences in comfort, convenience, scenery and other factors offered by alternative modes and routes, as well as in time, are disregarded. Questions about whether travel expenses are paid by employers, or recoverable from taxes, are also noticeably rare, despite their relevance.

Even so, cost-benefit analysts tend to use the results and to base advice about urban projects upon them. Several questions arise. A few of them are:

1 If a man values his leisure time in a way that depends on his wage-rate, how does a person whose income does not depend on work, such as an unemployed person, a child, or a pensioner value his leisure time?
2 Are sixty savings of one minute, ten savings of six minutes, two savings of half an hour and one saving of an hour, all by the same person, to be equally valued?
3 Even if we know precisely and indisputably how every person values a saving of his own time, is it right to say that a community decision based on cost-benefit evaluations should put the value of time saved as the aggregate of these personal valuations?

We leave the first two of these questions for the reader to try to answer. The third requires a little comment. It has been argued by some analysts that people on high incomes derive a lower marginal satisfaction from a single marginal pound than do people on low incomes. A pound is worth more to a pauper than it is to a millionaire. Before aggregating values of savings of time, we should therefore recalculate these values in a way that makes a pound worth the same to everybody. Apart from the fact that there is no universally agreed way of doing this, we must also ask whether the same technique is to be used for all personal valuations, including the value put on a piece of land by its owner?

There is, however, a more fundamental aspect of this question. We argued in Chapter 10 that different people may value the same thing differently. It seems likely that this is true in the case we are considering. I value a saving of one hour of my time (at a certain time of day when I am in specified circumstances) at £5. But why should anybody else value my saving of that hour of my time in that way? Perhaps somebody who wants to employ me does so, but there are many who are unmoved by whether I lose or save time. More convincingly, perhaps, we may note that if a man forces his way on to a bus, pushing off another, saying 'I am richer than you and therefore cannot waste so much time waiting' he is likely to be inconvenienced. In bus queues, or crowds, at least, people seem to place at least as great a value on their own time as on anybody else's, without questions about income: but there is no guarantee that they would employ the same concepts of values in other circumstances. The essential point is that while it is right to identify the costs and benefits falling on various individuals and sets of people, the decision-makers should still consider whether to value them according to the values placed upon them by those who experience them, or according to the way in which the community at large seems to value the costs or benefits it imposes on some of its own members.

A full, or even a fair, analysis of these and other points would occupy more space than we have. All that can reasonably be inferred from the comments just made is that the evaluation of savings of travel time is fraught with philosophical as well as with methodological problems; and that consequently any cost-benefit analysis whose conclusion would be different if the value given to time-savings were (say) 25 per cent higher or lower should be looked upon as inconclusive. Here the figure of 25 per cent is a purely personal guideline. In some cases it would be too low, while in others, perhaps, too high.

What is sometimes forgotten is that, because the costs and benefits arise in the future, the pertinent question is not how we at this moment value a benefit such as a saving in travel time, but how the people who will experience that benefit some years in the future will then value it. This means that there will inevitably be assumptions about the tastes and preferences that people will have some years from now; and these assumptions will introduce further uncertainties. However difficult it may be to decide on how we now value a present cost or benefit, it is even more difficult to determine how people will do so in future.

Discounting

The fifth area of difficulty is in deciding how the present decision makers should value the values that other people will in the future put on costs and benefits when they arise. The essential idea is that a cost or benefit arising in ten years time and then valued at £1 million is, for purposes of present decision-making, to be valued at less than a cost or benefit arising in five years time and then valued at the same sum of £1 million. This idea, closely related to the concepts of discounting and net present worth used in the appraisal of private investment decisions, must now be considered more carefully than it sometimes is.

First let us simplify by assuming away all of the uncertainties that we have mentioned. We assume that we can measure and predict accurately, and that we know exactly what values various groups of people will put on the costs and benefits that we know they will experience in the future. We will suppose that in a year t years from now the authority will have to pay out a cash amount of E_t and will receeive a cash revenue of R_t. We will also suppose that a set of people S will experience costs and benefits in year t to which they give a net value of V_{St}. (If benefits exceed costs this is positive, but in the contrary case it is negative).

Clearly if, for every value of t and S, $R_t - E_t$ is positive and V_{St} is also positive then every affected set gains and there is no problem in making the decision. This, however, is not a very common occurrence.

An approach to the more common problem can be obtained if we begin by assuming temporarily that every $V_{St} = 0$, so that no set experiences net social costs or benefits. The municipal council has simply to consider its financial outgoings and returns. We consider first the question of whether it should spend £1 million now on a venture that will produce an annual revenue of £80,000 indefinitely. The answer is not quite as simple as it may appear to be.

If the municipal authority has £1 million it can use it in several ways. One of concern to us now is that it could lend it to some person or institution at a rate of interest. If this exceeds 8 per cent then it secures an annual revenue greater than £80,000 for the life of the loan. Clearly, therefore, the answer to the question we are considering depends to some extent on the rate of interest. This conclusion is also reached if the authority has to borrow the money, for then, if the interest rate exceeds 8 per cent, it will have to repay in interest more than it receives in revenue.

Another possibility open to an authority that has or can borrow £1 million is that it should lower its level of local taxes. The choice between this action and the investment in a revenue-earning project highlights the issues that are really involved.

The authority that has accumulated cash may have done so deliberately or accidentally, but in retrospect it is true to say that taxes in the recent past could have been lower without causing the authority to be in debt. Whatever benefits may be derived by future taxpayers as a result of this cash will have been made possible by recent taxpayers. This presents existing decision-makers with a moral value-judgement as well as with an economic problem. Clearly, if the money is to be used for the benefit of future taxpayers it would be wrong to invest it in a project that will earn less than the interest that could be obtained by lending it. But should it be so used? Is it right for the decision makers to deprive current taxpayers (of whom many will also have been recent taxpayers) of a tax-rebate in order to provide a rebate for future taxpayers (of whom fewer and fewer will have been recent taxpayers)?

The question can be answered only if it is put more precisely. Suppose that there are at present T taxpayers, and that in n years time only $T(1 - nd)$ of them will still be locally resident, where d represents an annual diminution due to deaths and emigration. There will also be new taxpayers due to immigration and growing up at a rate i. We suppose that in consequence the total number of taxpayers will be $T(1 + (i - d)n)$.

Let the annual sum (or interest or revenue) available from the proposed investment for the reduction of taxes in future years be R.

If we look at things simply from the viewpoint of existing taxpayers we have that in n years time presently existing taxpayers will be only a fraction of then existing taxpayers, and this fraction will be

$$\frac{1 - nd}{1 + (i - n)d}$$

Thus the money available in n years time to reduce the taxes of existing taxpayers will be not R but the lesser sum

$$\frac{1-nd}{1+(i-n)d}R$$

Present taxpayers may argue thatt this is the only sum that is relevant to them as a set. If they do so then various tenable arguments are open to them.

1 According to our assumption about death and emigration, none of the existing taxpayers will be in the town in $1/d$ years. If existing taxpayers want a stream of income for those who remain, given by

$$\frac{1-nd}{1+(i-n)d}R$$

each year, and becoming zero when their own number is zero, then they could get it by lending a sum of money that was repaid in annual instalments, with interest at r per cent on the outstanding balance, over a period of $1/d$ years. It is easily shown that this sum of money is given by

$$S = \sum_{n=0}^{1/d} \frac{1-nd}{1+(i-n)d} \frac{1}{(1+r)^n} R$$

Some idea of the effect of this calculation is given by the fact that if $d = 0.05$ (so that 5 per cent of the original taxpayers disappear every year), while i, (the growth rate before allowing for these disappearances) is 0.08, and r the rate of interest is also 8 per cent then $S = 8.3R$. In other words, an annual tax reduction in future years of £80,000 would be valued at about £664,000. This has to be compared with a sum of about $13.5R = £1,081,000$ which is the value that would be put on a perpetual income of this value by a person, firm or community that paid no regard to the identity of the recipient.

2 Existing taxpayers could also argue in more personal terms, with each taxpayer estimating the worth to him, personally, of his share of the future income.

3 Alternatively existing taxpayers might place a different value on benefits received by others than those received by themselves, rather than a zero value, but still be unaffected by prospects of incomes after 20 years time.

4 Yet another possibility is that they will value benefits receivable by anybody, at any time, as a result of their actions.

We could go on listing possibilities, and performing calculations along the lines of that done in the first example. The obvious point to emerge is that if the municipal authority's decision-makers ignore the complication of questions of the 'who pays and who gains?' type then investing £1 million for a perpetual annual income of £80,000 is just worth it: but it is not worth it if they look at it simply in terms of gains accruing to members of the set who finance it, and it may not be worth it if they look at it in terms of other arguments based on the attitudes of those who pay to future benefits for themselves or others. Thus, even when there are none of the problems associated with the identification, measurement, prediction and evaluation of social costs and benefits, this single problem of determining whether to invest out of accumulated capital in return for a perpetual income has no single demonstrably correct answer.

If we consider a more common problem, of whether a municipality should borrow money now in order to finance a project that will bring an annual income, we have a similar problem, but the overlapping between memberships of the set who pay and of the set who benefit is likely to be greater. The decision-makers may consider the returns on the investment to those who finance it, and argue more or less as we have done above but allow for the fact that new taxpayers will share the burden of paying. Alternatively they may pay no attention to membership of sets. Yet another possibility is that they may attempt to maximize the returns for members of the set to which they are directly responsible, or who elected them to power, and to push the burden of repayment on to some other larger or more remote set of future taxpayers. The application of conventional techniques for discounting future costs and benefits tends to bias decisions in the same way, as we now show.

First we may observe that all items, be they costs or benefits, arising in the future have a lower present value than they would have if they arose now and had the same valuation put upon them. This means that a scheme that produces benefits in early years and involves payments in later years will appear better in cost-benefit terms than one that has the reverse pattern. For example, if we apply discounting at the rate of 10 per cent per annum a scheme producing costs and benefits as in Scheme A below would have a present net benefit of £735, but Scheme B would show a present net cost of exactly the same amount. This is obviously a simplified example, but if present decision-makers choose Scheme A rather than Scheme B because of cost-benefit considerations then they are deciding that in years 1, 2, and 3 there will be benefits in exchange for costs in years 4, 5 and 6. It is likely that these costs will fall onto a set of people that includes some who do not enjoy the benefits arising in years 1, 2 and 3. Moreover, if these costs could have been postponed until years 14, 15 and 16, then the present net worth would have been even higher. In that case this new scheme would have been chosen, producing current benefits in 'exchange' for costs that would almost certainly be borne very largely by a different set of people. The further ahead you can postpone payment the greater is the likelihood of it being borne by somebody else, if the process is one of community payment.

Year	Cost	Benefit	Present worth	Year	Cost	Benefit	Present worth
1		1000	+1000	1	1000		−1000
2		1000	+900	2	1000		−900
3		1000	+810	3	1000		−810
4	1000		−729	4		1000	+729
5	1000		−656	5		1000	+656
6	1000		−590	6		1000	+590
Total Present Net Worth			+735	Total Present Net Worth			−735
		Scheme A				Scheme B	

This leads us to an interesting conclusion. Cost-benefit calculations involving discounting of future costs and benefits lead to the selection of schemes that most enable the burden of repayment to be passed to future taxpayers who may themselves derive little benefit. For example, if a scheme involves spending £1 million every year for the next seven years, in order to produce benefits for every year thereafter, perpetually, of the same £1 million per annum, then a discount rate of 10 per cent would show it to be unjustified. On the other hand, if we could derive benefits of £1 million each year for the next seven years, and cause posterity to pay for them with a perpetual annual payment of this amount, in cost-benefit terms we should go ahead. Whether this is morally justifiable is not an economic question, but we may note that it is an action that is at strange variance with public attitudes towards planning and towards pollution. A principal public argument for planning is that it enables us to adopt long-term approaches, lest that which brings us a short-lived benefit now produce ills later. We also spend money now in order not to build up problems for future generations. We build sewage works so that in ten years time a river will not be so polluted that fish cannot live in it. Similarly we incur expense conserving certain fuels, or developing alternative sources, in the interests of people not yet born. Yet if we apply cost-benefit discounting techniques to these activities then, if the benefits are sufficiently far away, or the discount rate high enough, they fail the test.

When all of these points are considered it is difficult to escape from the conclusion that simply to discount all future costs and benefits at some rate inspired by consideration of the currently held views about interest rates and their likely movements is a gross oversimplification.

The role of the analyst

We have argued that cost-benefit analyses often rest on very doubtful data, assumptions and techniques. There may be poor data or inadequate measurement, faulty prediction, erroneous evaluation, and dubious discounting. Does all of this mean that cost-benefit analysis should not be used? The answer must be a very definite negative. Making decisions about urban projects and policies is an extremely difficult matter, and the decision-makers need to use the kind of careful analysis that well conducted cost-benefit work contains. The cost-benefit approach, of identifying all of the costs and benefits, and listing them according to their incidence, should be an essential part of any decision-making. So should attempts to quantify these, and to predict them. If we stop there the decision-maker is faced with lists of predicted quantities of costs and benefits affecting different sets of people. Somehow he has to weigh one against the other. How can he do so?

The attempts to put monetary values on all of these costs and benefits, and to discount these to present monetary values, are simply parts of an attempt to answer this question. There have been other approaches, such as ranking alternative schemes according to various criteria and then committing the mathematically invalid step of combining the ranks, with or without the apparent sophistication of weighting. Here the problems of monetary evaluation and of discounting may be avoided but the conclusion that emerges is dependent on the judgement of the analyst compounded by the accidents of spurious arithmetic. If different costs and benefits have to be weighed against each other then either they must be expressed in common units or the decision-maker has to perform the balancing move by what he feels in his bones than by the fruits of computations. The great merit of the monetary approach is that it is a logically valid one. The demerit is more an attribute of the user than of the approach itself. It is simply that the monetary evaluations are commonly endowed with a greater reliability than they should have, and sometimes ascribed to costs and benefits that are probably best left described but unvalued.

One less objectionable method of proceeding is to use surveys or other techniques to determine how different sectors of the community value various costs and benefits, possibly obtaining the results as probability distributions. In other words, just as every prediction of a magnitude should have with it a statement of its probable error, or be expressed as a range within which the truth has a high chance of being, so should many values. A statement that there is a 95 per cent chance that between 7000 and 10,000 people will save between 8 and 10 minutes a day, and that there is a 95 per cent chance that these people will value savings of that magnitude at between 40p and 60p per person per day is not as clear cut as the statement that 8500 people will save 9 minutes, and value this saving at 50p per day. But it does honestly admit the uncertainty.

This kind of approach, which has yet to be properly developed, is important. Suppose that in some simple scheme, there is a 95 per cent chance that the costs falling on certain people are between £1.7 million and £2.3 million, while there is a 95 per cent chance of benefits lying between £1.9 million and £2.5 million. To transmit this finding as a statement that costs are expected to be £2 million and benefits £2.2 million is a convenient piece of averaging but is completely misleading. The role of the analyst is to wring what he can from the data, but not to make decisions or to conceal uncertainties and chances of error. If the decision-maker chooses to ignore the uncertainties and to opt for averages he may be entitled to do so: but his advisers are not. It is perhaps unfortunate that cost-benefit analysts have been so concerned with recommending a particular decision rather than with marshalling conclusions that summarize the evidence. On the other hand it must be conceded that often the blame for this lies partly with the decision-makers who 'insist' on a precise single-figure answer, or a positive statement that X is best. In this way the decision-makers can choose either to implement a policy on the grounds that 'the experts' have shown it to be the right policy, and it is their duty to do what is right, or to reject the policy on the grounds that they are sure that the arid arithmetic of the experts cannot contain everything that is valuable to the community. The more precise the advice they receive the easier it is for them to avoid the unpopular consequences of having made that decision.

The analysis of consequences

The truth is that urban decision-makers have to make choices about matters whose consequences they usually do not fully understand. The main reason for this is that in one way or another societies have placed responsibilities upon them, but failed to recognize the difficulties of the task, the complexities of the issues, and the extent of ignorance about matters with which even the experts are endowed. This is as true of the economic consequences, and the authors of economics books, as it is about other matters. We are all inadequately informed.

Yet while we cannot hope ever to have the understanding and knowledge that will enable us confidently to predict the economic consequences of urban decisions, we can improve our ability to do so. One technique that has been applied fairly widely is that of modelling. Here we attempt to provide some set of formulae, rules or computer instructions that represent some simplified aspect of reality and translate assumed or known information into estimates of unknown information. In the remainder of this chapter we shall consider briefly some matters concerning the uses of models to provide decision-makers with better information about the economic consequences of their contemplated actions. If this can be achieved then clearly the identification of costs and benefits becomes easier.

The main purposes for which models are used in urban analysis (as opposed to urban planning in which models may also have other uses) are the prediction of population, household formation, journey-to-work, shopping trips, car-ownership and road traffic. The first two of these have obvious economic implications in such matters as labour supply, levels of demand for houses, schools and other services, demands for goods, and so on. The journey-to-work predictions may affect spending on roads, vehicles and railways. They also provide data for the evaluation of time-saving in cost-benefit studies. Knowledge of shopping trips can be of similar value, and help to indicate the volume of business that various shopping centres can expect to attract. Car-ownership, obviously determined in part by economic factors, will also have economic consequences over a wide range of matters from the levels of house prices in areas where public transport is poor and the demands for car-parking spaces, to the volume of imports by the set of residents. Patterns of road traffic, including investment needs, congestion levels and so on are clearly of concern to economists. There are, of course, many other reasons why the economist should be concerned with prediction of the variables we have listed; and there are other equally important variables that require his attention. What matters now is that we recognize that the urban economist needs better information if he is better to advise the decision makers.

The models that are intended to give this better information are of varying quality. Some of them are manifestly over simplified for useful prediction at the level that decision makers require. Others are very complicated and their inventors and users try to make them both realistic and useful. Unfortunately, however, many of the models are based on the assumption that certain observed quantitative relationships that appear to have existed in the past will continue to exist in the future, and lack adequate exploration of the nature and causes of these relationships and the conditions under which they may cease to be valid. Two instances may be cited. A relationship between the rate of growth of population, the rate of growth of incomes, and the level of car-ownership during a period of low petrol prices (or of uncongested roads) may cease to be valid if petrol prices rise (or road congestion appears). Similarly, a statistical model predicting the numbers of houses that will be built, and based on data for a period when there was a substantial historic shortage of houses, may not be valid when the shortage disappears. Statistical analysis that is not based on an understanding of the processes and phenomena concerned will often be better than no analysis: but it will certainly be better if understanding is improved.

If we do attempt to base our predictions on a better understanding then we soon see another defect in much urban modelling. Essentially it is a parallel to the time-honoured *ceteris paribus* assumption of economic theorists. Almost all urban models are models that are essentially concerned with but one part of the urban system, and either ignore or are based on assumed constancies or simple trends in the other parts. Obviously every model must simplify, and to some extent ignore, but a 'retailing model' that ignores the impact of retail trips on traffic, and of traffic in decisions about where to shop and where to locate shops, is not very satisfactory. Nor is a retailing model that ignores changes in incomes, population, rents or wage-rates. Yet these are closely affected by other factors. In short, if we are to progress in our knowledge of towns and our ability to make useful predictions we need to take greater account of the interactions between the various parts of the urban system. We need a model of a town, or models of towns, in which retailing, housing, employment, traffic and all the other major components are integrated.

If we attempt to construct such a model, and keep in mind the desirability of attempting to base it on an understanding of the processes involved, we seem to be led almost inevitably to a model that attempts to reconstruct the principal decisions reached by various sets of people, and the decision processes they use. It is through decisions reached by property owners, prospective and actual tenants, employees, shoppers, employers, builders, and others that an event has its impact, economic or otherwise, on different aspects of urban life. A model that is based on this approach is currently being completed in the University of Manchester. Its purpose is to help the decision-maker to examine the probable consequences of various decisions; but in its construction the paucity of information about how decisions are made has become all too evident. It is probably in this area that future research will be able to make its most important contributions. In the next chapter we consider the matter a little further.

13

Urban decisions

In this chapter we consider in more detail two closely related matters on which we have touched several times: decision making and power. We then consider their importance in an analysis of urban economics. In Chapters 1 and 2 we remarked upon ways in which the fabric and activities of a town are affected by decisions made by a variety of sets of people. We also argued that decisions made by sets could not be guaranteed to be consistent. In subsequent chapters we explored some of the ways in which different sets of people had their economies, or certain aspects of their economies, affected by decisions about retailing, housing, transport and other matters, but we rarely extended the analysis far beyond the subject area of the decision. Now we must show how this can be done.

In Chapter 2 we also touched upon the fact that an imbalance between imports and exports could lead to one set having some form of power over another, but the idea has yet to be integrated into our study of urban economics. In this last chapter we shall show how power, possibly derived through such an imbalance (and therefore economic in its origin), enters into decision-making, and so affects the economies of various sets.

Finally we indicate how a more detailed examination of decision-making helps us to study economic aspects of the town.

The identity of decisions

First we have to consider whether two decisions made by different people can be called identical, or whether they must be looked upon as different decisions simply because they have been made by different people. Clearly the answer depends on

207

how we define our terms: and as long as we are clear about it and do not apply conclusions based on one definition to a case where the definition does not apply we can define our terms in any convenient way. For the analysis that follows it is convenient to define decisions to be different if they have different outcomes. Thus whether P or Q decides to dig a hole in a road, the outcome of a hole having been dug is the same. If, however, P insists on adding a notice saying 'P dug this hole', then the outcome is not the same as if Q dug it. Similarly, if two people decide to become world chess champion, there are different decisions, since there would be different champions. There are obvious difficulties in this approach, as frequently the fact that a decision has been made by P endows it with an authority or significance that it would lack if it had been made by Q. One way of coping with this is to consider that P (or Q) has made two decisions – one that a hole shall be built, and the other that that decision shall be enforced or implemented by him. The decision is thus split into a pair of decisions, one impersonal and the other personal. This is a device to which we may sometimes have to resort, but its greatest use to us now is that it indicates how to modify, where necessary, conclusions based on the simpler approach that two decisions having the same outcome are the same.

Influence and power

Let us now suppose that there are two sets of people, A and X. They may or may not have members in common. We will denote the set of all the decisions that might conceivably be made by A by D_A, and represent it by the enclosed space D_A in Figure 13.1. Similarly D_X represents all the decisions that might conceivably be made by X. We may note that the intersection of these sets of decisions contains all decisions that might be made by either A or X. There are also decisions corresponding to the space lying outside the union of D_A and D_X which could not conceivably be made by either set.

The set A is able to exert some influence over various decisions. Obviously every set can exert some influence over decisions made by itself; but there may also be influence over decisions made by others. We will consider that all the decisions over which A may have some influence, other than decisions made by itself, are represented by C_A.

All decisions over which X has some influence (except its own decisions) are shown by C_X.

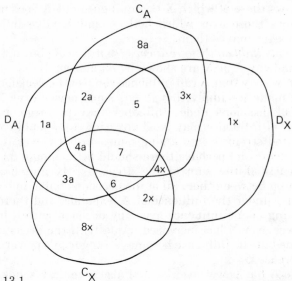

Figure 13.1

In Figure 13.1 we have numbered the various spaces. There is also the space lying outside the union of $D_A + D_X + C_A + C_X$ which corresponds to decisions over which neither set has any influence and which neither set would make. We must now comment on the decisions represented by each space.

Decisions liable to be made by A but not by X, are shown in spaces 1a, 2a, 3a and 4a. The different spaces subdivide these decisions according to:

1a Not under the influence of X, and such that if made by non-A then not under the influence of A.

2a Not under the influence of X, but under the influence of A, even if made by non-A.

3a Under the influence of X, but not of A when made by non-A.

4a Under the influence of both A and X, by whomever it is made.

Decisions liable to be made by X but not A are denoted by 1x, 2x, 3x and 4x, which may be described similarly.

Decisions liable to be made by A or X are shown by spaces 5, 6, 7.

5 shows decisions over which X has no influence if they are made by non-X, but A has influence if they are made by non-A (or A).

6 shows those of which X has influence but A does not.

7 shows those over which both A and X have influence, whoever makes them.

Decisions liable only to influence from A or X, but not liable to be made by A or X are shown by 8a and 8x.

When we say that A can influence some of the decisions that X may make we imply that A has some power over X. The extent of decisions under influence may be large, but the strength of influence may be slight. How we should combine extent and strength into a single measure of power is by no means clear; and perhaps there should be no single measure. But clearly if the sum of the areas 3x, 4x and 5 and 7, containing between them all of the decisions liable to be made by X and under the influence of A, expands, and there is no weakening of A's influence over any decision within it, then A's power over X has increased. Equally, if the areas remain the same but the influence becomes stronger, A's power over X has increased.

While A has power over X, it is also true that X has power over A. The extent of X's influence over A's decisions is indicated by the sum of the areas 3a, 4a, 6 and 7, but this tells us nothing about the strength of the influence.

Clearly area 7, where each set may make the decision, and where each has influence over the decision if made by the other set, is an area where direct conflict may arise, or where one set may support the other. In determing whether A or X is likely to win in the event of conflict within area 7 we have to take account of the relative extents and strengths of A's influence over the areas 3x, 4x and 5, and X's influence over 3a, 4a and 6. This is because A may decide to let X make a decision in area 7, contrary to its own wishes, lest X should intervene in some decision in one of the other areas. We also have to take account of the importance of a decision to A and to X.

This is not the place to develop much further an abstract theory of influence and power, but a few points need to be made. First we may note that a set may be unaware of the true extent and strength of its influence. At the same time other sets may be well aware of it. In some cases this may mean that A's knowledge that X has the ability to influence a decision will cause A to modify it, or to modify some other decision, in deference not to any overt expression by X but to its perception of X.

Secondly we may note that some sets will seek deliberately to increase their power, either generally or directly over a specified set, by extending and strengthening their influence. Thus A may attempt to expand C_A until it contains the whole of D_X. It will also try to reduce the extent of 3a, 4a, 6 and 7, by shifting the boundary of C_X.

Another point to keep in mind is that as the membership of a set changes so may the boundaries of the sets of conceivable decisions and decision influence. Obviously some members of a set may be virtually powerless to affect certain decisions made by that set. In that case they may (consciously or otherwise) form a sub-set which may behave relatively to its complementary sub-set in much the same way as A and X in our example, with each sub-set attempting to be more influential in determining the decisions made in the name of the set. One way of doing that may be to increase their numerical strength.

Many other points may be made, but for us the important one is that gain or loss of power may have important economic causes, as well as consequences. We now consider this more fully.

Power and the balance of payments

In Chapter 2 we argued that if any set of people was in a long-term balance-of-payments deficit arising out of some form of charity, subsidy or donation from a second set, then it would be to some extent under the power of this second set. In an extreme example, set A could either withdraw its help from set X, or even insist on repayment of an accumulated debt, unless A made certain decisions in accord with the wishes of X. Clearly, if the amount of money involved is trivial, the power due to it is not great; but if the debtor set would have difficulty in managing its economy without that aid, or in making the repayment, then the creditor set could have great power over it. Power of an economic kind will be related to the possessions of the set. A set whose members own considerable assets is going to be more able to run a balance of payment deficit, or to withstand economic pressures, than one whose members own little.

While such a power is rooted in the economies of the creditor and debtor set, it may not require any conventional economic transaction to reduce it. For example, a property company may have allowed a tenant to pay rent informally at a reduced rate, on the understanding that the tenant, who is a member of the municipal council, votes in favour of development schemes proposed by the company. Here the property company has some power over the tenant, and it arises out of a financial subsidy. But if the tenant discovers that the chairman of the company has a disreputable past he can shift the extent of the company's influence over him by threatening disclosure. In terms of our approach, he extends his influence over the company chairman, and therefore over those company decisions that are under the influence of the chairman. Indirectly this weakens the company's influence over his voting decision. Thus, in due course, the company may be compelled, through the power of the tenant over its influential chairman, to continue the rent subsidy that at one time gave it power. One way in which it could perhaps recover that power would be to remove itself from the influence of its chairman.

In urban affairs the interplay of economic and other power is commonplace. It is compounded by the multiple membership of sets, and by deliberate trading of power, and the exercise of power. Frequently the extent and strength of the power of one set over certain decisions, or the decisions of another set, will be known by very few; and frequently it will be virtually impossible to prove its existence. In countries where bribery is openly accepted as part of the decision system the trading of power and decisions is probably easier to follow than in a country where the trading is done more by unwritten and even unspoken agreements to trade one decision for another. Yet this kind of trading is probably an inevitable aspect of urban decision-making. It means that the causes of a decision are frequently not what they seem to be; and that often the consequences of a decision include some other decision apparently unrelated to it. In other words, a study of the economics of a decision is likely frequently to be a study of only part of the economics.

A decision framework

Although we have considered sets of decisions and of influences over them, we have not yet looked at the decision-making process. In order to see more clearly how power – economic or other – enters this process, and to develop a general approach to the study of the economic and other consequences of decisions, we now develop a schematic framework.

We will consider that every set of people exists in what we will call its *actual environment*. This includes not only its physical environment but also all of the cultural, social, economic and other factors that help to define the ways in which its members can live and in which they perceive themselves, their opportunities and others. In most cases this actual environment will differ from the *desired environment* of the set. Here we are not talking of Utopia unless the set happens to consist of Utopians. A cricket club will wish to modify its actual environment by having a new pavilion. Residents of a street will want to do so by having through traffic abolished and a scrapyard closed down. In short, we here define desired environments to be environments that can be formed by making a small number of changes to the actual environment. These changes form what we will call the *environmental imbalance*.

Whether the set tries to do anything about this imbalance will depend upon many factors. Its members know that it has various controls imposed on its activities by national and local government, and possibly by other public or private sets who are able to call upon the law, if necessary, to help them to enforce the controls. Residents of a street may be forbidden to park their cars in it, and possibly it is that very control that constitutes their environmental imbalance. There will also be other controls, such as a law that effectively prevents the residents from painting over the double yellow lines, which will not constitute the imbalance but will limit the actions that they can take in regard to it. Every prohibitive law or regulation enforceable upon members of the set by authority of any constitution to which members of the set subscribe may form a control.

Apart from these controls, there will be other constraints on their activities. These may be economic, as when a cricket club is unable to afford a new pavilion. There may also be social, cultural, physical or other constraints, distinguished from controls by the fact that they do not arise directly out of legally enforceable requirements. In some cases these constraints will be important, or thought to be important, only if some other set is in a position to enforce them. In other words, the constraints will correspond to the areas of influence that we have just been considering. One set exerts its power over another by enforcing a constraint, or a control.

We must also mention another factor. A set may be very tolerant of an environmental imbalance, because of lethargy, kindness or some other factor. The greater its tolerance the less likely is it to act.

We can now consider a set endowed with a certain tolerance, subject to various constraints and controls, reacting to its environmental imbalance by making a decision. This may be a decision to do nothing, and may be made by default, for no set is continuously making decisions actively. If, however, there is a decision to do something then it leads to an action, which has various consequences. By intention it will affect the actual environment, and it may be intended also to affect the constraints and controls. Yet all of these may also be affected unintentionally, as may the desired environment. Moreover, the action may affect the actual and desired environments of other sets, and the controls and constraints that concern them.

The analysis of the decision making process can conveniently be illustrated as in Figure 13.2. We may imagine first of all that this diagram relates to a single set, whose actual environment contains various constraints, controls and power balances, which we have also shown separately, linking them to the actual environment by two-way arrows. The actual environment, weighed against the desired environment, produces the environmental imbalance. Subject to the constraints and controls, and to the set's tolerance which may be affected by these, there is a decision leading to action which changes the actual environment.

But every single set has such a framework, and decision made by one set affect another. In order to remind ourselves of the impacts made by this set on others we have introduced hollow arrows, leading from five of the boxes. The solid arrows remind us of the areas where decisions of other sets may affect the one we are considering. We must also keep in mind the historical factor, which helps to define the actual environment and tolerance.

The scheme that we have just outlined has a usefulness going beyond the concern of urban economics, but also provides urban economics with a context. It emphasizes that, whatever has led to its causative decision, every action by every set may alter the constraints and controls that limit decisions made by other sets. Every such action may also alter the environments of other sets, often by providing new opportunities or removing existing ones; and in the latter case a consequence may be that the former actual environment becomes the present desired environment. The constraints on a set may also be affected by others, as when a set possessing great wealth has a wealth tax imposed on its members, so that it is more constrained than formerly by financial considerations.

Even the simplified scheme of Figure 13.2 helps us in our analysis. If, for example, we consider a single control, such as a parking control in a specified street, we can usefully go backwards through the diagram asking what action led to it, and what the other consequences of this action have been on (a) those whose decision led to it and (b) others. We can then consider the environmental imbalance that prompted the decision. What does it imply about the perception of the actual environment and the formulation of the desired environment? What were the essential aspects of constraints, controls, and tolerance that enabled this decision to be reached? And how did these come about?

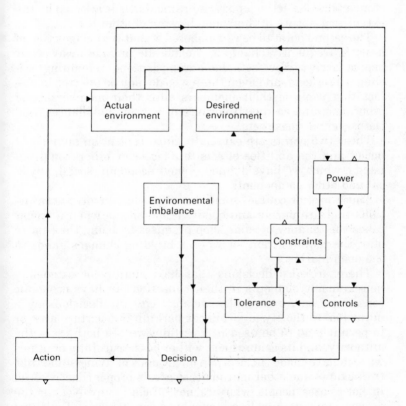

Figure 13.2

We can also move forwards through the diagram. How does this control affect the actual environment, the desired environment and the decision limits of this set and of other sets?

In all of these matters two more important points must be kept in mind. One is that most people belong to a variety of sets, and this affects their decisions. Thus residents of a street may, as residents, consider introduction of a one-way traffic system which will reduce the noise and nuisance of traffic in their street. But if that system would also reduce access for non-residents to a nearby shopping precinct, then those residents who are shopkeepers would probably oppose the scheme. Any poll of residents would reveal a greater tolerance of the existing traffic than might be expected. In short, the tolerance of members of a set to a particular imbalance is affected by the extent and nature of their membership of other sets.

The second point to be remembered is that the composition of a set is frequently changing. People die or fade away. New people arrive. Few sets have compositions remaining unchanged for long, and even those who do may be affected by the fact that some of their members alter their membership of other sets, and so their tolerance of various imbalances, and the powers of these sets.

These two points are especially important in an analysis of power and the abilities of sets to affect each others' environments, which we have defined to have economic, social, physical and other components.

There are, of course, some decisions that involve transactions that are purely and openly economic, as when a trader takes the tenancy of some shop premises by being the first to offer the required rent, or when a building changes hands in the open market.

There are also decisions that have mainly or ostensibly non-economic elements in their causation but have economic consequences. As examples we may cite the decisions by a municipal authority to forbid car parking in a certain area or to permit land to be used in a certain way. In both cases the authority, and its committees, will profess, truthfully or otherwise, to have made the decision on grounds of living standards, traffic flows and other matters that are its proper concern. And in both cases people who are not officially involved in the decision may gain or lose money as a consequence of it. Land values may change, both in the vicinity concerned and elsewhere; and traders may gain or lose custom. We also know that sometimes those who stand to gain or lose may seek to persuade officials or others who help to make the decision, by offering them money, favours, friendship or support. We must now consider this more formally within our decision-making scheme.

The two decisions instanced are of very different types. The decision about car parking can easily be accommodated in our framework by positing that the municipal authority considers the existing traffic pattern to be part of the actual environment, which it wants to alter. In short the initiative for the decision comes from the decision-maker. But the decision to permit land to be used in a certain way is in response to an initiative from elsewhere. There are in fact two closely related decisions. Those seeking permission to use the land have an environmental imbalance between the present land use and the desired land use. This leads to a decision to apply for permission to change the use. Remembering our very wide definition of environment, we can consider this application to form part of the new actual environment of the municipal authority (or its land-use control department). Its desired environment includes removing the application from the undecided to the decided tray, but because of the repercussions of the decision in this matter on the use of land, which is also part of the authority's environment, the desired environment has to include not just a decided, rather than an undecided, application, but one that has been decided in the right way. The application has, in fact, altered the actual and the desired environments, for it compels the municipal council to choose between an environment embracing the consequences of its refusal and an environment embracing the consequences of its being granted.

We have cited these two examples of decisions that have non-economic origins in order to explore some of their consequences. We shall note especially their economic consequences and argue that these should be foreseen and considered as part of the decision-making process.

The decision to restrict car parking leads to the formulation and enforcement of a control that affects the actual environments of several sets of people. It may also affect some desired environments. The sets whose environments we have to consider include:

1 occupiers of property in the restricted area
2 drivers who wish to visit these occupiers
3 other drivers for whom it is a convenient parking place
4 drivers who wish to drive along the restricted streets

5 pedestrians in the restricted streets
6 occupiers of near-by property outside the restricted area
7 drivers who wish to visit these occupiers
8 other drivers for whom these places are convenient for parking
9 people associated with similar areas where there are not yet restrictions.

The immediate local effect is experienced by sets 1–5. While we have put occupiers in the first set, much of the effect on their environment depends on how the other sets respond to their altered environments, and so we first consider these. In order to give a little more precision to the argument we will consider that the restrictions apply to a shopping street. The effects will depend on what alternative provisions or exceptions are made, but we may here suppose that these come through subsequent decisions made in response to environmental imbalances generated or increased by the decision we are considering.

Drivers who wish to visit a shopping street may be customers, drivers who are delivering goods, or people such as sales-representatives, government shop inspectors and others who have business to conduct.

In all cases their actual environment is affected, and in some cases the desired environments may also change. Customers, and some sales representatives, may have it within their power to decide to go instead to other places. Whether they do so will depend upon what they want to buy, where they can get it, the accessibility of alternative places of purchase by car and foot, price differences and other factors. But other drivers wanting to park outside the premises in the street may have no option but to visit it. For them, in one way or another, there is inconvenience, which may be reflected in higher charges to the shopkeepers, poorer service to them, or an attempt to reduce their own inconvenience by passing some of it on to the shopkeeper or others. In these ways the environments of shopkeepers and others become affected.

The other drivers for whom the street is a convenient parking place also have their actual, and possibly their desired, environments affected. They may react in only three ways. Either they visit the same locations but use some other form of transport; or they continue to drive but visit other locations; or they park elsewhere and walk what is probably a greater distance. We may suppose that in all cases this is not what they would prefer to do, and that in behaving differently they affect the environments of others, of whom some may be neighbouring shopkeepers.

Through drivers find it easier to pass through the area. Since the actual environment of every driver includes the opportunities open to him, then in fact every driver finds that it is now easier to make this trip, and some of those who previously avoided the street now use it, unless other schemes make this undesirable. In short, the street is likely, in the absence of deterrents, to acquire more through traffic, with consequential impacts on the environments of others.

Some of these others will be pedestrians visiting the street. Their environments will be affected by the abolition of parked cars, and their manoeuvring, and an increased volume of probably faster through traffic. The net effect may cause a decline or an increase in their numbers (as the environments of potential pedestrians in the street are also affected), once again affecting the environments of the shopkeepers, and of other shopkeepers elsewhere.

Thus we are brought to the effect of the control on the environments of those who occupy the shops. They may be affected directly by being unable to park their own cars there, but most shopkeepers would in any case not park in a place that is attractive to their customers. The greater impact is through decisions made by other sets in response to the impacts of the control on them. They will experience the reactions of those who deliver to them, call on them and buy from them. While some of these reactions will certainly add to their environmental imbalances, as by making deliveries uncertain, others may add to or subtract from them, depending on whether their customers decline or increase. In general terms there is no way of telling which of these will happen, as it depends on the precise circumstances. The important point to notice, however, is that in one way or the other the incomes of the shopkeepers are likely to be affected. If they go up then the shop profits are likely to rise, and to do so by a higher percentage than the takings rise (as we recall from Chapter 6). This may lead to increased employment, and is very likely to lead to higher rents at the next rent review. Thus part of the financial gain experienced by the shopkeepers is passed on to the property owners.

On the other hand trade may fall. We may recall that in that case there is a possibility of profits turning into losses, with consequences discussed in Chapter 6.

But this is not the end of the story. Apart from the sets numbered 6–9 above, we have to recognize that if, for example, the shops in the street get more trade then some shops elsewhere will get less. One possible effect of this can be seen if we imagine two shopping streets in an area whose total trade is not growing. If car-parking controls shift trade from street A to street B then when rent reviews arise, rents in street B are likely to increase, but rents in street A are more likely to be held level than to decrease – especially if (as is common in some countries) the legal contract species that rent reviews will be upwards. Thus the set of shop-property owners will obtain a net increase in their income, even though trade will have been constant. It is possible that this will cause the set of shopkeepers to raise prices; but the temptation to do so will be greatest on the part of those whose profit is falling, and this may reduce their competitive powers.

Instead of exploring this landlord-shopkeeper-customer relationship further we may pass to sets 6–9. One aspect of set 6 has already been covered. Some occupiers of nearby property outside the restricted area may be shopkeepers, who gain or lose trade in the way we have described. Whether parking in that other street becomes greater depends on how great it was previously; but it certainly is likely to become more difficult, with consequent effects on sets 7 and 8, and perhaps through these on set 6. In general there is a round of secondary effects that can be analysed in detail along the lines already indicated.

Finally we come to set 9. Here the effect of the control and the decisions emanating from it is to provide information that may serve to confirm or to alter the desired environment. This would result perhaps in a greater attempt to exert power over similar decisions contemplated by road-traffic managers, or even to a request to the municipality to introduce controls elsewhere.

This possibility brings us to the second kind of decision, which we instanced as the decision about an application for permission to develop some land in a certain way. Here there are two obvious economic effects to be considered, and probably others that are less obvious. The economy of the landowner is likely to be dependent to some extent on whether that land use is permitted; and the economy of the intending land-user (who may be the same person) is also likely to be affected. To some extent we have discussed these matters in earlier chapters. Other economic consequences will depend on how the actual and desired environments of people elsewhere are affected by such diverse matters as, for example, traffic, landscape, employment prospects, trade and other factors that may to some extent be influenced by the decision.

Our purpose is not the impossible one of exploring the economic consequences of all possible urban decisions, but the more realistic one of pointing out how they can be analysed with the help of the decision-making framework depicted in Figure 13.2, and attention to the economies and environments of various sets of people. In the parking control example we identified these sets in the first instance by considering the users of the land, of neighbouring land, and more distant places. We could, in fact, think of the local effects, the overspill effects, and what might be called the 'emulation effect'. In the land-use example we again identified two sets associated with the land, and could have then looked at owners and users of neighbouring land, and at owners and users of similar land elsewhere. Instead we indicated an alternative approach by looking at various physical and economic consequences of the decision, and the impacts of these on sets of people. But even here these impacts need then to be analysed within the decision-making framework. A thorough analysis of the economic consequences of a decision may need the use of both approaches, and even perhaps of others. Every approach that adds to our understanding of the consequences is an essential part of well-informed analysis and decision-making.

14

Conclusion

We have argued that the concept of 'an urban economy' is too vague and ambiguous for it to be the basis of any rigorous analysis. Instead we must look at the economies of various overlapping sets who have identifiable associations with the town. Every set has its imports and exports, a multiplier mechanism, and a balance of payments, which may embody some form of power as well as the more conventional economic variables. This means that sets of people who, for economic or other reasons, are in the power of other sets may not be able to make their decisions as freely as they would wish, and may even be forced to reach decisions that appear not to be in their best interests – economic or otherwise. In any case, there is no reason why those economic decisions that are made by sets of rational people, acting subject to or free from constraint, should necessarily be consistent. It follows that an analysis of economic behaviour in an urban context must take account of these matters, and cannot safely rest on assumptions that exclude them.

The decision-making framework developed in this last chapter provides the basis of an approach to urban economic analysis that is based on the economies of sets, and on the relationships between sets. It needs a great deal of development, but even as it stands it helps us to see the extent and nature of the economic interdependencies that arise in a town. The earlier chapters are concerned essentially with more detailed analyses of certain sectors and activities; but in every case the interdependence of these and other sectors and activities has always to be kept in mind.

We have also seen that the techniques available to decision-makers for the assessment of various ideas are very imperfect, and at times credited with a reliability that they do not have. When we add to this the complexity of the urban system we are forced to concede that when we examine the probable consequences of decisions, be they economic or otherwise, we are still using tools that are far too crude for their purpose.

To understand towns we have to understand the economies of the sets of people who are associated with them; and to understand these economies we have to understand the complex pattern of interactions, and the processes of decision-making. Neither urban economics nor urban activity analysis can be a free-standing study. Each supports the other, and must go hand in hand with studies of urban sociology, urban politics, and other facets of urban life. Until we have studied further the ways in which decisions are made, and in which one activity interacts with another, our study of urban economics is in danger of being unreal.

Bibliographical note

Most books have both strengths and weaknesses. The strength of this book is the emphasis that it places on the set approach, and on the decision processes. Its weaknesses would probably take more space to list, and would be assessed differently by different people. Since I know of no other book that emphasizes sets and decision processes to the extent that I have done, I must consider this lack of emphasis to be a major weakness of all the books that I know: but many of them have compensating strengths. In a developing, but still young, subject every author presents his contribution of good and bad, leaving posterity to make its selection and its synthesis. In this note I mention some of the books that are likely to contribute in some way to this synthesis, or to a sound understanding of the subject, even though what I have written implies disagreement with some of what they say. All books, including this one, should be read critically and appreciatively, to learn from what is good and from what is bad.

A nowadays neglected volume is R. F. Ratcliff's *Urban Land Economics* (New York, 1949). Other general books of merit, some of them containing useful detailed bibliographies, are Wilbur R. Thompson *A Preface to Urban Economics* (Baltimore, 1965), B. Goodall's *The Economics of Urban Areas* (Oxford, 1972), D. W. Rasmussen *Urban Economics* (New York, 1973), K. J. Button *Urban Economics: Theory and Policy* (London, 1976) and P. N. Balchin and J. L. Kieve *Urban Land Economics* (London, 1977). Useful collections of readings include H. S. Perloff and L. Wingo Jr. (eds) *Issues in Urban Economics* (Baltimore, 1968), D. Rasmussen and C. T. Howarth (eds) *The Modern City, Readings in Urban Economics* (New York, 1973) and W. H. Leaky, D. L. McKee and R. D. Dean (eds) *Urban Economics* (New York, 1970). Another volume of readings, not exclusively economic, but important is Murray Stewart (ed) *The City: Problems of Planning* (London, 1972). In particular, the papers in it by Alonso (1960), Burgess (1925), Rothenberg (1967) and D. Harvey (1971) are important for their economic content. The volume also contains useful treatments of social issues and of power.

Part of Chapter 4 is based on arguments in 'The Layfield Report', more properly called Report of the Committee of Enquiry into Local Government Finance (HMSO, 1976). The writings of Ursula Hicks, including *Public Finance* (Cambridge, 1947) and *The Large City: A World Problem* (London, 1974) are valuable.

Much has been written on the economics of housing. Apart from the contribution in the books already listed Margaret Reid, *Housing and Income* (Chicago, 1962), A. A. Nevitt, *Housing, Taxation and Subsidies* (London, 1966), and Leland S. Burns and Leo Grebler *The Housing of Nations* (London, 1977) particularly merit attention. The last is particularly good on undeveloped countries. Another useful volume is A. A. Nevitt (ed) *The Economic Problems of Housing* (London, 1967) which contains the proceedings of an international conference. A great deal of useful information is contained in P. A. Stone *Housing, Town Development, Land and Costs* (London, 1962). This also touches on matters considered by us in Chapter 10, for which the more mathematical work in Richard Muth, *Cities and Housing: The Spatial Pattern of Urban Residential Use* (Chicago, 1969) and Alan W. Evans, *The Economics of Residential Location* (London, 1973) are important. The demographic aspects of housing, and their interaction with economic matters, are considered in my own book *Building Cycles and Britain's Growth* (London, 1965). A broader and particularly well argued appraisal of them appears in Brinley Thomas *Migration and Urban Development* (London, 1972). Some aspects of the finance of house building are considered in a contribution by myself to H. Richards (ed) *Population, Factor Movements and Economic Development: Studies presented to Brinley Thomas* (Cardiff, 1976). A valuable review of housing finance in various countries is Centre d'Information et d'Étude du Crédit *Le Financement Du Logement en France et à l'Étranger* (Paris, 1966). The books mentioned at the beginning of this note make comparatively brief reference to retailing, whose economic problems at the urban level have not received wide treatment. They contain useful bibliographies on the economics of urban transport, and of matters considered in our

Chapter 8. Here we should note the light shed on office location and interacting activities in John H. Dunning and E. Victor Morgan (ed) *An Economic Study of the City of London* (London, 1971). The treatment of obsolescence in Chapter 9 is based on G. C. F. Capper and J. Parry Lewis 'Decay, Development and Land Values' in *Manchester School*, XXXII (1964), and then developed in D. F. Medhurst and J. Parry Lewis *Urban Decay: An Analysis and a Policy* (London, 1969) and in my book on building cycles. Other books of interest to readers of Chapters 8–11 are P. A. Stone *The Structure, Size and Costs of Urban Settlements* (Cambridge, 1973), H. Darin-Drabkin, *Land Policy and Urban Growth* (Oxford, 1977) and the particularly balanced appraisal in A. J. Harrison *Economics & Land Use Planning* (London, 1970).

Cost-benefit analysis and other techniques have attracted many writers. Nathaniel Lichfield, Peter Kettle and Michael Whitbread's *Evaluation in the Planning Process* (Oxford, 1975) provides a good account of these techniques even though it is too prone to claiming too much for them. A more modest, and very valuable, approach is in Robert Sugden and Alan Williams *The Principles of Practical Cost Benefit Analysis* (Oxford, 1978). Both books contain useful bibliographies. A classic in this field is the article by A. R. Prest and R. Turvey, 'Cost-Benefit Analysis: a survey', *Economic Journal*, 1965. Amongst the many books and articles relevant to the last two chapters are Stephen L. Elkin *Politics and Land Use Planning* (Cambridge, 1974) and, again, Murray Stewarts *The City* (London, 1972).

Finally we must note the development of a mathematically powerful theory of urban development, by such writers as Alonso, Muth, Mills and others. A masterly survey and appraisal of this is provided in H. W. Richardson, *The New Urban Economics: and Alternatives* (London, 1977). Students who wish to pursue it and have difficulty with the mathematics will probably find help in the second edition of my book *An Introduction to Mathematics for Students of Economics* (London, 1969).

Index